Redesigning the Financial Aid System

Redesigning the Financial Aid System

Why Colleges and Universities
Should Switch Roles with
the Federal Government

Robert B. Archibald

The Johns Hopkins University Press
Baltimore and London

The Johns Hopkins University Press
2715 North Charles Street
Baltimore, Maryland 21218-4363
www.press.jhup.edu

Library of Congress Cataloging-in-Publication Data

Archibald, Robert B., 1946–
Redesigning the financial aid system : why colleges and universities
should switch roles with the federal government / Robert B. Archibald.
    p.   cm.
Includes bibliographical references (p.   ) and index.
ISBN 0-8018-7123-9 (hardcover : alk. paper)
    1. Student financial aid administration—United States. 2. Government
aid to higher education—United States. I. Title.
LB2340.5 .A73 2002
378.3′0973—dc21   2002001841

A catalog record for this book is available from the British Library

For my wife, Nancy, and
my children, Brian and Emily

Contents

Tables and Figures

Tables

Figures

Preface and Acknowledgments

A college education is a prominent feature in the modern version of the American dream. In older versions of this dream a bright young person (most likely male) overcomes an impoverished background and makes something of himself through hard work and initiative. According to the American dream, a person's background need not define his or her options; barriers of class and station should not stand in the way of industry and intelligence. Despite some obvious counterexamples—Bill Gates, for example, dropped out of Harvard—in modern America the dream is normally beyond the grasp of young people (male or female) who do not have a college degree.

The importance of higher education in the American dream is relatively new. It began just after World War II, with the GI Bill, and has been growing rapidly ever since. As the crucial role of a college education became clearer, first private colleges and universities, through the formation of the College Scholarship Service in 1954, and then the federal government, with the Higher Education Act of 1965, created a financial aid system to provide need-based aid to students who could not otherwise manage the expense of higher education. In essence, financial aid was designed to keep the American dream alive, and for a great number of students, it has done just that.

Through the years, the system has evolved with changes in funding levels, adjustments in rules, and the addition of programs. For the most part, this evolution has been unplanned. On occasion, programs have been changed with no thought to how other programs might be affected. In some instances, new programs have been created to fix shortcomings in an existing program without removing the old program. The funding required for a smoothly running financial aid system has often been absent, and financial aid administrators have simply had to make do. The financial aid system of today resembles something that has been patched up many times with duct tape, bailing wire, clothespins, and spit. It is dizzyingly complex, and it is not doing its job efficiently. Many students who should take advantage of the financial aid system are unable to do so, and often the students who do receive financial aid receive less aid than they need. A thoroughgoing redesign of the financial aid system is in order. I am by no means alone in pointing out deficiencies in the financial aid system. Its flaws are easy to document. Still, it has been difficult to fix the system. In part, this is because its failings are unspectacular (some students who could benefit from a college education do not receive one, and some students leave college with excessive debt burdens), and its achievements are substantial (many students receive critical assistance from the existing system). People are wary of making changes. It is much easier to lobby for increases in funding that will alleviate current problems than to consider more permanent fixes. Nevertheless, I think that the financial aid system can and should undergo a major overhaul. Americans should not be satisfied with a system that underperforms as consistently as the financial aid system does.

From its beginnings in 1965, the federal financial aid system has been a partnership between institutions of higher education and the federal government. My analysis of this partnership suggests, among other things, that from the outset the roles were not correctly assigned. Colleges and universities, not the federal government, should provide loan guarantees. Similarly, allowing institutions of higher education to share the duty of providing grants to students gives them an inappropriate role. The system would perform much better if the federal government provided all grants. This switch in roles, coupled with several other changes, would lead to a much more effective financial aid system.

The changes suggested in this book are big changes, and people are uncomfortable with big changes. Generally, the initial response I receive when I present my reform ideas is "Too radical—never happen." Perhaps this is an accurate forecast. It is possible that the only politically feasible changes in financial aid are more modest incremental changes. Even if this is true—and at the moment I am unwilling to concede the point—I am uncomfortable when the discussion turns quickly to political feasibility. My purpose in writing this book is to present an analysis of the financial aid system and some suggested remedies for the system's deficiencies. The first order of business should be to discover whether my analysis and remedies are correct. If, ultimately, people decide that I have not correctly analyzed the financial aid system or that I have not designed the best remedies for the present system's flaws, my proposals should be politically infeasible. If, on the other hand, I have it right, the magnitude of the suggested changes should not be a sufficient reason to oppose them.

Determining whether my suggested remedies are the best ones is not an easy task. Many changes in financial aid policies involve trade-offs; a change that causes us to gain ground in one objective causes us to lose ground on another objective. Because reasonable people can place different values on objectives, it is not likely that any proposal will gain unanimous support. Nevertheless, it is better to face the trade-offs and discuss them than to ignore them. I am convinced that the financial aid system is in sorry shape, and one way or another it should be fixed. It is critical to keep a focus on the failings of the current system and have a vigorous discussion of potential solutions. Owing in some measure to the current performance of the financial aid system, the American dream is dying for a large number of young people. This is an unacceptable state of affairs. The ideal the American dream represents should not be discarded.

I can trace the start of this book to May 1996. I was flattered when a group of my colleagues asked me if they could recommend me to serve as interim dean of the Faculty of Arts and Sciences at the College of William and Mary. I was willing to have my name entered on the list because my colleagues assured me that the obvious candidate's name was also on the list. As I saw it, I was in no real jeopardy of being appointed interim dean because I was confident that the obvious candidate would be selected and that he would accept the position. A call from the provost a few days later informed me that, indeed, the obvious candidate had been selected, but he had declined the position. With little warning and no mental preparation, I thus became the interim dean of the faculty.

Before serving as an administrator, I had little interest in college finances or financial aid, though I had filled out financial aid forms—my son, Brian, was in college, and my daughter, Emily, would follow in a year. During my stint as interim dean, I managed a considerable amount of money and spent quite a bit of time learning about college budgets, and over the course of the year I developed a fascination with the subject of higher education finance. Upon leaving the dean's office, I became involved in research on the financing of state-supported colleges and universities in Virginia (see Archibald and BeVier 1998). The more I learned about college finances, the more I came to believe that financial aid played a critical role in most decisions about college attendance. As I began to look closely at the current financial aid system, I found its performance surprisingly unsatisfactory. This book is the result of combining my natural tendency to try to fix things with this investigation of the financial aid system.

Several of my colleagues deserve credit for helping me formulate the good ideas in this book but deserve none of the blame for any errors. I want especially to thank my fellow William and Mary economists and collaborators David Finifter and David Feldman, who listened to my ideas evolve and read portions of the manuscript. Michael BeVier of Charlottesville, another of my collaborators, was very helpful at an early stage of the development of my ideas. Morton Owen Schapiro, the president of Williams College, was kind enough to read an early version of the book and provided useful comments. I presented the ideas in this book to the social and political philosophy discussion group organized by David Dessler of William and Mary's Government Department and received a good dose of the noneconomists' perspective. Two referees for the Johns Hopkins University Press provided valuable comments on drafts of the manuscripts; I am indebted to them for finding errors and letting me know where I had to strengthen my arguments. Finally, my wife, Nancy, showed tremendous patience and skill editing the many incarnations of the manuscript. This is just one of the many ways I am indebted to her.

Redesigning the Financial Aid System

Introduction

This book presents options for the reform of the financial aid system in the United States. In the interest of accuracy, I have not titled the book *The Solution to the Crisis in Financial Aid,* because there is no crisis. No one will fall off a cliff if the financial aid system is not fixed properly. It is more accurate to say that the financial aid system is poorly designed and, as a result, chronically underperforms. Because "crisis" is much more exciting than "chronic underperformance," the failures of the financial aid system do not get the attention they deserve. Nevertheless, the costs of a poorly running financial aid system are real: despite a significant commitment of public funds, some students are not able to obtain a higher education, and others face severely limited choices.

The Dutch scholar Frans J. de Vijlder has colorfully described the financial aid system thus: "Postsecondary education funding in the United States is like a landscape in which architects from successive eras have constructed roads, viaducts, and buildings, each in its own style. Some features have been demolished, altered, or incorporated into new structures but generally, once something is built, it remains standing; and the longer something has been part of the landscape, the more it appears to be a permanent feature" (de Vijlder 1994). Rather than a well-coordinated system designed by a single author, the financial aid system is a hodgepodge of programs involving a number of participants with diverse interests. Instead of improving things, the system's most recent innovations have caused its performance to deteriorate. When a system chronically underperforms and recent changes cause its performance to deteriorate rather than to improve, it is time for reform.

Many leaders in higher education are worried about the state of the financial aid system. Michael S. McPherson and Morton Owen Schapiro have expressed concern over the growing use of financial aid as a recruiting device: "It is increasingly clear that, unchecked, that trend will lead to growing stratification in U.S. higher education and increasing inequality of income and opportunity in society at large" (McPherson and Schapiro 1999).[1] In a similar vein, an article reporting on a meeting of the National Association of College and University Business Officers notes that "many of the roughly 100 financial-aid directors, finance vice presidents, enrollment managers, and consultants in attendance expressed deep frustration and anxiety over the current aid environment—in which an increasing proportion of scholarships are going to students from middle- and upper-middle-income families" (Gose 2000). Finally, the February 2001 report of the Advisory Committee on Student Financial Assistance warns that "powerful demographic forces already at work will dramatically increase college enrollment of 18- to 24-year-olds by 1.6 million by 2015. . . . This rapidly expanding pool of needy students has already begun to strain current federal, state, and institutional financial aid programs and threatens to precipitate an access crisis for this new generation of college students" (Advisory Committee on Student Financial Assistance 2001, v).

A clear sense of urgency is evident in comments about "growing stratification," "deep frustration and anxiety," and a coming "access crisis." The need for reform in the financial aid system is evident to many. The difficulty is deciding on a set of reform proposals acceptable to all the participants in the financial aid system.

Here as elsewhere, problems are best dealt with before they reach crisis proportions. My hope is that this book will focus attention on the underlying problems in the financial aid system and the changes required for their solution. In my view, continuation of the status quo, even with considerably more funding, will not allow the financial aid system to meet its legitimate objectives. Its performance can be improved only through a recognition of its shortcomings and the creation of an agenda for change. As in most cases, it is unlikely that unanimous agreement for a reform plan can be achieved. The objective of this book is to describe the redesign options and the factors that should guide the reform of the financial aid system.

The Need for Reform

The function of a financial aid system should be to reduce the effect of low income as a barrier to college attendance. It does so by providing assistance to students with financial need. *Financial need* is defined as the difference between the cost of attending a college or university and the amount the student and his or her parents can be reasonably expected to contribute toward these costs; *unmet financial need* is the difference between financial need and all forms of financial aid (including subsidized loans) available to the student. Figure 1.1 charts the relation between unmet need and family income for dependent students, using data from a survey of students attending college in the 1995–96 academic year.[2] In these data, unmet need is truncated at zero. If negative values for unmet need had been allowed, the line would surely be below the horizontal axis at very high incomes.

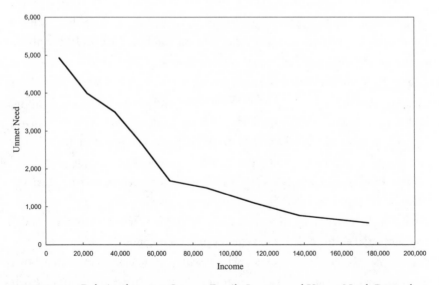

FIGURE 1.1. Relation between Current Family Income and Unmet Need, Dependent Students, 1995–1996 (dollars). *Source:* Data from U.S. Department of Education, NCES 1998.

As the figure illustrates, the average unmet financial need of students decreased at higher levels of household income. The figure is disturbing: the line for unmet need does not hug the horizontal axis as it should; rather, it slopes sharply downward at the beginning of the distribution, where household incomes are low. If the financial aid system were accomplishing its task, the left-hand portion of the line would be much flatter—that is, the unmet need of all students would be similar, regardless of household income.[3] The shape of the line in the figure seems to indicate that the existing financial aid system has not eliminated the income barrier to college attendance. I equivocate in the preceding sentence because it is possible that, despite unmet need, students from low-income households are as likely to attend college as high-income students. After all, the figure is based on data from students attending college; and so the low-income students represented by the left-hand portion of the line somehow overcame the problem of unmet need—their parents dug deeper, or they got serious jobs, or they borrowed larger amounts of money. It is important to ask, however, whether other low-income students who might otherwise have gone to college found the problem of unmet need an insurmountable barrier.

In a 1999 report prepared for the National Center for Education Statistics, Susan P. Choy presents data from the 1994 follow-up to the National Education Longitudinal Study of 1988. Her data indicate that in 1994 only 52 percent of college-qualified students from families with incomes of less than $25,000 attended college, compared with an attendance rate of 62 percent for qualified students from families with incomes between $25,000 and $75,000 and an 83 percent rate for qualified students from families with incomes of $75,000 or more (Choy 1999, 9).[4] Low income appears to be a significant barrier to college attendance even for students who do well in high school.[5] In combination with figure 1.1, Choy's data are strong evidence that under the present financial aid system, aid is not going where it needs to go.

On the other hand, any complex system goes through changes, and a redesign is called for only if the system is performing poorly and is not able to correct its deficiencies. The evidence presented in figure 1.1 and in Choy's analysis might be snapshots of a pendulum in an extreme position, and it is possible that changes within the system as it now exists might mitigate the need for redesign. In the case of the financial aid system, however, the recent significant changes have failed to improve its performance. Two examples make this clear.

First, the most recent innovations in federal financial aid, the Hope Scholarship and the Lifetime Learning tax credits enacted in 1997, break a long-standing precedent according to which all federal financial aid, both grants and subsidized loans, is granted on the basis of demonstrated financial need. Eligibility for tuition tax credits is based on income, not on need, so some of the credits go to families without financial need. Perhaps more important, tax credits are of no benefit to the many families with incomes so low that they do not pay income tax. Second, the most significant change in financial aid offered by states and institutions is the decided shift toward merit-based financial aid. The HOPE Scholarship Program, initiated in Georgia in 1993, is the nation's largest merit-based program, and it has spawned a number of imitators. The increasing popularity of these programs has cut into state funds available for need-based aid. Merit-based programs accounted for roughly 22 percent of all state financial aid spending in 1999–2000 compared with only 15 percent in 1994–95.[6] A similar trend is occurring in the financial aid offered by institutions (see chapter 5).

The increase in merit-based financial aid is likely to have a perverse effect on the shape of the line in figure 1.1. At best, merit-based grants would be randomly spread across the income distribution; more likely, however, given the positive correlation between academic performance (as determined by standardized test scores and grade point averages) and income, merit-based grants will be won disproportionately by students from high-income families. If we add to this the likelihood that merit-based grants are financed by reductions in need-based grants, the net effect of the shift toward merit-based financial aid by states and institutions has to be a deterioration in the distribution of financial aid.

The Components of the Financial Aid System

The first step in redesigning any complex system is to understand its component parts. The basic components of the current financial aid system are the four types of financial aid—grants, loans, work-study, and tax privileges for educational expenses—and the eligibility rules that determine who receives that aid.

Grants

A grant is a gift of money a student can use to defray the expenses associated with higher education.[7] There is a vast array of different kinds of grants, and they are distinguished by who gives the grant, the reason for the grant, and the portability of the grant.

Grants are provided by four groups: the federal government, state governments, institutions of higher education, and private groups and individuals. The first two sources require no further explanation, but the activities of various foundations associated with colleges and universities make the distinction between the third and fourth categories unclear. I include a foundation associated with a college as part of the institution if the grants it gives can be used only at the institution in question. I include in private groups and individuals those entities—such as the local Rotary Club, the National Merit Corporation, or the Ford Motor Company—that award grants that can be used at any institution. A student's parents or other relatives are excluded from private groups and individuals.

Grants are awarded on the basis of need or on the basis of merit. In general, need-based grants are given to students who do not otherwise have sufficient financial resources to attend college, and merit-based grants are given to students in recognition of particular talents or abilities. A vast array of talents are rewarded with merit-based grants, including noteworthy ability in athletics, academics, music, and leadership.[8] The distinction between need-based and merit-based grants is at times less than clear. It is quite possible that a merit-based grant could be awarded to a student with financial need; a football player receiving an athletic scholarship, for example, may come from a poor family. The presence of financial need, however, does not in itself transform the grant from a merit-based grant to a need-based grant. If financial need is not a consideration in determining eligibility for the grant, it is not a need-based grant. Some institutions do not have funds sufficient to meet the full need of all students. Often these institutions award their limited need-based funds on the basis of merit.[9] In this case the grant is still a need-based grant because, though merit plays a role in its allocation, it is available only to a student with financial need.

The existence of two kinds of grants and four kinds of entities giving grants yields a taxonomy with eight possible combinations. It is easy to find examples for six of the eight combinations. The two grants provided by the federal government, the Pell Grant and the Supplemental Educational Opportunity Grant (SEOG), are need based. With the exception of the implicit grant to students who attend military academies, there are no merit-based federal grants.

Most states offer both need-based and merit-based awards. As noted earlier, the success of the HOPE Scholarship Program initiated in Georgia has led to a shift toward merit-based state grants. Nevertheless, for the 1999–2000 academic year the total state spending on need-based grants of $3.2 billion was still much larger than the total state spending on merit-based grants of $0.9 billion. Three states (Alaska, Georgia, and South Dakota) offer no need-based grants, whereas fourteen states (Arkansas, California, Hawaii, Maine, Michigan, Nebraska, Nevada, Oregon, Pennsylvania, Rhode Island, South Dakota, Texas, West Virginia, and Wyoming) and the District of Columbia offer no merit-based grants (Schmidt 2001).[10] The remaining thirty-four states offer both need-based and merit-based grants.

Institutions also offer both types of grants. Some, notably those in the Ivy League, award only need-based grants, while most others offer both types. Institutional grants are growing rapidly in relative importance. Data in the College Board's *Trends in Student Aid, 1999,* indicate that in the ten years from the 1988–89 academic year to the 1998–99 academic year, institutional and other grants grew by 126 percent in constant dollars,[11] far exceeding the 65 percent growth in state grants and the 17 percent growth in federal grants (College Board 1999b). As a result of this rapid growth, grants from institutions and private groups and individuals, which totaled much less than federal grants throughout the 1980s, exceeded federal grants by more than $4 billion in 1998–99.

The grants awarded by private groups are almost exclusively merit based. The best known of these grants, those awarded by the National Merit Corporation, are based on the results of a national competition. Less well known grants are available in almost every community. Community organizations and businesses award these grants to local high school students based on academic achievement, though on occasion larger grants are slanted toward students with greater financial need.

The final characteristic of grants I want to emphasize is their portability. A grant is portable if it can be used at any institution the student chooses to attend. The portability of grants does not map conveniently into a taxonomy based on who gives the grant and whether it is awarded on the basis of need or merit. This is clear in the case of federal government grants. The SEOG program, for example, is a campus-based program. Following broad guidelines, institutions have discretion in how they spend these federal grant funds. These grants are therefore not portable. They can be used only at the institution awarding the grant. The Federal Pell Grant Program is different. A student who qualifies for the Pell Grant can use the award at the institution of his or her choice. In essence, students can take Pell Grants wherever they want; hence, the grants are portable.

State grants have varying degrees of portability. Some state grant funds, like those administered through the federal SEOG program, are campus based and are not portable. Others, for example Georgia's HOPE Scholarships, have limited portability. HOPE Scholarships can be used at any college or university in Georgia. Much less common are state grants with unlimited portability—that is, grants that can be used at out-of-state as well as in-state institutions.

Institutional grants are almost by definition not portable. Institutions use financial aid to attract students, not to make higher education in general more affordable for students. On the other hand, grants offered by private entities other than institutions of higher education are generally portable. I have used National Merit Scholarships funded by the National Merit Corporation as my example of these private grants. These grants are portable; students can take them to any institution. National Merit Scholarships funded by a particular institution, on the other hand, are not portable; a student receives this grant only if he or she attends the institution funding the grant.

Guaranteed Student Loans

In terms of dollars made available to students to cover higher education expenses, guaranteed student loans are much larger than grants. In the 1998–99 academic year, federal loan programs channeled $34.7 billion to students, almost four and a half times the $7.9 billion spent for Pell Grants and the SEOGs. Federal loan programs dominate lending to students. In 1998–99, small state loan programs lent a total of $438 million, and a somewhat larger private loan sector lent a total of $1.98 billion.

Although guaranteed student loans are traditionally considered to be financial aid, they have at best a tenuous claim to the label. Obtaining a loan does not reduce the price of a college education as a grant does; it simply allows the student to delay payment. Nevertheless, guaranteed student loans are considered financial aid for two reasons. First, the loan guarantee is crucial. Borrowers with no collateral and nonexistent credit ratings—a category that includes most college students—have a difficult time obtaining loans, so the government loan guarantees open credit markets to students. Second, most student loans are offered at subsidized interest rates. This does provide an indirect price break to college students.

Federal student loans come in five varieties. The Perkins Loan is available on some campuses and, like the SEOG, is controlled by the institution. The much larger, more generally available student loans, typically called Stafford Loans, come in four varieties. The first distinction depends upon who provides the loan funds. Starting in the 1994–95 academic year, the federal government made loans directly to students under the William D. Ford Direct Loan Program. Before that, private lenders had made all guaranteed student loans. The Federal Family Education Loan Program, which uses private lenders, still makes most guaranteed student loans. The second distinction involves the interest subsidy. Some student loans have subsidized interest rates and others do not. This creates four types of federal student loans in addition to Perkins Loans: subsidized Ford Direct Loans, unsubsidized Ford Direct Loans, subsidized Federal Family Education Loans, and unsubsidized Federal Family Education Loans.

One additional federal higher education loan program, Parent Loans for

Undergraduate Students, makes loans to parents, not to students. These loans are typically used when a student's eligibility for Stafford Loans has been exhausted in any year and are available in both the Ford Direct Loan and the Federal Family Education Loan Programs.

Work-Study

Until relatively late in the twentieth century, campus-based jobs for needy college students accounted for the vast majority of need-based financial aid awarded. Work-study now represents a small fraction of federal financial aid awards—$1.0 billion compared with $7.9 billion in grants and $34.7 billion in student loans in 1998–99. Funds from the Federal Work-Study Program are used by institutions to provide on-campus employment for students with demonstrated financial need. Like the SEOG and Perkins Loan Programs, the work-study program is administered entirely on campus.

Tax Privileges

The 1997 federal tax legislation introduced three types of tax privileges for higher education expenses: tax credits for tuition payments, special tax privileges for state-sponsored college savings plans, and the deductibility of interest payments on student loans.

Perhaps surprisingly, proposals for tax credits for college and university tuition are as old as the federal role in financial aid, but before 1997 they had not mustered majority support in Congress. Two federal tax credits are currently available: The Hope Scholarship Credit applies to the first two years a student is in college and gives a 100 percent tax credit for the first $1,000 paid toward tuition and required fees (less grants, scholarships, and other tax-free educational assistance) and a 50 percent tax credit on the second $1,000. The Lifetime Learning Credit covers the junior and senior years in college as well as continuing education for adults returning to college and provides a tax credit of 20 percent of the first $5,000 paid in tuition and fees. Both tax credits are phased out as family income increases, starting with joint filers with adjusted gross incomes above $80,000 ($40,000 for single filers), and are completely phased out for joint filers with incomes above $100,000 ($50,000 for single filers).[12] The revenue forgone from these tax credits is considerable: the estimates for the fiscal year 1999 tax expenditures for these credits is $7.5 billion dollars, just slightly less than the $7.9 billion the federal government spent on grants in the 1998–99 academic year.[13]

In 1997, Congress also introduced two additional tax privileges affecting higher education expenses. Section 529 of the Internal Revenue Code allows families to defer taxes on the earnings on state-sponsored college savings plans. In addition, at such time as the funds in these plans are used to pay college expenses, their earnings are taxed at the child's tax rate, despite the fact that the college savings plans are property of the parent or parents. The final tax privilege is the deductibility of interest payments on student loans. Interestingly, these two tax privileges send conflicting messages to students and their parents. Section 529 encourages savings for college expenses, whereas the deductibility of interest on student loans encourages borrowing to cover these expenses.

Eligibility Rules

For many types of private and institutional grants the eligibility rules are quite straightforward. Grants from the local Rotary Club, for example, are given to students selected from the senior class at the local high school, and the merit-based grants awarded by a given university are based on a selection made by the university from among all admitted or continuing students. The eligibility rules for federal financial aid and need-based aid given by institutions are more complex. The eligibility rules for need-based aid are contained in what is typically called the needs analysis system.

The needs analysis system relies on income information from federal income tax returns, information on assets, and information on the structure of the family. Both the student and his or her parents or legal guardians are required to provide this information. The federal government gathers this information on the Free Application for Federal Student Aid, or FAFSA. The needs analysis system applies various formulas to the information provided on the FAFSA to determine the expected family contribution. If the cost of attendance, including tuition and fees, room and board, and an allowance for books, supplies, and travel, exceeds the expected family contribution, a student is eligible for federal financial aid.

For the purposes of determining eligibility for institutional need-based financial aid, some colleges and universities ask students and parents to provide additional information. This information is collected using either institutionally provided forms or a form provided by the College Scholarship Service of the College Board. Typically, these institutions ask for information on assets beyond the limited set covered by the FAFSA. These institutions then use their own formulas to determine the expected family contribution for the purposes of awarding their own need-based aid.

The Objectives of a Financial Aid System

An effective financial aid system enables students to overcome financial barriers to college attendance, thereby improving access to education. For access to be more than minimal, however, it must also provide students with an element of choice. One of the strengths of the higher education system in the United States is that it offers a broad range of educational opportunities to students. A properly running financial aid system should provide each student with the financial means to take advantage of the opportunity that best suits him or her. Access and choice, therefore, are the core goals of a well-functioning financial aid system.

In addition, I have chosen four secondary objectives for my redesign. First, the new system should be simpler than the existing system, making it easier for participants to understand what is required of them and what they stand to gain for their efforts. Second, the rapid rate of increase in college tuition is a major national concern, and the redesigned system should minimize the contribution that financial aid makes to this problem. Third, it should provide the appropriate incentives to its participants. Fourth, it should encourage families to make evenhanded decisions about how parents and students share college expenses.

Simplicity

Properly understood, simplicity is part of the choice goal for a financial aid system. The choice goal has two parts: students must have sufficient funds to be able to afford the options for which they qualify, and they must have sufficient information to make wise choices. Often, analyses of the financial aid system focus exclusively on providing funds sufficient for choice. I emphasize simplicity here because simplifying the financial aid system will make it easier for students to make wise choices.

The existing financial aid system is unnecessarily complex. The needs analysis system is full of arcane rules, and the large number of financial aid programs creates confusion. Federal financial aid alone includes two grant programs, three student loan programs awarding both subsidized and unsubsidized loans, and the federal work-study program. The financial aid programs at state governments, institutions of higher education, and at private groups and individuals add further layers.

The complexity of the financial aid system is not one of its selling points. If college is to be made a viable choice for low-income students, they should begin early in their high school career to explore the financial options available to them. Thus the system should be simple enough to be understood by a sophomore in high school and his or her parents—many of whom will be unfamiliar with the college experience. Currently, this is almost impossible. The financial aid system is so confusing that it has spawned shelves full of books and an industry of consultants to guide students and parents. One of the objectives of any redesign should be to simplify the system, making it easier for prospective students and their parents to understand.

The current complexity arises in part because the variety of participants have different, and sometimes conflicting, objectives. Innovators in the past have made changes to shift outcomes in their desired direction. Unfortunately, the result has been a system that is quite incoherent as a whole. Some participants will be unhappy with a redesign that unravels past changes. Unless some of those agents are willing to give up some autonomy, however, it will be difficult to design a system that will not quickly evolve into a system as complex as the one we are trying to simplify.

Financial Aid and Rising Tuition

Concern over the rate of increase of college tuition over the 1990s was such that in 1997 Congress created a commission to study its causes (see National Commission on the Cost of Higher Education 1998). Although the public generally holds the higher education sector in high regard, the creation of the commission suggests some slippage in this relationship. A number of individuals, in Congress and in the public at large, feel that the recent rapid increases in tuition are the result of an abuse of the public trust on the part of colleges and universities. Draconian controls that might come from federal interference in setting tuition rates would most likely be counterproductive to colleges and universities.

There are many factors behind the escalation of college tuition, and financial aid practices are only a part of the story (see, for example, Ehrenberg 2000 and Clotfelter 1996). The relation between institutional financial aid expenditures and college tuition is complex. Clearly, other things being equal, increases in tuition create increases in financial need: more students become eligible for financial aid, and those eligible for financial aid are eligible for larger awards. In this way, budgets permitting, increases in tuition lead to increases in both federal and institutional financial aid spending. If this were the only connection between tuition and financial aid expenditures, it would not be sensible to blame any of the increase in tuition on financial aid.

The causation, however, also works in the opposite direction. An institution that wants to increase its financial aid spending, either by increasing merit-based aid to attract more high-quality students or by increasing need-based aid to meet a larger percentage of the financial need of its current and prospective student body, can finance the increased spending in two ways: by decreasing spending elsewhere in its budget or by raising tuition. There is considerable evidence that the second option, raising tuition, has been used by a great number of institutions. To the extent that this is true, increases in institutionally funded financial aid create increases in list prices. These increases in list price allow the institution to selectively cut the price for students in high demand without suffering a decrease in revenue. In essence, institutions mark up prices so that they can discount them for some students. As the process has evolved, the prevalence of discounts has increased. At several colleges and universities, almost every student receives some type of institutional grant—that is, a price discount. When every student gets a price discount, the list price is rendered completely meaningless.[14]

The redesigned financial aid system should try to weaken this second link between financial aid and tuition. Under some circumstances, the practice of raising list-price tuition and increasing financial aid for some students does not affect the average net price of attending the institution in question. One could argue, then, that institutional financial aid spending has no effect on the average cost of attending college. Nevertheless, it was the rise in list-price tuition that caught the public's attention and compelled Congress to study college and university pricing. Perceptions, after all, are sometimes as important as reality.

Incentives in the Financial Aid System

The financial aid system can be redesigned in several ways to improve incentives. For example, the needs analysis system itself creates disincentives for families to save; a redesign of the formulas determining grants could also increase incentives for colleges and universities to control their costs. Federally guaranteed student loans have their own particular disincentives.

Student loans are difficult products for lenders. Few students have established credit ratings; there is no way to "repossess" a higher education; and few students can offer physical collateral. Lenders are loath to become involved with borrowers without a credit rating or good collateral. Under the current system, federal loan guarantees overcome the reluctance of lenders. Although there is a clear need for loan guarantees, assigning this role to the federal government does not provide the proper incentives.

There is an inherent moral hazard problem in federal loan guarantees. The college, university, or trade school that does a shoddy job of educating a student is not harmed by its own failure; it has already been paid. If a student does not repay the loan, it becomes the government's problem. In a case like this, the forecast is clear: either loan default rates or the government's monitoring costs will be high.[15]

One solution to the moral hazard problem is to assign the task of guaranteeing loans to colleges and universities. Under this arrangement, institutions will have added incentive to provide a good education. Because it is more expensive, even with loan guarantees, to service a group of loans with a high default rate,[16] lenders will have strong incentives to take a close look at institutions. Institutions clearly able to meet their loan guarantee commitments and institutions with good default rate histories will be able to attract more lenders and offer better interest rates to their students. Such a system provides the correct set of incentives. It rewards an institution for keeping its financial house in order and for providing a good education.

As with other design proposals, the suggestion to shift responsibility for loan guarantees is not perfect. This arrangement introduces an incentive for an institution to reduce its default risk by admitting only students who are unlikely to take out large loans. This is not a reason to close the door on the proposal, however. The proposal to shift loan guarantee responsibilities from the federal government to the institutions creates incentives for institutions to practice need-aware admissions, but this is not a big change. The current system has incentives that lead to this same result. In fact, only a small number of institutions currently practice need-blind admissions. We are therefore comparing two flawed systems. Finding a flaw in a proposal is not sufficient to eliminate it from serious consideration.

A More Evenhanded Intergenerational Approach

McPherson and Schapiro (1991) note the two fundamental ways of financing a college education: by using a parental responsibility system, in which parents save and pay for their children's education, or by using a student responsibility system, in which children borrow to pay for their education and repay the loans out of the incomes they earn after college.[17] In both systems one generation has to forgo consumption to pay for higher education. In the first case, parents forgo present consumption to pay for their children's college expenses. In the second case, children agree to forgo future consumption to repay the debts they accumulated in attending college.

Currently, the financial aid system is essentially a parental responsibility system: it assumes that the costs of college fall primarily on parents. All federal financial aid and some of the financial aid offered by institutions is based on financial need, defined as the difference between the cost of attendance and the expected family contribution. The terminology is telling; the family—basically, the parents—are "expected" to pay for college expenses. The implicit assumption is that all college-bound students have parents who will assume a large part of the responsibility of paying for their higher education. The "expected" family contribution determines the amount that parents are able to pay and assumes they are willing to pay that amount. Willing parents, however, are not always present; and in many cases students start or continue their higher education after becoming independent of their parents. The current financial aid system does make allowances for independent students, but for fear of creating incentives for parents to abandon financial responsibility for their children, it does not award aid as generously to independent students as to dependent students.[18] In other cases, parents are unwilling to alter their lifestyle to help their dependent children obtain a higher education. When willing parents are absent, students who still want to pursue a higher education have two choices: they can attend low-cost institutions, or they can leave college with much larger debts than other students.

Given that willing parents are not always present, it is tempting to suggest a switch to a student responsibility system. This is not a feasible plan, however. Many parents are willing to help their children, and there is no way to force these parents not to contribute to their children's college expenses. The conclusion has to be that a pure system of either kind is impossible. Some students will have parents who are able and willing to help pay for college. A parental responsibility system works for these students, and they will leave college with few debts. Other students will not have parents or will have parents who are unwilling or unable to help them pay for college. These students will, by default, use a student responsibility system, and they will leave college with significant debt. Probably the vast majority of students will use some mix of parental and student responsibility.

This discussion suggests two objectives for a redesigned financial aid system: it must be neutral with respect to the choice of payment system, and it must be sensitive to those who have a student responsibility system thrust upon them. The current financial aid system does not do well on either count. The way the needs analysis system treats accumulated assets and the subsidization of student loans create disincentives to use a parental responsibility system by saving. Recently enacted special tax treatment for college savings programs has lessened this bias somewhat, but on net the financial aid system discourages savings. The small income-contingent repayment program is the current system's most significant attempt to deal with the problem of students with uncooperative parents.

Adding the objectives that the financial aid system be simple, not contribute to rising tuition, have the proper incentives, and be evenhanded across generations to the traditional objectives of access and choice creates some difficulty. Reform proposals that promote one objective might make it more difficult to reach others. The evaluation of proposals will have to account for how they affect all objectives, and it will be difficult to find a proposal that is unambiguously an improvement. A requirement of unanimous agreement for change, however, would result in a tyranny of the status quo.

The Switch in Roles

Under the current financial aid system, both institutions of higher education and the federal government provide grants, with institutions playing the larger role and the federal government providing loan guarantees. I have already introduced the proposal that the responsibility for loan guarantees be transferred from the federal government to colleges and universities. A case can also be made for colleges and universities to minimize the number and amount of grants they provide, shifting the responsibility for grants to the federal government.

The desire to simplify the financial aid system and to reduce the role financial aid plays in the problem of rising tuition provides the rationale for minimizing institutional grants. First, a system that relies heavily on institutional grants is, by necessity, complicated. In such a system, the difference between the price listed in a college's catalogue and the price a student actually has to pay can be quite large and will vary considerably from institution to institution. Unfortunately, for most students, the price confusion introduced by institutional grants is resolved very late in the decision-making process. Students get full information on the price they must pay only after they are admitted to an institution and receive notice of a financial aid award.

At this point in the process, because applying to a college or university is costly in both time and money, students may well have eliminated an institution that would have been their first choice had they had full information on costs. The price confusion caused by institutional grants is a serious drawback for many students.

Moreover, because institutional financial aid offers are based on private information provided by students and their families, it is difficult for the general public to obtain an accurate picture of the actual net price of attending college. Thus the list-price tuition—the tuition advertised in the catalogue—is the price information with which the general public is most familiar. As a result, many families now feel that a college education is beyond their reach, and many students are discouraged from even considering college. It is ironic that increases in institutional financial aid spending are part of the reason for higher list-price tuition. The use of institutional funds to reduce the price to some students inadvertently increases the perception that college is too expensive.

A system that relies much more heavily on the federal Pell Grants would eliminate these problems. Pell Grants are portable, so they do not create confusion about net prices. Students can learn about their Pell Grant eligibility early, and their eligibility is not affected by their choice of institution. The size of the maximum Pell Grant can and should be widely publicized. The increased assistance from the federal government should help allay the fears of some low-income families. Finally, a substitution of larger Pell Grants for institutional spending on grants should allow many institutions to reduce their list-price tuition significantly. This too should allay fears about the high price of attending college.

The proposal that the federal government should take a much larger role in providing grants could be seen as a plea for more spending for financial aid. More spending for financial aid is a good idea, one I want to encourage. Nevertheless, in the balance, if the roles were reversed on both dimensions—the institutions taking primary responsibility for loan guarantees and the government for grants—the need for additional federal spending would be reduced. The interest subsidies, the payments to cover loan defaults, and the money required to administer the loan programs are significant, more than the federal government currently spends on Pell Grants. Giving up the responsibility for the current government loan programs would free up a considerable amount of revenue that could be redirected toward Pell Grants. Moreover, if colleges and universities reduce their list-price tuition as they eliminate spending on institutional grants, the average student's financial need should decrease. These two changes will result in much less unmet need than we see in the current system.

Some of the proposals presented in the remainder of this book will be thought radical by some readers. Not surprisingly, these proposals, while they have some appealing properties, are unable to meet all of the objectives I have laid out for a financial aid system. The analysis of the proposals uncovers trade-offs inherent in any financial aid system and suggests ways in which the proposals might be amended.

The History of Financial Aid in the United States

Let me begin this chapter by telling a story. At his first service the new pastor of a church in New England was puzzled when his congregation entered and all sat on the right-hand side of the sanctuary. Obviously, he thought, he must not know the local customs. The pastor proceeded with the service, and things transpired in their normal fashion. About two-thirds of the way through the service, however, during the singing of the Doxology, the entire congregation moved over to the left-hand side of the sanctuary, where they remained through the rest of the service. The pastor later learned that many years before, the sanctuary had been heated with a potbellied stove that sat on the right-hand side of the sanctuary. The congregation would come in and sit close to the stove to warm themselves. Eventually they would become too hot, and so, during the Doxology, they would shift to the other side of the sanctuary. The church now has central heat, but the congregation retains the custom of switching sides during the service.[1]

The moral of the story about the new pastor is that history matters. Some customs have their roots in a peculiarity of the past, unrelated to present-day reality. This is true for financial aid policy. Often, what we do today is a result not so much of careful analysis and planning as of past changes and past battles.

The federal government spends a considerable amount of money supporting higher education. Most of this spending goes toward student aid. Surprisingly, the notion that federal funds should be put to this purpose is a relatively new idea. There was a short-lived federal financial aid program during the Great Depression, but the programs that currently exist were initiated in 1958, 1964, 1965, and 1972. The Higher Education Act of 1965 represents the major shift in policy. With this act, the federal government inaugurated programs designed to reduce economic barriers that had kept many poor students from obtaining the best possible higher education.

What took so long? Why was a political consensus that it is in the public interest for the federal government to support access to higher education so late in coming? The Higher Education Act of 1965 introduced an important new participant in the financing of higher education, bringing about changes both in federal policy and in college and university finances.

Financial Aid before the Higher Education Act of 1965

Harvard University was founded in 1636, only sixteen years after the landing of the Mayflower. Just seven years later, in 1643, Lady Anne Mowlson, whose maiden name was Radcliffe, contributed £100 to a scholarship fund to allow needy young men to attend Harvard (Morison 1936, 12). Mowlson's gift was an exception to the rule, however; financial aid for needy students was not common in the first three centuries of higher education in America. In fact, a college education was not at all common until the twentieth century. Figure 2.1 illustrates the percentage of the United States population holding bachelor's degrees each year from 1650 to 1998. Mass higher education is clearly a twentieth-century phenomenon.

During the first two centuries following the founding of Harvard, the few who did obtain a college education were either very wealthy or interested in becoming clergymen. During the colonial period all of the colleges in what was to become the United States were church supported.[2] Colleges, or the church in some instances, gave direct support to needy students who were training for the ministry, but financial aid for anyone else was essentially nonexistent (Rudolph 1990, 183).

During the Constitutional Convention of 1787, Charles Pinckney of South Carolina and James Madison of Virginia moved that Congress be empowered "to establish a university, in which no preference or distinctions

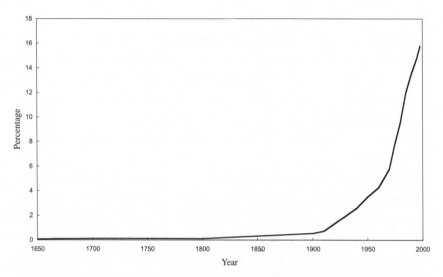

FIGURE 2.1. Baccalaureate Degree Holders in the United States, 1650–1998 (as percentage of population). *Source:* Data from Eells 1958 and Bureau of the Census 1960–98.

Note: Eells 1958 gives the percentage of the population with a baccalaureate degree through 1950, making every effort to adjust the earlier data so that the degrees are the equivalent of a modern bachelor's degree. Bureau of the Census 1960–98 give the percentage of the population over the age of twenty-five who had completed four or more years of college in 1960 and later years. The later data are adjusted to be comparable to the earlier data.

should be allowed on account of religion" (quoted in Farrand 1911, 616). The motion failed on a vote of four delegations in favor, six opposed, and one divided. There is no mention of education in the U.S. Constitution; the Founding Fathers left this matter entirely up to the states. President George Washington, in his first message to Congress on January 8, 1790, recommended that Congress set up a national university, but the idea met with considerable resistance. Congress clearly felt that education should be a state function, and the president did not get his university.[3]

The idea that a college education should be made more widely available emerged with the new attitudes surrounding the election of Andrew Jackson to the presidency in 1828. "In an atmosphere of expanding universal manhood suffrage, of unlimited belief in the inevitability of material and moral progress, the Jacksonians were overwhelmingly persuasive. When they were finished, almost everyone either was a Jacksonian or sounded like one" (Rudolph 1990, 202). The response to this change in attitudes was a concerted, if at times belated, effort on the part of colleges to dispel their image as preserves for the rich.[4] Harvard established a loan fund in 1838, and in 1852 the first endowments permanently earmarked for scholarships were raised through a fund-raising effort by the Harvard Alumni Association.[5] In 1853, Princeton initiated a fund-raising drive to endow one hundred scholarships of $60 each (Wertenbaker 1946, 271).

The balance of supply and demand was precarious in higher education in the nineteenth century. One of the reasons for the imbalance was the rapid increase in the number of institutions. In 1800, 35 institutions of higher education had the power to grant degrees (Eells 1958, 3–14). By 1900, the number had risen to 977 (Bureau of the Census 1975, series H 689, 382). In the competitive environment that resulted from this rapid expansion, colleges and universities were hard pressed to meet their budgets, let alone provide generous scholarships to needy students. Many private institutions resorted to appeals to state legislatures for support, and some succeeded (Rudolph 1990, 185). Other institutions experimented with new funding schemes. Many colleges and universities, for example, authorized the sale of perpetual scholarships, which were sold at a fixed price and allowed the owners or their designees to attend the institution at any time for no charge.[6] If the institutions had priced these perpetual scholarships correctly and prudently invested the proceeds from their sale, this might have been an attractive funding devise. As it happened, however, most of the colleges used the funds for current expenses and thus only postponed their financial troubles.

Land Grant Colleges and Universities

Representative Justin Smith Morrill of Vermont was the driving force behind the growth of state-supported higher education in the latter half of the nineteenth century. Morrill first introduced his land grant college bill in December 1857. The bill granted each state twenty thousand acres of land for each senator and member of Congress representing the state. For states without public lands, the bill provided scrip for an equal amount of land in an unoccupied area of states with public land; the land would provide an endowment to support at least one college that would focus on "such branches of learning as are related to agriculture and the mechanical arts" (Rainsford 1972, 85).

The educational objectives of Morrill's bill raised relatively few objections. However, the bill was opposed by members of Congress from western states, who had other ideas about how to dispose of public lands, and by members of Congress from southern states, who questioned the constitutionality of federal support for education, which they considered a state issue. The bill passed Congress in 1859 with slim margins in both houses, but it was ultimately vetoed by President James Buchanan, who considered it unconstitutional.

The political balance in Congress changed after the secession of the southern states. With the help of Senator Benjamin F. Wade of Ohio, Morrill introduced a similar bill. The Morrill-Wade Land Grant College Act passed Congress with sizable margins and was signed by President Abraham Lincoln on July 2, 1862. The bill required that states act within two years to receive the grant. Seventeen states met this deadline. For various reasons the deadline was extended frequently, and by 1929 sixty-nine land grant colleges and universities had been established. Only two of these institutions, Massachusetts Institute of Technology and Cornell, were privately supported. The other sixty-seven formed the backbone of state-supported higher education in the United States.

The Late Nineteenth and Early Twentieth Centuries

Late in the nineteenth century as the national economy weakened, the already precarious financial situation of colleges and universities worsened. Although the number of institutions of higher education actually peaked in 1890 at 998, it fell over the next two decades, to 977 in 1900 and 951 in 1910 (Bureau of the Census 1975, series H 689, 382). For most institutions the financial picture did not improve until well after the conclusion of World War I. Even the elite institutions did not fare well during this time period. Yale University, for example, was not able to raise its tuition for nearly thirty years

(Levine 1986, 16). This environment was not conducive to offers of financial aid. The institutions were operating with tight budgets, and the concerns of needy students did not get much attention.

Conditions improved for colleges and universities after World War I, and there was an enrollment boom in the 1920s. Following earlier expansions of high school education, the idea of mass higher education took hold during this decade. For the first time in the nation's history people started to think of a college education as a vehicle for economic and social mobility rather than an activity reserved for the rich. Many colleges and universities took advantage of this increase in demand to increase prices. For the most part, the effect of these tuition increases on the opportunities for the less well to do was ignored. The lack of concern for poor students, at least among the well-established private colleges and universities, was not surprising given the discrimination most of them practiced against everyone except upper-crust white male Protestants (ibid., 137–61; U.S. President's Commission on Higher Education 1947, 25–44).

Despite the tuition increases and the dearth of financial aid, the 1920s was a decade of expanding access to higher education. College attendance increased 84.1 percent over the 1920s, from 598,000 students in 1920 to 1,101,000 students in 1930 (from 4.7% to 7.2% of the eighteen-to-twenty-four-year-old population). The increase in college attendance was primarily the result of the growth in state-supported institutions. State-supported institutions charged low tuition, if any at all, and many of them were junior colleges located in or close to population centers. Although access increased, the available choices for many students were limited. In almost every case, during the 1920s and 1930s the only affordable option for a poor student, even an academically talented one, was the local state-supported school.

The enrollment expansion in state-supported institutions in the 1920s came from three sources. First, because most states already had one or more state universities, part of the enrollment increase came from expansions of these institutions. Second, the rapid expansion of junior colleges played a significant role. In 1918 only 4,500 students—1.9 percent of all college students—attended junior colleges. By 1938 that number had increased to 237,700 students—17.6 percent of all college students (Levine 1986, 162). Third, the transformation of normal schools into state teacher colleges and the broadening of the curriculum at these institutions were contributing factors in many states. In most states the result of this expansion was a system of state-supported institutions that offered considerable variety to its residents.

The most well known attempt to rationalize the expansion of state-supported higher education occurred in California. Based on a 1932 report of the Carnegie Foundation for the Advancement of Teaching, California developed a three-tier system (Carnegie Foundation for the Advancement of Teaching 1932). On the top tier were the branch campuses of the University of California. At the second tier were the California state colleges, and at the third tier the junior colleges. This plan essentially made explicit what was happening in many of the other states. State higher education was becoming a differentiated system. Most states had at least one flagship institution, a number of second-tier four-year institutions, and a number of two-year institutions. The flagship institutions had the highest admission standards, received the most funding per student, and had important research roles in their states. The second-tier four-year institutions had lower admission standards, received less funding per student, and had minimal research roles. The two-year institutions usually had open admissions and combined traditional college courses with vocational education.

Not surprisingly, the Great Depression caused severe hardship for many institutions of higher education. Nevertheless, most colleges and universities survived. In fact, fueled by the expansion of state systems, the percentage of the eighteen-to-twenty-four-year-old population who were resident students in institutions of higher education was higher in 1938 (8.3%) than it had been in 1930 (7.2%) (Bureau of the Census 1975, series H 707, 383). One of the reasons for their survival was the assistance of the federal government. In the spring of 1934, the Federal Emergency Relief Administration established a federally funded work-study program for 65,000 students (Levine 1986, 196). In June 1935 the program was transferred to the National Youth Administration (NYA). Over the course of its existence (from 1935 to 1943), the NYA work-study program spent $93,860,000 assisting approximately 620,000 students from 1,651 participating institutions of higher education (U.S. President's Commission on Higher Education 1947, 48). At its peak it provided assistance to roughly 12 percent of the national undergraduate student body (Levine 1986, 199).

Although the NYA program is considered one of the successes of the New Deal, at the time it clearly was considered a relief program, not a model for a financial aid program. At the highest levels of the government, there was no support for federal aid to improve access to college. In fact, President Franklin D. Roosevelt seemed to be hostile to financial aid for higher education. In July 1939, in a conversation with Treasury Secretary Henry Morgenthau Jr., Roosevelt commented that "just because a boy wants to go to college is no reason we should finance it" (quoted in Blum 1965, 42).

After World War II

The Servicemen's Readjustment Act of 1944, more typically called the GI Bill, had a profound effect on higher education in the United States. The bill provided a variety of veteran's benefits. For our purposes the most important of these was a grant to cover tuition, books, and living expenses for one year of full-time schooling plus an additional month for each month a student had served in the armed forces. This allowed a veteran with two years of active service to finance thirty-six months of full-time study—in many cases sufficient time to earn a bachelor's degree. Nearly one-half of the 15 million veterans participated in GI Bill programs, roughly 4.4 million of them going to college (Cohen 1998, 182). The GI Bill is widely credited with starting an era of mass education in the United States. Many of the veterans who took advantage of the GI Bill were not from the kind of families that typically sent their children to college.

Was the GI Bill the start of federal financial aid in the United States? Without denying its importance in the history of higher education, the answer has to be no. The GI Bill was deferred compensation for the soldiers and sailors who had fought in World War II. It was not designed to be generally available, and although it was resurrected for the veterans of the Korean and Vietnam Wars, it was originally scheduled to end when World War II veterans had exhausted their benefits. Federal programs that were generally available to prospective college students did not appear until 1965.

Although the GI Bill did not represent a real federal financial aid program, there was considerable interest in starting a more general federal financial aid program in the second half of the 1940s. Reports of two commissions chartered to study possibilities for financial aid indicate the thinking of that time. First, the Committee on Student Personnel Work of the American Council on Education Studies concluded in 1946 that "today, the American public assumes that in a democracy, every mother's son (and every mother's daughter) is born with the inalienable right of opportunity to obtain a bachelor's degree or a diploma from the more recent junior colleges, regardless of his ability to pay for it" (Sharpe et al. 1946, 3–4). Despite this sentiment, the commission report recommended only that colleges and universities become more systematic and professional in the way they handled financial aid. Interestingly, work-study, not loans or grants, was the focus of this report. The authors of the report clearly thought of financial aid as an opportunity for the recipients to work their way through college.[7]

One year later, in 1947, a group with a different view of the potential for financial aid, the President's Commission on Higher Education, published its report. This commission saw equal educational opportunity "without regard to economic status, race, creed, color, sex, national origin, or ancestry" as "a major goal of American democracy" (U.S. President's Commission on Higher Education 1947, 3). The commission was convinced that existing financial aid practices were not meeting this goal. Moreover, the success of the students on the GI Bill convinced the commission that a higher percentage of the nation's youth could benefit from higher education. The commission was clear as to why many young people who would benefit from a college education were not getting one. "It must always be remembered that at least as many young people who have the same or greater intellectual ability than those now in college do not enroll because of low family income. This is the single most outstanding factor in the whole situation" (ibid., 6). The commission recommended a federally funded national scholarship program in which "the primary basis for determining the award of the scholarship to an individual student should be his financial need" (ibid., 54). As we know, this recommendation did not find its way into legislation for many years.

The College Scholarship Service

In 1953 and 1954, although the federal government was doing little to redress inequalities in educational opportunity, a group of colleges and universities acting together as members of the College Entrance Examination Board made considerable progress. In 1954 the College Board formed the College Scholarship Service (CSS) as a clearinghouse for information on the financial need of college students. The 155 member colleges and universities of the College Board included most of the private institutions with national reputations, and their decision to gather systematic financial information from college students and their parents represented an important step in the development of the current financial aid system. The speed with which the CSS was founded indicates that needs analysis was an idea whose time had come.[8] The first discussion in a symposium on scholarships took place in 1953, and the CSS was announced and in operation in 1954 (Fels 1954, 428–29).

The formation of the CSS was a major step for private institutions. The information it collected on the finances of the student and his or her parents allowed the CSS to determine the student's financial need. The CSS worked with the institutions to develop a common methodology for this calculation. In principle, if the colleges to which a student had applied used the CSS formulas to determine financial need and provided financial aid awards commensurate with this need, financial considerations would be removed from the student's decision about which college to attend. This represented the ideal for the colleges and universities that founded the CSS—to remove financial considerations from the college admission and college choice process. Under this plan, admissions would be based solely upon the academic qualifications of the student, and the college would provide a financial aid offer—a combination of grants, loans, and work-study—sufficient to meet all of the student's financial need.

The CSS system achieves the dual goals of a financial aid system—meeting need and rewarding talent (McPherson and Schapiro 1998, 5–14). The role of the CSS process in meeting need is obvious. Its role in rewarding talent relies on selective admissions. To the extent that the colleges and universities that attract the most applicants are the most well endowed institutions and provide the best educational opportunities, a selective admissions policy rewards the most talented students with admission to these institutions. The less talented students will be relegated to the less selective institutions. Thus, even without merit-based scholarships, there is a reward for the meritorious in this system.

The financial aid strategy for state-supported institutions is different from the private school model, which is frequently called the "high-tuition high-aid" model. In the "low-tuition low-aid" model of state schools, tuition is set so low that few students have financial need, and those students who do have financial need can be funded relatively easily. In essence, the low tuition in itself goes a long way toward meeting need.[9] The differences among the state-supported institutions combined with selective admissions allow this model to reward talent. The California system provides an example. The most talented students in California are rewarded with spaces at one of the campuses of the University of California (with some talent differentiation, probably favoring the Berkeley and Los Angeles campuses). Students with less talent are relegated to the Cal State system, and the junior colleges are on the bottom rung. The differences among the state-supported institutions are not as clear in many other states, but students in a particular state usually have an accurate understanding of the quality ranking of the state-supported institutions.

Unfortunately, both the high-tuition high-aid private institution model and the low-tuition low-aid public institution model represent ideals that are seldom met in actual practice. Only a few private colleges or universities are well enough endowed both to practice a need-blind admissions policy and to meet all of financial need of their students. Institutions react to their financial limitations one of two ways: Some maintain need-blind admissions and then make financial aid offers that do not meet all of a student's need. If the student still chooses to attend the institution, he or she, or his or her parents, either have to make a much larger than normal adjustment in their standard of living or incur a much larger than normal debt over the student's college career. Other institutions abandon need-blind admissions in favor of what is called a "need-aware" admission policy. In this situation, other things being equal, a student who does not apply for financial aid has a higher chance of admission than a student who does apply for financial aid.

State-supported institutions have different problems. The low-tuition low-aid ideal works only when both parts of the formula are present. Some states adopt policies that can be summarized as low-tuition no-aid policies. For some students the cost of room and board, books, and transportation generates a need for considerable aid. For these students, low tuition, or even no tuition, is not enough to make college affordable, and without financial aid these students face severely constrained choices. Other states have adopted policies that can be best summarized as high-tuition low-aid policies. In these states, state-supported colleges and universities are allowed to set tuition charges that rival those of private institutions, but they have meager financial aid budgets. These institutions have the same choices as private institutions with low financial aid budgets: either they must fail to meet all the financial need or they must adopt need-aware admissions. In either case, the system does not do a good job of eliminating economic considerations from the college attendance decision.

One reason the shift to a federal role in aiding students took so long is that it required a significant change in long-held attitudes. First, the prevalent notion of financial aid, to the extent that there was one, was based upon helping students get jobs to enable them to work their way through school. The sentiments behind Roosevelt's statement, "Just because a boy wants to go to college is no reason we [the federal government] should finance it," were common. Education was widely thought to be the financial responsibility of the person receiving the education. Second, and this was important in Congress, higher education, like primary and secondary education, was considered a state concern. George Washington had failed in his attempt to charter a national university. The Morrill-Wade Land Grant College Act of 1862 had had to fight off serious constitutional challenges. Federal programs that did benefit college students, such as the National Youth Administration work-study program during the depression or the GI Bill, had not been viewed as aid to education; the work-study program was part of a general relief effort, and the benefits of the GI Bill represented deferred compensation for veterans. Most people simply did not see a federal role in higher education.

Given these roadblocks, perhaps the proper question is not what took so long but rather what changed to bring about federal financial aid. There were four important factors. First, as the rhetoric of the 1947 report of the President's Commission on Higher Education indicates, some national leaders were willing to strongly espouse the notion of federal support for equal opportunity in higher education. Second, the demand for a college education grew dramatically in the postwar period. In 1946, 12.5 percent of eighteen- to twenty-four-year-olds were in college. By 1960 that number had grown to 22.2 percent (Bureau of the Census 1975, series H 701, 383). The consequences of this expansion were hard for members of Congress to ignore. Plainly, they would find themselves in greater and greater electoral peril if they ignored the problems of colleges and universities and their students and families.

Third, in 1958 Congress again became involved in financial aid, though through a back door. The launch of *Sputnik* by the Soviet Union in 1957 raised the fear that Americans were falling behind in science and engineering education. Congress responded with the National Defense Education Act of 1958, which created the National Defense Student Loan Program. (National Defense Student Loans are now called Perkins Loans.) Despite its small size, this program represents the first generally available student aid program. Finally, the landslide election of Lyndon B. Johnson as president and the Democratic Party to a substantial congressional majority in 1964 placed equal opportunity at center stage in the legislative agenda. The Equal Opportunity Act, which started the War on Poverty, passed in 1964, and 1965 saw passage of the Voting Rights Act, Medicare authorization, and the Elementary and Secondary Education Act as well as the Higher Education Act (Mumper 1996, 77).

From the Higher Education Act of 1965 to the Present

The Higher Education Act of 1965 is a complex bill containing eight titles: Community Service and Continuing Education Programs (Title I), College Library Assistance and Library Training and Research (Title II), Strengthening Developing Institutions (Title III), Student Assistance (Title IV), Teacher Programs (Title V), Financial Assistance for the Improvement of Undergraduate Instruction (Title VI), Amendments to the Higher Education Facilities Act of 1963 (Title VII), and General Provisions (Title VIII).

Title IV, with which we are concerned here, consists of four parts. Part A established Educational Opportunity Grants to "assist in making available the benefits of higher education to qualified high school graduates of exceptional financial need" (Public Law 89-329, Nov. 8, 1965, sec. 401). Although the federal government provided these grants, it was left to institutions to administer them, select the student recipients, and determine the amount of the grant, within certain limits.

Part B established the Guaranteed Student Loan Program, which included loan guarantees and interest subsidies. The actual loans were made by the private sector, but the federal government provided the lenders insurance in the case of default. Moreover, the government paid any interest on a Guaranteed Student Loan that accrued while a student was in college, and after the student left college the government paid the difference between the low interest rate set on the loan and the market interest rate. This interest subsidy eventually became quite expensive. In 1965, only students whose family incomes were below $15,000 could qualify for this aid.

Part C transferred the authority for the work-study program, established under Title I of the Economic Opportunity Act of 1964, from the Office of Economic Opportunity to the commissioner of education. Part D amended the National Defense Education Act of 1958, reauthorizing and expanding the National Defense Student Loan Program.

Debates Surrounding the Higher Education Act

Although the Higher Education Act of 1965 represented a major change in federal policy toward higher education finance, it marked the start of a process more than a completed policy.[10] The act embraced competing views of how higher education should be financed. One debate focused on the distinction between student aid and institutional aid. Most of the titles of the act provided institutional aid for particular purposes, for example, libraries and facilities; only Title IV provided aid to students. In fiscal year 1966, 68 percent of Higher Education Act funds were devoted to institutional aid and 32 percent to student aid (U.S. House of Representatives 1985).

A vigorous debate centering on student aid versus institutional aid continued after the passage of the Higher Education Act of 1965.[11] Even within the two camps there was considerable debate. Advocates of institutional aid argued over whether it should be categorical aid—for specific projects—or general aid—used at the institutions' discretion. Advocates of student aid argued over the mix of grants, loans, and work-study.

Participants also debated the relative merits of institutional and student aid—the approach taken in the Higher Education Act of 1965—as opposed to tax credits for educational expenses. One argument against tax credits is that they offer no help to the most needy families; they defray educational costs only for those with tax liabilities. Nevertheless, middle-class families were also concerned about the rising costs of higher education, and middle-class families represent a significant proportion of the vote in any election. During the debates over the Higher Education Act in 1965, there was considerable pressure for tax cuts. Senator Abraham Ribicoff of Connecticut had introduced a bill authorizing tax credits for tuition payments. Modern observers generally agree that the Guaranteed Student Loan Program was established to gain support from members of Congress sympathetic to the difficulties of middle-class families—the same group to which tax credits had considerable appeal. Guaranteed student loans were "designed by the Johnson Administration and incorporated in the Higher Education Act as a way to help defuse the tax credit movement, led by Senator Abraham Ribicoff of Connecticut" (Gladieux and Wolanin 1976, 41).

The debate over institutional aid versus student aid was complex and at times convoluted. Individuals often favored more than one kind of aid. The short papers from a symposium on financing higher education sponsored by the Carnegie Commission on Higher Education in 1968 provide interesting examples of the thinking at the time. Clark Kerr, the former president of the University of California at Berkeley and a participant in the conference, summarizes his thinking as follows: "I would presently suggest rejection of two alternatives (tax relief, grants to states), acceptance of two others (aid to students, categorical programs), and careful study of the fifth (aid to institutions-as-such)" (Kerr 1968, 103).

Others showed more enthusiasm for general aid to institutions. Charles J. Hitch, at the time the president of the University of California at Berkeley, argued that a "federal subsidy for each student could be made to the institution" (Hitch 1968, 126–27). Malcolm Moos (1968), the president of the University of Minnesota, and David B. Truman (1968), the provost at Columbia University, also favored general grants to institutions. Milton Friedman, a professor of economics at the University of Chicago, James S. Coleman, a professor of social relations at Johns Hopkins University, and Roger E. Bolton, a professor of economics at Williams College, all supported student aid but not general aid for institutions (Truman 1968; Friedman 1968; Coleman 1968; Bolton 1968). Interestingly, a 1972 report of the Carnegie Commission on Higher Education recommends a federal support package that includes general aid (Carnegie Commission on Higher Education 1972).

In the long run the proponents of student aid won the debate. Some categorical institutional aid remains in the Higher Education Act, but the federal government has not become involved in general aid to institutions of higher education. There are several reasons for this victory. First, an argument based on economic efficiency makes a strong case against general aid. According to this view the fundamental question concerns the benefits of education. The benefits of an education flow to the individual being educated and to the society in differing amounts, depending upon the level of the education. Basic economics suggests that if the benefits of education accrue mostly to the individual, in terms of enjoyment of the education and higher future earnings, then the individual should bear most of the cost of the education. In contrast, if most of the benefits flow to the society, in terms of creating a literate, law-abiding citizenry able to participate in a democracy, then most of the costs should fall on the citizens as taxpayers. Although there is not unanimity about the magnitudes involved, most evidence suggests that the benefits of higher education accrue primarily to the individual, whereas the benefits of primary and secondary education accrue more to society.[12] Following this logic, large general public subsidies to primary and secondary education are efficient, but large general public subsidies to higher education are not.

The efficiency argument recognizes that some of the benefits of higher education do in fact accrue to the society. In this case, a system relying solely on private decision making would lead to less than the optimal amount of higher education. This suggests some government subsidies for higher education. Advocates of need-based student aid argue that the government subsidies should be targeted so as to have the maximal effect in expanding higher education. General subsidies to institutions allow the institutions to offer the education at a lower price, spreading the government subsidy broadly. In this case, many of the individuals receiving the government subsidy would have been more than willing to pay the unsubsidized price of a higher education.[13] These individuals receive a benefit from the government subsidy, but the government subsidy does not change their behavior. Because many of the recipients of need-based financial aid would not have gone to college without it, government funds used in this way affect behavior in the desired way.

These efficiency arguments can be similarly applied to state support for higher education. Unlike the federal government, most state governments give general aid to institutions. The low-tuition low-aid strategies pursued by many states rely on large amounts of general aid for state-supported institutions. Many have pointed out the problems involved with this approach. Milton Friedman asks, "Why should the families in Watts pay taxes to subsidize the families in Beverly Hills who send their children to UCLA?" (Friedman 1968, 108). Why did the federal government decide not to provide general aid to institutions while many states made just the opposite decision?

The answer to this question probably has more to do with politics than policy analysis. First, in most political situations the status quo has the advantage. Once benefits to voters are in place, it is difficult for governments to take them away. By chartering and supporting institutions in their states, states had, from the very start, provided general subsidies. In contrast, the federal government had no history of general subsidies. Second, student aid skirts some thorny political issues at the federal level. Given the large number of church-related colleges and universities, direct federal support of all colleges and universities would raise difficult issues of the separation of church and state. Direct state support of state institutions avoids this difficulty. Moreover, to the extent that direct federal aid to colleges and universities involved federal control of how those dollars are spent, the federal government could have been accused of infringing on state prerogatives. Finally, direct federal aid would have required choices among institutions, and such choices would have been politically perilous (Finn 1978, 61–62).

Of course, as is the case with most political victories, the victory of student aid over institutional aid was not complete. In fiscal year 1966, 32 percent of the authorizations in the Higher Education Act were for student aid. By fiscal year 1986 this percentage was 90 percent (Keppel 1987, 56). The institutional aid that remained was narrowly targeted aid for particular purposes, not general aid.

Flaws in the 1965 Act

As the time for the debate on the reauthorization of the Higher Education Act approached in 1972, there were several concerns about the way in which the student assistance programs were working. Title IV used a campus-based model for financial aid. The act details how federal funds are to be allocated to individual institutions, both state supported and private (nonprofit). Decisions about the recipients and the actual amount of loans or grants, though constrained by limits written into the law, were made on the campus.

The flaws in this campus-based model became apparent as policy makers observed it in action. The model created a short-term problem for many institutions. To use the federal funds, institutions had to be able to determine the financial need of their students. This required little if any work for the private institutions that participated in the programs of the College Scholarship Service, but other institutions had to set up financial aid bureaucracies on campus. Determining students' and their parents' ability to pay is a complex matter, and, not surprisingly, institutions used different criteria to determine financial need. This caused concern because a particular student could be treated quite differently by different institutions.

Second, with campus-based financial aid, a student had to be admitted to a college or university before he or she could determine how much and what kind of financial aid would be available. A 1969 report from the Department of Health, Education, and Welfare saw this as a major flaw.

Moreover, these programs [Title IV] contain a more fundamental limitation which cannot be removed without changes in their structure: They do not dramatically and clearly indicate that the Federal Government has established a policy of removing financial barriers to college attendance. Under existing programs lower-income students must first apply to specific schools in order to try to qualify for aid, yet we know that high school performance (and graduation) is affected by students' perceptions of college costs while they are still in the early grades of high school. (U.S. Department of Health, Education, and Welfare 1969, 9)

The third flaw in the campus-based programs is that the funds were allocated to the states for distribution to the colleges and universities within the state based upon the percentage of the national full-time college enrollment from that state (Public Law 89-329, Nov. 8, 1965, sec. 405). This mechanism does not take need into consideration. Because there was considerable variation in average income from one state to another, the percentage of financial need covered by the state's allocation varied across states. With this design, federal aid covered a lower percentage of the need of a poor student from a poor state than that of a poor student from a rich state.

The 1972 Reauthorization

Senator Claiborne Pell, the chair of the Senate Subcommittee on the Arts and Humanities, took the lead in the reauthorization process in 1972 by proposing a new type of grant. The Basic Economic Opportunity Grant, which in 1980 became known as the Pell Grant, was larger than the old Educational Opportunity Grant and was administered in Washington, not on institution campuses. The design of the Pell Grant addressed the three problems noted above. All decisions about need were made centrally; a student could know about Pell Grant eligibility before applying to college; and the amount of federal student aid from this source flowing to a state was related to the need of the students in that state. In 1972, the maximum for the Pell Grant was set at $1,400. In addition, no student could receive a grant larger than one-half of the cost of attendance, which was calculated as the combined cost of room and board, books, transportation, tuition, and fees.

In the 1972 reauthorization, Congress decided to retain the existing campus-based programs. The reauthorization combined the existing programs with the Pell Grants in much the same fashion that in 1965 the existing National Defense Student Loans and the work-study program had been combined with the new programs. The only change in the campus-based programs was that the grant was renamed the Supplemental Educational Opportunity Grant (SEOG) to distinguish it from the Basic Educational Opportunity Grant (BEOG), the original name for the Pell Grant.

The 1972 bill also established the State Student Incentive Grant Program (SSIG). The program, which provided matching funds for state-operated need-based financial aid programs, enjoyed a considerable degree of success: "In 1965, only about ten states had programs which provided aid to low-income students. Under the stimulus of the SSIG, such state aid increased rapidly. By 1975, all fifty states were operating student aid programs that would qualify for federal SSIG grants" (Mumper 1996, 84).

The 1972 reauthorization also broadened the eligibility for Title IV programs by substituting the term *postsecondary education* for the term *higher education*. "The intent was to break the stereotype that education beyond high school meant full-time attendance in a four-year academic program leading to a baccalaureate degree" (Gladieux and Hauptman 1995, 16). This represented more than a change in language, as proprietary trade schools thereby became eligible for all the Title IV programs. This change had a profound effect on the trade school sector. Moreover, the requirement that federal aid recipients had to be high school graduates was eliminated, giving a large boost to these schools.

Changes in Federal Programs after 1972

With the reauthorization of the Higher Education Act in 1972 the major student aid programs that currently exist were in place. Some names were changed along the way, honoring various members of Congress: the BEOG became the Pell Grant, the Guaranteed Student Loan became the Stafford Loan, and the National Defense Student Loan became the Perkins Loan.

In 1980, with the initiation of the Parent Loans for Undergraduate Students Program, parents as well as students became eligible for government-subsidized loans for education. In the same year, graduate and undergraduate students not financially dependent on their parents could get government-subsidized loans from the Supplemental Loans for Students Program. Other than these changes, since 1972 the debates over student aid, though at times heated, have involved modifications in detail, not wholesale changes.

The Middle-Income Student Assistance Act (MISAA) of 1978 was the Carter administration's response to yet another tuition tax credit plan that had developed momentum in Congress. The MISAA was being considered at the same time as the tax credit bill, and the competition between the two proposals yielded generous benefits to the middle class. The MISAA widened the eligibility for Pell Grants, increasing the limit on family income to $26,000 from the previous limit of $15,000, and removed the income ceiling for guaranteed student loans, making all students eligible.

The election of Ronald Reagan in 1980 brought changes in student aid just as it did to many other domestic spending programs. In 1981 need was reintroduced into the guaranteed student loan program, and a 5 percent origination fee for these loans was imposed. As part of the Reagan administration's attack on all domestic spending, total spending for student aid leveled off in the early 1980s.

The combination of the slowing of the growth of student aid spending and continued growth in the demand for Stafford Loans caused an increase in the ratio of loan spending to grant spending. This shift toward loans away from grants was a natural part of the budgetary process. Francis Keppel, a former U.S. commissioner of education, explains the effects of the increases in student loans as follows: "The budgetary process required that costs of loan eligibility be joined with annual appropriations for the Title IV program in calculating the total appropriation for student aid. It was inevitable that the uncontrollable costs of loans (because of their less predictable long-term costs to government) would affect the controllable appropriations for grants or other aid" (Keppel 1987, 57).

In effect, Keppel's claim is that this budgetary process makes Stafford Loans an entitlement and accomplishes a transfer from the poor to the middle class. As the government has to allocate more of a fixed budget to cover loans for which many students from middle-class families qualify, the portion of the budget left over for the grants that are needed by students from poor families shrinks. High tuition increases combined with growing college participation rates clearly have driven up the demand for loans. The data since 1980 indicate the result of the budgetary process, a shift from grants toward loans. This fact has been the subject of considerable concern.[14]

The Antitrust Investigation of the Overlap Group

In 1958, four years after the founding of the College Scholarship Service, twenty-three institutions formed what became known as the Overlap Group.[15] These institutions met annually to compare the financial aid offers made to students who had been admitted to more than one of the institutions. The objective of the group was to eliminate differences in financial aid offers so that such offers would be made entirely on the basis of need. In the view of the U.S. Department of Justice, the members of the Overlap Group were fixing prices in violation of the Sherman Antitrust Act, and in July 1989, the department's Antitrust Division initiated an investigation of the group.

In March 1991, under pressure from the Justice Department, the Overlap Group decided to suspend its annual spring meeting. In May of the same year, the eight members of the Ivy League, all members of the Overlap Group, agreed to stop sharing financial aid information on students—on the same day the Justice Department formally charged Massachusetts Institute of Technology (MIT) with violations of the antitrust laws. In June 1992, a trial on the charges against MIT began in federal district court in Philadelphia, and in September, Judge Louis C. Bechtle ruled against MIT.[16] MIT appealed Judge Bechtle's decision, and the following September, in 1993, the appeals court ruled that the Judge Bechtle had "not adequately considered MIT's arguments about the benefits of the [Overlap] group" (Jaschik 1993, A25). The judges on the appeals court did, however, reject MIT's claim that its tuition setting and financial aid policies should be exempt from federal antitrust laws. In the new trial MIT had to argue that the Overlap Group process was the only way to achieve its goals. The case was finally settled with an agreement that allowed institutions to communicate with one another about financial aid policy but explicitly excluded discussions of financial aid awards to individual students.

The downfall of the Overlap Group has been blamed for the advent of a much more competitive environment in financial aid among selective institutions (Gose 2000). Many commentators point to the antitrust case as one of the factors that has lead to increases in the amount of merit-based aid used by private institutions. From the perspective of the antitrust laws, this competition is just what was desired. Ronald Ehrenberg gives an interesting example of how the competition works: "By the late 1990s, several [institutions], including Harvard and Carnegie-Mellon, actually were inviting accepted applicants to inform them about offers elsewhere. During 1997–98, Carnegie-Mellon had about 800 competitive offers faxed to it, and it responded by increasing the size of the grant that it offered in about 460 cases. Dialing for dollars, the shopping around to get institutions to improve their financial aid offers, has become a widely practiced strategy by admitted students and their families" (Ehrenberg 2000, 78). From the viewpoint of many college administrators, this is precisely the outcome they had feared.

The 568 Presidents' Working Group

In 1992, under Section 568 of the Improving America's Schools Act, Congress allowed colleges and universities to get together to discuss financial aid policy. Since then, a group of college and university presidents from private institutions that practice need-blind admissions have been meeting for several years to discuss financial aid policy. This group calls itself the 568 Presidents' Working Group (see Burd 2001).

In July 2001, the 568 Presidents' Working Group announced that twenty-eight of its member institutions had agreed to adopt a common set of rules for determining financial need (Hoover 2001).[17] This contract addresses part of the competition that cropped up after the breakup of the Overlap Group. The institutions agreeing to the common rules for financial need are quite different from those in the Overlap Group. Only eleven of the Overlap Group members—Amherst, Bowdoin, Columbia, Cornell, MIT, Middlebury, Penn, Wellesley, Wesleyan, Williams, and Yale—are in the new group.[18] Interestingly, four of the Ivy League members of the Overlap Group—Brown, Dartmouth, Harvard, and Princeton—are not in the new group. The Overlap Group included only New England institutions, but the 568 Presidents' Working Group has much more geographical diversity. It will be interesting to see if the number of institutions who eventually adopt the common rules for determining financial need grows or shrinks as time passes.

Federal Programs in the 1990s

Three changes in 1992 are worth noting. First, the 1992 legislation increased the limits on the amount a student could borrow and created unsubsidized Stafford Loans. These loans were designed to give more access to credit to students who did not qualify for need-based subsidized Stafford Loans. The new loans were similar to the old, with two exceptions: the government did not pay the interest cost when the borrower was in school, and the borrower had to pay market interest rates. Second, the legislation established a consolidated federal methodology for determining need, one that applied to all Title IV programs. The new methodology dramatically reduced the expected family and student contributions, making many more students eligible for aid. One of the ways in which this liberalization was accomplished was by eliminating the value of the family's principal residence from assets in the formula determining the expected family contribution. Third, Congress authorized a small demonstration project involving direct government loans in contrast with the system in place, under which the loans were made by private financial institutions.

The net effect of the first three changes—increased loan limits, the new unsubsidized loans, and the changes in the expected student and family contribution—was another increase in the demand for loans. Because there had been only limited increases in the overall funding for Title IV programs, this increase in demand led to a further shift in the program mix toward loans. Figure 2.2 tracks the share of loans, grants, and work-study as a percentage of total federal financial aid awarded from 1971 to 1999. The widening of the gap between loans and grants has been pronounced, especially at two points. The first accompanied the passage of the MISAA in 1978, which broadened the eligibility for Pell Grants and extended loan eligibility to all students; the second occurred in 1993, after the increase in borrowing limits and the advent of unsubsidized loans.

The Student Loan Reform Act of 1993 required the Department of Education to offer income-contingent loans. In essence, this program makes the percentage of the loan that a student repays contingent on his or her postcollege income, with high-income students repaying more of their loans than low-income students. This program has never been widely used.

Tax Credits

In 1997, tax credits for higher education expenses finally became law. The Clinton administration and Congress created the Hope Scholarship Credit for the first two years of higher education and Lifetime Learning Credits for the remaining years of higher education. As noted in chapter 1, these two tax credits represent the first generally available federal financial aid that

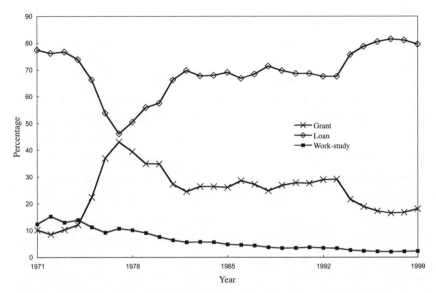

FIGURE 2.2. Federal Financial Aid Awards as Loans, Grants, and Work-Study, 1971–1999. *Source:* Data from College Board 1999b.

is not need based. In addition, the 1997 tax credit legislation made interest payments on student loans tax deductible.

The 1998 reauthorization of the Higher Education Act made no fundamental changes in the structure of financial aid. The 1992 demonstration program for direct government loans, which had become the William D. Ford Direct Loan Program, now shares student loans with the Stafford Loan program. Before the reauthorization there had been some fear that congressional Republicans, who favored the traditional approach using private lenders, and the Clinton administration, which favored the direct loans, might clash, but the parties reached a compromise early in the reauthorization process (Burd 1998b). The reauthorization raised the maximum Pell Grant dramatically, from $3,000 a year to an eventual $5,800 a year for 2003–4. The reauthorization also reduced the interest rates on new Stafford and Ford Loans. Otherwise the changes were minor.[19]

State Merit Scholarships

A final significant change in the financial aid system has been the rise of merit-based scholarships financed by state governments. Georgia started this practice in 1993 with its HOPE Scholarship Program, which awards a scholarship covering full tuition at state-supported college or university to any Georgia student who has a certain minimum grade point average. By 2001 thirteen states had similar broad-based merit scholarship programs.[20]

These merit-based scholarships are politically popular. Several other states are considering the institution of similar programs. These programs are partly an expansion of financial aid, but there is considerable evidence that they are also squeezing out need-based aid. Jeffrey Selingo (2001) estimates that these thirteen states are spending roughly twice as much on these programs as they do on need-based financial aid programs. McPherson and Schapiro present data that suggest that these state plans are part of a broader growth in merit-based financial aid throughout the higher education system (McPherson and Schapiro 1998, 119).

Conclusions and a Look Ahead

Many commentators have marveled at the variety of ways in which financial aid is provided in the United States. The financial aid system, if one can use that word, is an amalgam of state programs, federal programs and tax credits, practices of private institutions, and programs of some private foundations and charities. The result is a bewildering maze of programs and options. Janet S. Hansen is too kind when she says the system is "not the result of a grand design"; Charles T. Clotfelter is closer in likening the financial aid system to "a Rube Goldberg machine" (Hansen 1991, 6; Clotfelter 1991, 90).

Since 1965 the federal government has played an increasing role in financial aid for higher education. Clearly, part of the complexity of the system derives from the government's unwillingness to consolidate programs. In large measure, the rationale for the 1972 creation of the Pell Grant was that would cure widely recognized flaws in the Economic Opportunity Grants created in 1965. One might expect that the birth of the Pell Grant would thus have coincided with the death of the Economic Opportunity Grant; but one would be wrong. Economic Opportunity Grants continued; they simply changed their name to Supplemental Economic Opportunity Grants. In addition, the 1972 legislation created a third set of grant programs encouraging states to give grants that would be matched with federal dollars in the form of State Student Incentive Grants. A similar situation obtains with federal loans, of which there are now four different types: the Perkins Loan, the Family Education Loan, the Parent Loan for Undergraduate Students, and the William D. Ford Direct Loan. Finally, in 1997, tax credits were added to the mix.

State financial aid practices add a further layer of complexity. States have widely divergent tuition and financial aid policies. Some have generous financial aid systems that provide aid to students attending both public and private institutions in the state; others provide aid only to students attending state-supported institutions. In most cases, most aid awarded by state governments is in the form of general institutional aid, not direct financial aid to students. This general institutional aid allows the state-supported institution to offer an education at a tuition that represents a significant discount over the cost of providing the education.

There is considerable variation in the way private colleges and universities use financial aid. The premier institutions, the Ivy League and other well-endowed institutions, practice need-blind admissions and provide student aid that meets all financial need. The downfall of the Overlap Group made this effort much less well coordinated than it had been, and there is some evidence that the need-only philosophy of some of these schools is breaking down. Other private institutions follow different financial aid strategies. Increasingly, some are using financial aid strategically to manage the size of their student bodies and, with the use of merit-based aid, to attempt to increase the quality of their student bodies.[21] Financial aid is a major expense of private institutions no matter what type of strategy they employ. In addition, private institutions almost always have endowments, though a small number hold the major part of endowment funds. The earnings on these endowments are used in much the same way that state-supported institutions use state appropriations. Endowment earnings are a general subsidy that allows the institutions to charge tuition that is less than the cost of providing the education.[22]

The final players, who are often ignored in discussions of financial aid policy, are the private foundations and other charities that sponsor scholarships. Many local groups, some businesses, and a few national foundations offer scholarships mostly to students with exceptional merit. National Merit Scholarships are the most well known, but there are many more. For example, civic organizations such as Rotary Clubs and Lions Clubs award scholarships to meritorious high school graduates in almost every community in the United States. A number of firms have scholarships for the children of their workers. Often these scholarships are not large, but they can be important for the recipient.

Despite its complexity, the current financial aid system does operate. Does it do a good job of providing aid to students? In the chapter that follows I highlight two studies that clearly demonstrate that the answer is no. This look at the poor performance of the system guides the suggestions for redesign given in subsequent chapters.

The Financial Aid System: How It Works and How Well It Works

In broad outline, the financial aid decision process is straightforward. A student applying for financial aid provides information on income and assets. The government and institutions use this information to determine how much the student, and his or her family, can be expected to contribute toward college costs. If the cost of attendance exceeds the expected family contribution, the financial aid officer makes a financial aid offer to the student. Because the federal government is a major contributor in the financial aid process, specific federal rules and definitions constrain the process. Nevertheless, an institution's financial aid officer has considerable latitude for action.

Determining the Expected Family Contribution

In 1992, Congress established a consolidated methodology for determining the expected family contribution (EFC). This methodology is used to determine eligibility for all of the federal financial aid programs: Perkins Loans, Stafford Loans, Pell Grants, Supplemental Educational Opportunity Grants, and Work-Study. The calculations use the information collected on the Free Application for Federal Student Aid (FAFSA), which asks questions about the composition of the family, the parents' and student's income, and the parents' and student's assets. Because the FAFSA contains questions that can be answered only after the respondent has calculated his or her federal income taxes, it is normally completed in January or February for financial aid to be received in the following academic year.

For the purpose of making financial aid awards with their own funds, some institutions require information in addition to that queried on the FAFSA. To gather this information, these institutions use forms provided by the College Scholarship Service or their own financial aid applications. In most cases, the additional information relates to the family's assets; there is very little detailed asset information on the FAFSA.

The appendix at the end of this chapter contains a description of the federal methodology for calculation of the EFC.[1] The calculations are designed to determine the amount a family can contribute for the student's college expenses from the income and assets of the parents and the student. The calculation for income deducts an amount to account for normal expenses such as taxes, family upkeep, and expenses involved with employment. The calculation for assets starts with the net worth of the parents and deducts an "education savings and asset protection allowance"; it then determines a contribution from assets as 12 percent of the difference. The final calculation combines available income and the contribution from assets to arrive at the adjusted available income. The parents' contribution to the EFC is based upon a progressive formula.[2] Student's income and assets are treated in a similar fashion except that greater percentages of student income—50 percent of income after allowances—and a greater percentage of assets—35 percent of net worth—are included in the expected contribution of the student. A family's EFC is the sum of the expected contribution of the parents and the student.[3]

Figure 3.1 illustrates the results of EFC calculations. The graph lines represent income and asset combinations that yield a particular EFC for the academic year 1999–2000. The example used for these calculations is a family made up of two working forty-five-year-old parents who earn equal incomes and a student who has no income and no assets. This family was assumed to take the standard deduction on their federal income tax and to live in Virginia (for the purpose of determining the allowance for state taxes). The lines are downward sloping because as income increases, the amount of assets required to yield a particular EFC declines. Each line has a kink at an asset level of $42,500, the asset protection allowance for a family in which the age of the oldest parent is forty-five. Such a family has to have assets above $42,500

Assets = house, car, any other things

So where is that defined on an aid applicant?

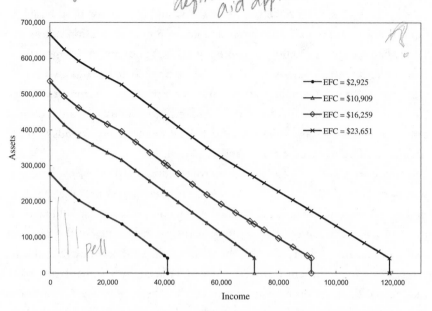

pell

FIGURE 3.1. Contours of Equal Expected Family Contribution, 1999 (dollars),
Source: Data from U.S. Department of Education 1999a; College Board 1999a, 5.

Note: The EFC cutoffs are determined as follows: $2,925 is the highest EFC at which a student was eligible for a Pell Grant for the 1999–2000 academic year; $10,909 was the average budget for an in-state resident student at a four-year public institution; $16,259 was the average budget for an out-of-state resident student at a four-year public institution; and $23,651 was the average budget for a resident student at a four-year private institution.

before assets affect the EFC. Changes in the federal income tax rates, state tax rates, and the effect of additional income in the EFC formula cause the other changes in the slopes in the lines (see the appendix for more details).

The lowest line in the figure represents an estimated family contribution of $2,925, the threshold for Pell Grant eligibility. Students from families with income and asset combinations below or to the left of this line were eligible for a Pell Grant, and students from families with income and asset combinations above or to the right of this line were not. The other lines are contours for higher EFC values.

Income data help put the figure's contours in context. The estimated median family income for 1998–99 was $47,193 (College Board 1999a, 15). A student from a family with this income would not qualify for a Pell Grant.

As the figure illustrates, however, he or she would qualify for need-based financial aid as an in-state student at a state-supported institution unless the family had roughly $150,000 in qualifying assets.[4] The contours demonstrate that students with incomes well above the median income can qualify for federal financial aid, particularly if they attend a private institution or a state-supported institution as an out-of-state student. Federal financial aid is clearly not reserved for the poor. Eligibility for federal financial aid extends to middle-class and upper-middle-class families as well.

As Aaron S. Edlin (1993) and Martin Feldstein (1995) emphasize, one way to think of the EFC is as a tax system. The government uses the EFC formulas to determine how much of a family's income and assets should be used to cover college expenses. A quick look at the marginal rates of this tax system is informative.[5] First, consider the effect on the EFC of an extra dollar of assets. For purposes of illustration, assume that the family has qualifying assets that exceed the asset protection allowance, that these assets earn on average 6 percent in interest or dividend income, and that their income is high enough that they face the highest marginal effect of resources on EFC. With these assumptions, the marginal tax rate on an extra dollar of assets is 8.46 percent.[6] For lower incomes, the marginal effect of asset increases is less than 8.46 percent. This is the marginal tax rate on assets for the first year the student is in college. The assets will also be taxed the second, third, and fourth year the student is in college. Thus a dollar in assets will fall to 91.54 cents after the first year, 83.80 cents after the second year, 76.71 cents after the third year, and 70.22 cents after the fourth year.[7] This process would continue if the family had the misfortune to have another child who entered college as the first one left.

The tax rates on parent's assets are low, however, compared with the tax rates on student assets. The student's contribution from assets is 35 percent of net worth, compared with the 12 percent for parents, and it is added directly to the EFC—that is, it is not affected by the progressive formulas applied to parents' income and assets.[8] As a result, the increase in the EFC for a one-dollar increase in student assets is much larger than the effect of a one-dollar increase in parental assets. This tax rate would apply every year the student is in college. Clearly, a parent who understood the EFC formula would think

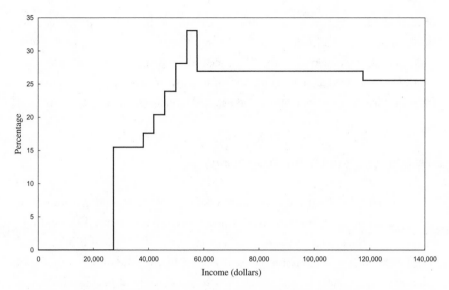

FIGURE 3.2. Effect of Income Increases on Expected Family Contribution, 1999
Source: Data from U.S. Department of Education 1999a, EFC formula for
1999–2000.

twice about saving for college expenses in a savings account in his or her student's name.[9]

Figure 3.2 shows the effect of an extra dollar of income on the EFC for various income levels based on the same example used to construct figure 3.1.[10] The shape of the graph line is unusual. Up to $57,550 in income, it is what one would expect: the marginal effect of an increase in income on EFC is zero for low incomes and then increases sharply as income begins to increase. In this example, the highest marginal effect of 33.06 percent applies to incomes between $53,845 and $57,550. This represents a very high marginal tax rate. Within this income range, every extra dollar earned reduces the potential financial aid award of a student by 33 cents. The reduction in the marginal effects at higher incomes results from increases in federal income tax rates. Federal income tax payments are an allowable expense, and as allowable expenses go up, the EFC goes down.

Federal financial aid is based on the financial need of the student, and financial need depends, in part, on the cost of attendance.[11] For the purposes of the federal programs, the major components of the cost of attendance are tuition and fees; an allowance for books, supplies, transportation, and miscellaneous personal expenses;[12] an allowance for room and board; and cost of dependent care if needed. The regulations also allow for special circumstances—for example, the extra expenses of a disabled student or the extra expenses of a student studying abroad.

Determining a Financial Aid Package

The difference between the cost of attendance and the student's resources is the financial need of the student. A student's resources are the EFC and any financial aid the student has received. For example, if a student is a National Merit Scholar, the scholarship stipend is part of the student's resources. In addition, as the financial aid officer creates a financial aid package for a student, he or she has to include the aid already in the package as a resource in making decisions on further eligibility. According to the regulations that govern the various programs, the financial aid officer should make every effort to avoid making awards in excess of need, and they include provisions for repayments if such awards do occur.

Pell Grants

The Pell Grant is generally the first program a financial aid officer considers. For the 1999–2000 school year, all full-time students with an EFC of $2,925 or lower qualified for a Pell Grant. The Pell Grant payment schedule is designed to raise the resources available to the student (EFC plus Pell Grant) up to the cost of attendance or roughly $3,125, whichever is higher. The asset and income combinations that determine the threshold of eligibility for a Pell Grant are presented in figure 3.1.

The cost of attendance and the EFC alone determine the amount of a Pell Grant. Therefore, the Pell Grant program, unlike the other federal student aid programs, will tolerate awards in excess of need. In other words, the recipient of a large scholarship can still qualify for a Pell Grant even if the combination of the student's EFC, the Pell Grant, and the scholarship exceed the student's cost of attendance. The federal government usually is able to provide funds for all those who are eligible for Pell Grants, but in some years it has been unable to fund a Pell Grant as large as the specified maximum. In any case, institutions have every incentive to use as much as is available in the form of Pell Grants for all eligible students.

After determining Pell Grant eligibility, the order in which a financial aid officer builds a financial aid package varies considerably by institution. Each institution has its own sources of financial aid, some of which have specific requirements; some grants, for example, are reserved for students from a particular county or for students studying a particular major. After considering these special sources of aid, the institution develops the financial aid package that includes all of the federal sources at its disposal.

Stafford Loans

The Stafford Loan Program is the largest federal program. If the student's resources, EFC, and other financial aid total less than the cost of attendance, the student is eligible for a subsidized Stafford Loan. Stafford Loans are financed in two ways: as Federal Family Education Loans, which are made by private institutions, or as William D. Ford Direct Loans, which are made by the federal government. The regulations for these two programs are identical. For dependent undergraduates, subsidized Stafford Loans are limited to $2,625 for first-year students, $3,500 for second-year students, and $5,500 for those who have completed two years of study. Independent students and students whose parents do not qualify (because of poor credit ratings) for Parent Loans for Undergraduate Students (PLUS) can qualify for larger loan amounts, but the limits given above for dependent students are the limits for the amount of these loans that can be subsidized. Unsubsidized Stafford Loans are not based upon financial need, and they accrue interest while students are attending college. Students can avoid actually paying this interest while in college by having the interest capitalized in the loan value until they start to repay the loan upon graduation. The total debt a dependent undergraduate student can have in subsidized or unsubsidized Stafford Loans is limited to $23,000.[13]

Campus-Based Programs

The campus-based programs represent federal funds that are given to institutions. These funds are reserved for students with demonstrated financial need, and the programs limit the amount an individual student can receive. Within these constraints institutions are free to disburse funds in these programs as they see fit.

Supplemental Educational Opportunity Grants (SEOGs) are awarded to students with the most need. The program gives priority to those who have received Pell Grants and still have unmet financial need. The maximum grant from the SEOG program is $4,000. Because each institution has a fixed amount of money for these grants, there is no guarantee that every eligible student will be able to participate in this program.

Similarly, a college or university has a fixed budget for work-study. Most of the work-study jobs are on campus, though there are some jobs at nonprofit organizations or public agencies. There is no maximum for a work-study award, but a financial aid officer has to be sensitive to the amount of time that a full-time student can be expected to spend at a job.

Perkins Loans are heavily subsidized. They award a maximum of $3,000 a year and $15,000 over the course of an undergraduate career. Each institution participating in the program has a limited amount of funds that it can loan under this program. A student starts repaying any Perkins Loans nine months after he or she is graduated (or drops out of school or falls below half-time attendance).

Parent Loans

The other program students and parents need to consider, though it is technically not financial aid, is the PLUS program. Creditworthy parents can use this program to borrow up to the amount of unmet financial need—that is, the cost of attendance minus any financial aid award. The interest on PLUS loans is variable but is capped at 9 percent. Repayment of PLUS loans begins within sixty days after the final loan disbursement for the academic year.

TABLE 3.1.   Federal Financial Aid Awarded, 1998–1999

Program	Funds Awarded (millions of dollars)	Recipients (thousands)	Average Award (dollars)
Pell Grant	7,241	3,874	1,869
Stafford Loan			
Subsidized	18,009	5,174	3,499
Unsubsidized	12,256	3,154	3,886
Campus-based			
SEOG	591	1,109	533
Work-study	1,002	892	1,123
Perkins Loan	1,058	698	1,516
PLUS Loan	3,396	525	6,469

Source: Data from College Board 1999b, 6.

Size of the Federal Programs

Table 3.1 gives a review of the size of the various federal programs. Clearly, the loan programs are much larger than the grant programs. Both in terms of number of recipients and average award, the Pell Grant and Stafford Loans are much larger than the campus-based programs.

The emphasis on student loans in federal programs has been of great concern to public policy analysts, although its importance does not seem to be appreciated by the general public. A majority of the respondents to a survey conducted by the American Council on Education in 1998 thought of college financial aid as excluding student loans.[14] This result is consistent with the general level of ignorance about financial aid found in the survey. Stanley Ikenberry and Terry Hartle, reporting on the same survey, note that "many focus group participants were reluctant to see federal student loans as a form of financial aid. Even when they were told that the loans carried a subsidized interest rate that lowered costs to borrowers sharply, some still refused to see this as aid because it comes with a string attached" (Ikenberry and Hartle 1998, 10–11).

Maximum Federal Assistance

With the exception of the work-study program, each federal student aid program has a maximum benefit. Consider a first-year student with an EFC of zero. For the 1999–2000 academic year he or she was eligible for the maximum Pell Grant of $3,125, the maximum SEOG of $4,000, the maximum Perkins Loan of $3,000, and the maximum Stafford Loan of $2,625. The maximum federal loan and grant award to this student would have been $12,750.[15] If the student's cost of attendance exceeded $12,750, he or she would have had to make up the difference with work-study, some institutional source of financial aid, assistance from the student's state, a PLUS loan for his or her parents, or some other means of finance. Less than one-half of the total—only the $5,750 from the Pell Grant and the Stafford Loan—would have been guaranteed to the student.[16] Depending upon the other demands on the institution's funds, the SEOG and the Perkins Loan may not always be available.

The $5,750 is an important number; it is the base guarantee of federal financial aid system for a first-year student. Any full-time student with established financial need would have had a Pell Grant, or some combination of a Pell Grant and an expected family contribution of $3,125, and would also have qualified for a subsidized loan of $2,625. This guarantee of $5,750 should be compared with the average budgets of full-time students of $10,909 for an in-state resident student at a state-supported institution, $16,259 for an out-of-state student at a state-supported institution, and $23,651 for a student at a private institution. The base federal guarantee leaves a considerable gap in every case. Few students actually have an EFC of zero, but this guarantee represents the guarantee for all Pell Grant recipients, and in 1998–99 more than 3.8 million students received Pell Grants. Other financial assistance is clearly needed. The amount that a particular institution can add depends upon the student's need and the institution's resources from federal, state, and internal funds.

Grants at Private Institutions

The federal guarantee, or even the hypothetical maximum amount of federal aid, leaves a large gap for the student attending the average private institution. As a consequence of this large gap, the amount of financial aid given by private institutions has grown dramatically. Figure 3.3 presents the amount of grants awarded by institutions, state governments, and the federal government from 1971 to 1999. In 1971, institutions awarded considerably

do grants nued to be paid buck?

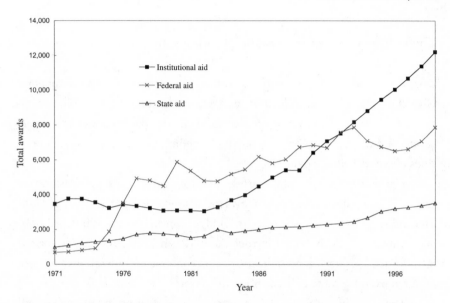

FIGURE 3.3. Institutional, Federal, and State Grants Awarded, 1971–1999 (millions of 1999 dollars). *Source:* Data from College Board 1999b.

more grant aid than either level of government. Beginning in 1976, as the Pell Grant program was phased in, the federal government passed institutions in grant aid awarded. From 1982, however, the rate of increase in institutional grants exceeded that in federal grants, and in 1992 institutional grants were again larger than federal grants. Despite a recovery in federal spending in the second half of the 1990s, the difference continued to grow after 1992. In 1999 institutions awarded $4.3 billion more in grants than did the federal government.[17]

Given that only roughly 20 percent of college students are enrolled in private institutions and that students enrolled in private institutions are eligible for federal grants (and some state grants), grant awards per student are much higher at private institutions than at state-supported institutions. The explosion of grants at private institutions in the 1990s makes the total system much less a federal system than would be suggested by many policy discussions. Private institutions, however, in almost all cases award grant funding to a student only after they have awarded any federal aid for which the student is eligible. This makes the federal rules and definitions important for private institutions as well as state-supported ones.

The Performance of the Financial Aid System

Does the financial aid system provide sufficient resources for college students? Given financial aid, what role do economic considerations play in college decisions? Unfortunately, for many students the current system does not provide enough aid to meet the goal of removing economic considerations from decisions about attending college.

Figure 3.4 presents data on student budgets for the entire postsecondary system. The top line in the graph shows the average cost of attendance for full-time, full-year dependent students by family income. This line is upward sloping because students in higher income quintiles generally attend higher-priced institutions. This itself is an indication that economic considerations have not been removed from the college choice decision.

The next line in figure 3.4 represents the cost of attendance minus all grant aid. Grant aid is clearly progressive. The difference between the top two lines is much larger for the lowest income quintile than for the highest income

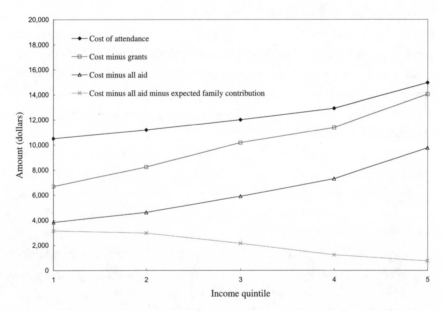

FIGURE 3.4. Student Budget and Cost of Attendance, 1995–1996, by Family Income Quintile. *Source:* Data from U.S. Department of Education, NCES 1998.

quintile. This second-highest line represents the amount of the total student budget that the student and his or her family has to finance, through loans, work-study, and the family contribution.

The third-highest line subtracts all aid from the cost of attendance. Student loans and work-study make up the difference between the second and third lines. These two lines appear to be almost parallel, indicating that the amount of aid in the form of loans and work-study does not vary much with income, though the raw data show that the amount of aid in the form of loans and work-study increases slightly with income. Nevertheless, despite the regressive nature of loan and work-study aid, this line is also upward sloping.

The fourth-highest line subtracts all aid and the expected family contribution from the cost of attendance. This line represents the unmet financial need. The difference between the third and fourth lines is the expected family contribution—a difference that clearly grows as income increases. This line indicates that the financial aid system is not fully funded. If it were, this line would lie on the horizontal axis—that is, there would be no unmet need.

It is important to remember that the data in figure 3.4 are for college students, so the word *need* is perhaps not quite appropriate. All of the students in this sample managed to enroll in college, many of them without the money "needed." Obviously they obtained the money somehow—through a job while in college, an additional loan through, for example, the PLUS program, or by a greater sacrifice on the part of the parents than envisioned by the EFC formula. Unmet need was not an insurmountable barrier for these students. It should be a concern to policy makers, however, because no doubt unmet need barred numbers of other students from pursuing higher education.

Perhaps more important than the level of unmet need is the relation between unmet need and income. Despite the fact that financial aid awards cause the second and third lines in figure 3.4 to increase as income increases, the amount of unmet need decreases as income increases. Although such a line would eventually have to become decreasing as income increased, a line that is always downward sloping is not the result one would hope for. If funding levels require unmet need, unmet need should be proportional to income if the funding burden is to be equitably shared. The fact that unmet need is decidedly downward sloping in absolute dollars is unfortunate. In percentage terms, the additional sacrifice that students and parents from low-income fam-

TABLE 3.2.   Student Budget and Family Income, 1995–1996, by Institution Type (dollars)

Income Quintile	Cost of Attendance	Cost Minus Grants	Cost Minus All Aid	Cost Minus All Aid Minus EFC
		Public non-doctorate-granting		
1	9,091	5,778	3,408	2,885
2	9,153	6,893	3,970	2,263
3	9,398	8,599	5,003	1,500
4	9,384	8,780	5,540	512
5	10,212	9,848	6,557	126
		Public doctorate-granting		
1	10,775	6,377	3,216	2,612
2	10,814	7,969	4,127	2,429
3	11,096	9,601	5,275	1,561
4	11,578	10,634	6,764	900
5	12,424	11,622	7,509	354
		Private non-doctorate-granting		
1	14,372	8,259	4,461	3,515
2	16,771	10,228	5,011	3,338
3	17,326	11,969	6,566	2,735
4	18,224	13,433	8,341	1,601
5	18,979	16,006	11,631	878
		Private doctorate-granting		
1	21,596	12,737	7,181	5,862
2	22,657	13,187	7,374	5,323
3	23,232	15,130	8,928	4,674
4	23,758	17,678	10,918	3,223
5	24,024	20,285	14,235	1,746

Source: U.S. Department of Education, NCES 1998.
Note: Only four-year institutions are included in the data. Proprietary (for-profit) institutions are excluded.

ilies have to make is much greater than that required of parents from high-income families.

Table 3.2 presents similar data for four different types of institutions: public four-year non-doctorate-granting, public four-year doctorate-granting, private nonprofit four-year non-doctorate-granting, and private nonprofit four-year doctorate-granting. In each case the pattern is the same as that seen in figure 3.4. The cost of attendance, the cost minus grants awarded, and the cost minus all aid all increase with income, but unmet need (the cost minus all aid minus the expected family contribution) decreases with rising income. The magnitudes are all larger for private institutions. Compare, for example, the figures for public and private non-doctorate-granting institutions for the average student from the lowest income quintile: In the private sector the average cost of attendance is $14,372 compared with $9,901 in the public sector. In the private sector the average grant is $6,113 ($14,372 – 8,259), the average loan is $3,798 ($8,259 – 4,461), and the average expected family contribution is $946 ($4,461 – 3,515), leaving unmet need of $3,515. In the public sector the average grant is $3,313 ($9,091 – 5,778), the average loan is $2,370 ($5,778 – 3,408), and the average EFC is $523 ($3,408 – 2,885), leaving unmet need of $2,885. The perverse relation between income and unmet financial need first observed for all postsecondary institutions, then, is not the result of the behavior of a single subsector. It is evident in each of the major institutional sectors.

Tax Credits

[handwritten note: If someone is in Quintle 1 they should be recieving more HELP than a student in 5 because they have less income right?]

The calculations in table 3.2 do not consider the effect of tax credits. Tax credits were initiated in 1997, after these data were collected. It is relatively easy, however, to simulate the effect of tax credits under the assumption that institutions do not adjust their charges or financial aid awards to account for the effects of the tax credits. The two tax credits are based on qualifying expenses—tuition and required fees minus grants, scholarships, and other tax free-educational assistance.[18] For each first- and second-year student, the Hope Scholarship tax credit is 100 percent of the first $1,000 in qualifying expenses and 50 percent of the next $1,000. For each third- and fourth-year student, the Lifetime Learning tax credit is 20 percent of the first $5,000 in qualifying expenses. The tax credit declines by 5 percent for every $1,000 in the family's adjusted gross income above $80,000. In this way the tax credit is completely eliminated for families with adjusted gross incomes above $100,000. Similarly, the tax credit declines by 10 percent for single taxpayers for every $1,000 in adjusted gross income above $40,000. In this case the tax credit is completely eliminated for single taxpayers with adjusted gross incomes above $50,000.

These tax credits are determined after the taxpayer has calculated his or her tax liability. The tax credit reduces the eventual tax liability by the amount of the tax credit or the calculated tax liability, whichever is smaller. In other words, the benefits of the tax credit are available only to those with tax liabilities. This means that the poorest students are unlikely to receive any benefits from the tax credits. Actually this happens for two reasons. First, the poorest students are unlikely to have income tax liabilities against which to take the tax credit, and if they do, the credit they can take will be very small. Only 29.92 percent of the families in the first income quintile of the 1995–96 National Postsecondary Student Aid Survey (NPSAS) had any income tax liability in 1994, and their average tax payment was only $234. Second, even if they have tax liabilities, the scholarships and fellowships they might receive diminish their qualifying expenses. For example, the student may have a full-tuition scholarship, resulting in no qualifying expenses. This student would still have room and board expenses, but these do not qualify for the tax credit. For these reasons, most of the benefits of the tax credits accrue to students from middle-class and upper-middle-class families, many of whom will not have financial need according to the standard formulas. For this reason, these tax credits are poorly targeted financial aid.

This criticism of tax credits is not at all new; the war between the proponents of tax credits and the proponents of need-based financial aid started with the battles surrounding the founding of federal financial aid in the Higher Education Act of 1965. This fact does not negate the criticism, however. To the extent that tax credits go to families without financial need or more than cover financial need, the revenue the government gives up in the tax credits could be spent much more efficiently elsewhere.

It is interesting to contrast tax credits with other federal financial aid. There is one glaring difference. As I mentioned earlier, other federal financial aid programs go to great lengths to avoid making awards in excess of need. If a financial aid officer awards financial aid to a student whose financial aid is already met through other aid, the award is invalid, and the excess aid must be repaid. No such provision applies to tax credits, however. If the tax credits were subject to the same prohibition, for many families either the tax credit could not be taken or some other forms of financial aid would be correspondingly reduced. The fact that this prohibition does not pertain to the tax credits is one of many inconsistencies in federal financial aid policy.

How poorly targeted are the tax credits? The NPSAS 1995–96 data for 1994 income taxes paid allow us to calculate the tax credit that would have been available to each student had the tax credits existed in 1994. Tax credits that played no role in meeting financial need were prevalent: A total of 40.11 percent of the tax credits went to students or families with no unmet need, and

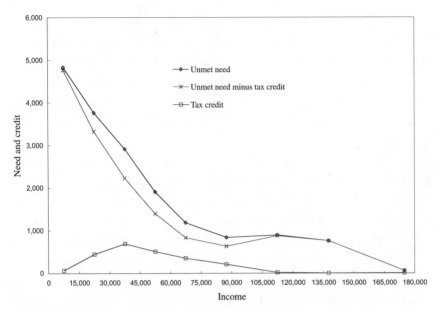

FIGURE 3.5. Unmet Need and Tax Credits, 1999, by Family Income (dollars).
Source: Data from U.S. Department of Education, NCES 1998.

another 8.18 percent of the tax credits went to families with so little need that with the application of the credit their financial need was more than completely met. Combining these two, the estimates suggest that just under one-half of the tax credits (48.29%) would qualify as awards in excess of need under the federal system.

Given that a substantial percentage of the tax credits play no role in meeting financial need, their place in the financial aid system is clearly questionable. This is only part of the problem, however. The other difficulty is that they do little to help where help is most needed. Figure 3.5 gives another view of the relation between unmet need and income for dependent students (the bottom line in figure 3.4). In this case I have used a larger number of income categories, so the shape of the unmet need lines in the two figures is not the same. Figure 3.5 also adds lines for unmet need minus the tax credit and the amount of the tax credit. In both cases I truncate unmet need at zero. These data are the average unmet need by income categories. Once again, unmet need declines as income increases. Subtracting the tax credit does not change the shape or direction of the line; it simply makes the line steeper. This happens because the average tax credit in the first income category (less than $15,000) is very small ($65). The average tax credit then expands in the second ($15,000–29,999) and third ($30,000–45,000) income categories and declines thereafter. Because a phase-out of the tax credit begins at family income of $80,000, unmet need minus the tax credit is actually upward sloping between the sixth ($75,000–99,999) and seventh ($100,000–124,999) income categories.

These effects of the tax credits are not surprising. As Jacqueline E. King concludes, "Most observers of higher education, if not all, agree that college affordability has become a central policy goal. Certainly, major new programs have been enacted recently at both the state and federal levels that are clearly targeted toward improving college affordability for middle-income students and their families" (King 1999, 198). Clearly, the students left behind are those from the poorest families. These data suggest that the Hope Scholarship and Lifetime Learning tax credits have increased affordability for the middle class but have done little to increase access to college.[19] Students from the lowest-income families face, in absolute and proportional terms, the highest financial barriers to attending college.

The unmet need lines in figure 3.5 should be seen as a thoroughgoing indictment of the current financial aid system and the current emphasis on affordability. Ideally, such lines should hug the horizontal axis; if funds are insufficient to yield this outcome, the line should be parallel at least for the first few income groups. It will eventually slope downward, as the expected family contribution is sufficient to pay a large percentage of the total costs. This cannot be avoided. The strong downward slope for the first few income groups, however, clearly can be avoided. The addition of tax credits makes the unmet need line slope downward more precipitously, a fact I take as evidence that the credits are a move in the wrong direction. One of the goals of my redesign proposal is to create a system that produces a line for unmet need that is flatter for the lowest income classes. The fact that the current line, including the effects of the tax credits, is so steep makes the need for reform all the more clear.

Is Low Income a Barrier to College Attendance?

In many ways, the question whether low income is a barrier to higher education is the most important question for a financial aid system. All of the data just reviewed were observations for college students. These individuals had found ways to overcome the barriers imposed by a highly inequitable system. The question I turn to now is whether other students have been discouraged from attending college by this system. Two recent studies, by Susan P. Choy and Thomas J. Kane, provide the answers.

Choy presents data from the Current Population Survey that indicate that the percentage of high school graduates enrolled in college in the year following graduation is strongly related to family income. Only 49 percent of high school graduates from families in the lowest income quintile were enrolled in college the year after high school, compared with 78 percent of students from families in the highest quintile (Choy 1999, 5).

This result should be treated with some caution. The rate at which those who complete high school enroll in college is related to students' academic qualifications and aspirations as well as family income. There are strong associations between family income and the parents' education level, between the parents' education level and a child's educational aspirations, and between a child's educational aspirations and the academic program he or she pursues as a high school student. Thus the percentages of students who aspire to go to college and who are qualified for college are strongly related to income. Although this is an unfortunate fact, it is not primarily a failure of higher education or of the financial aid system.

The associations among educational aspirations, educational preparation, and income are explained by strong social and familial interactions that the elementary and secondary educational system is not able to overcome. The financial aid system can play a role in lifting the aspirations of low-income high school students. However, even if more high school students were aware of the existence of need-based aid, it is unlikely that the link between parental education and the children's educational aspirations would be altered much, if at all.

Choy uses data from the third follow-up (conducted in 1994) to the 1988 National Educational Longitudinal Study to investigate these links. Table

TABLE 3.3   College Planning of High School Seniors, 1992, by Family Income (percentage)

| Category | Total | Family Income | | |
		Less than $25,000	$25,000 to $75,000	Greater than $75,000
College qualified	65	53	68	86
Expected a bachelor's degree	54	39	57	83
Planned to attend a four-year college	49	37	52	78
Had taken steps toward admission to a four-year college	47	33	50	78
Had been accepted at a four-year college	45	31	47	77
Was enrolled at a four-year college by 1994	40	28	42	71

Source: Data from Choy 1999, 9.

3.3 gives a summary of the data for the high school class of 1992. Sixty-five percent of the survey respondents were deemed to be qualified for college, based on high school grade point average, senior class rank, aptitude test scores, and a measure of the rigor of their high school curriculum. The data show a strong relation between family income and the likelihood that a student is college qualified. The table then illustrates students' participation in the progressive stages of the planning process, listing the percentage of respondents who expected to earn a bachelor's degree, planned to attend a four-year college, had taken steps toward admission to a four-year college, had been accepted to a four-year college, and had enrolled in a four-year college by 1994.

Table 3.3 allows us to investigate some of the reasons why low-income students attend college less frequently than their higher-income counterparts. Focusing on the lowest two income groups, there is a 14 percent gap (42% − 28%) in college attendance probability. Some of that gap is related to the fact that students in the lowest income group are the least likely to be "college qualified." To control for this effect, consider the conditional probability that a student attends college given that he or she is college qualified. For the lowest income group this probability is 52.8 percent (28%/53%), compared with 61.8 percent (42%/68%) for the middle income group. The gap in probabilities is now 9 percent (6.18% − 52.8%)—smaller than 14 percent but still considerable. Income still has an effect after controlling for the likelihood that a student is college qualified.

In like fashion, income still has an effect after controlling for aspirations as well as the qualifications of the student. The likelihood that a college-qualified student from the lowest family-income group who expects to receive a bachelor's degree and plans to attend a four-year college actually enrolls in college is 75.7 percent (28%/37%). This compares with 80.8 percent (42%/52%) for a student from a family with an income between $25,000 and $75,000. The probability gap shrinks again, this time to 5.1 percent (80.8% − 75.7%). Much of the effect of income is eliminated, but not all.

The effect of income is finally eliminated, at least for the first two income groups, after controlling for being college qualified, aspiring to go to college, and actually doing something about it. The likelihood that an individual who took steps toward admission to a four-year college was actually enrolled two years later is 84.8 percent (28%/33%) for family income of less $25,000 and 84.0 percent (42%/50%) for family income between $25,000 and $75,000. The student from a family with a family income greater than $75,000 who has taken steps toward admission to a four-year college still has a greater likelihood of actually attending such a college—91.0 percent (71%/78%).

How should this result be interpreted? At best it represents a partial success for the financial aid system. Essentially the data in table 3.3 suggest that low income is not a barrier for the students once they enter the higher education system. Before the student has taken some steps toward admission—typically, filled out an application—income is still a barrier. It appears that part of the reason for this is that low-income students, even those who are qualified for college, are wary of even trying to get involved with the higher education system. The percentage of college-qualified students who took steps toward admission to four-year colleges is strongly related to income—62 percent (33%/53%) for students with family incomes less than $25,000, 74 percent (50%/68%) for students with family incomes between $25,000 and $75,000, and 91 percent (78%/86%) for students with family incomes above $75,000.

Thomas Kane uses these same data and a slightly different methodology to come too much the same conclusion. Kane estimates regression equations designed to explain the likelihood that a student enrolls in any postsecondary training. His focus is, therefore, slightly different from Choy's. In addition, rather than accepting the survey's definition of college qualified and answers to questions about aspirations, as did Choy, Kane includes variables on the parental education, test scores, race, and state to control for these effects. Kane's results are clear: income is a statistically significant factor in determining the likelihood that a student will enroll for any postsecondary education. Those in the next-to-lowest income quintile are 6.4 percent more likely to be enrolled than those in the lowest income quintile, and the likelihood increases for each higher income quintile (Kane 1999a, 97).

As the previous analysis indicates, such evidence is insufficient to indicate that economic constraints rather than social dispositions correlated with income are driving the relation between income and the likelihood of college enrollment. In an attempt to isolate the economic factors, Kane estimates regressions in which he uses the average tuition at state-supported institutions and the state unemployment rate to measure the economic costs of postsecondary education. In his preferred specification, he finds that a $1,000 increase in the average tuition at a state-supported two-year institution decreases the likelihood of enrollment by 7.2 percent for low-income students (the bottom 40% of the income distribution) but by only 4.4 percent for high-income students (the top 60% of the income distribution) (ibid., 104). In addition, increases in the state unemployment rate, indicating a lower opportunity cost of attending college, has a statistically significant effect on enrollment likelihood for the low-income students but not for the high-income students. These results indicate that income is related to the likelihood of college attendance for economic as well as social reasons.

Kane's careful investigation of the relations among college attendance, tuition, and state unemployment convinces him that the elasticities involved are quite large. He compares these elasticities to the response in enrollment that has resulted from the increase in the labor market payoffs to higher education, which he finds to be quite low. He concludes that "this difference between the response to the cost of college, with large elasticities with respect to tuition variation and wide countercyclical swings in enrollment, and the comparatively muted response to the rise in the labor market value of a college education would be consistent with behavior in the presence of financing constraints" (ibid., 116). In other words, rational individuals make investment decisions, such as the decision to invest in human capital, based on net benefits. If they respond strongly to changes in the costs but not equally strongly to changes in the benefits, they must somehow feel constraints on the amount they can borrow. This result is perfectly consistent with the previous findings. Low-income families, those who are most likely to be constrained in financial markets, do not obtain as much higher education as they could take advantage of.

Choy's and Kane's results cover a period during which federal, state, and private financial aid was readily available. These results, therefore, suggest that the financial aid system has not succeeded. Low income is an economic barrier to higher education. Given the large amount of money the nation spends on need-based financial aid, this is an unfortunate finding.

There are several possible explanations for this failure. The data in table 3.3 indicate that low aspirations are part of the story. It could be that the low aspirations result from the student's belief that he or she could never afford a higher education. These students and their families may not be aware of the financial aid available to low-income college students. Many students think of college scholarships as something reserved for the highly talented, either athletically or academically. In response to the American Council on Education's 1998 survey question, "How much do you personally feel you know about where and how to get financial aid for college?," 59 percent of the respondents indicated "a little" or "almost nothing" (Ikenberry and Hartle 1998, 30).

If lack of knowledge about need-based financial aid is the problem, the solution would seem obvious. Colleges and universities should make every effort to make sure that in middle school or early in high school students and their families are aware of the financial aid that is available. It is not at all clear, however, that this strategy will work.

First, it is possible that student ignorance is not the problem. It may be that low-income students are aware of the financial aid available to them. It is unlikely that many have seen the data in figure 3.3 or table 3.2, showing that unmet need is highest for low-income students, but they may have heard anecdotes that suggest this result. Moreover, low-income high school students may be aware that much of the financial aid available is in the form of loans, and they may be daunted by the prospect of going into debt. Finally, it is possible that some students know of the difficulties with the financial aid system through the experience of older siblings.

Second, even if student ignorance is part of the problem, how easy will it be to give a description of the system that is understandable to young teenagers and their parents? The financial aid system encompasses a large number of programs, none of which has simple rules. The variation in the amount of financial aid that a student might get at different institutions is great. Much of the aid is in the form of loans. Finally, families have to be willing to fill out long complicated forms to find out if they will qualify for aid. It will not be easy to make a presentation that makes the present system appealing.

The bottom line is this: the current financial aid system is not working as well as it could. Institutions lack sufficient resources to meet all of the need of their students, let alone the need all of students who could benefit from higher education. As a result, low income is a barrier to receiving a higher education even among students who aspire to get a degree. Some would take this simply as evidence that the financial aid system is underfunded. More funding would probably help but would not address the fundamental problems. In the remainder of this book I explore the idea of redesigning the financial aid system to better meet the goal of educational access.

Appendix: The Calculation of the Expected Family Contribution for Dependent Students, 1999–2000

Three distinct formulas are used to calculate the EFC: one for dependent students, one for independent students without dependents other than spouse, and one for independent students with dependents other than spouse. The formula for dependent students includes six calculations: parents' income, parents' assets, parents' contribution (based on a combination of information from parents' income with information from parents' assets), student's income, student's assets, and family contribution (based on a combination of information on the student's income and assets with information on the parents' contribution). All of the information required for these calculations is provided to the government on the FAFSA.

Parents' income. Income is defined as the sum of taxable income—either adjusted gross income, for tax filers, or the sum of the earned income of the two parents, for nonfilers—and untaxed income, including contributions to

TABLE 3.4.   Determination of Parents' Contribution, 1999–2000

Adjusted Available Income	Parents' Contribution
Less than –$3,409	–$750
–$3,409–$11,000	22% of AAI
$11,001–$13,700	$2,420 plus 25% of AAI above $11,000
$13,701–$16,500	$3,095 plus 29% of AAI above $13,700
$16,501–$19,300	$3,907 plus 34% of AAI above $16,500
$19,301–$22,100	$4,859 plus 40% of AAI above $19,300
$22,101 or more	$5,979 plus 47% of AAI above $22,100

Source: U.S. Department of Education 1999a.

individual retirement accounts (IRAs), contributions to 401(k) and 403(b) plans, tax-exempt interest, and child support payments received. There are six types of allowances against parents' income: federal income taxes; state and other taxes; father's social security tax; mother's social security tax; the income protection allowance, which depends upon the number of family members and the number of college students in the family; and the employment expense allowance, if all parents work. The available income is the difference between the income and the allowances against parents' income. Available income can be a negative number, and given a minimum income protection allowance of $12,260 (for a two-person family with one college student), for many low-income families it will be.

Parents' assets. For the purposes of the EFC, the parents' net worth includes cash, savings, checking account balances, and the net worth of real estate and investments (excluding the net worth of the student's home and the value of IRAs, annuities, and pension funds) plus the adjusted net worth of businesses and farms. An education savings and asset protection allowance is subtracted from net worth to determine discretionary net worth. The education savings and asset protection allowance increases with the age of the older parent; for a two-parent family with a forty-five year old as the oldest parent, it is $42,500. Finally, the contribution from assets is 12 percent of positive discretionary net worth. (If discretionary net worth is zero or negative, the contribution from assets is zero.)

Parents' contribution from income and assets. The sum of the available income, which may be negative, and the contribution from assets, which is either zero or positive, is called the adjusted available income. The parents' contribution is estimated according to the progressive formula presented in table 3.4. As the table indicates, the result can be a negative number. This negative number is combined with the student's contribution in the final step. If the final result is a negative number, the EFC is set at zero.

Student's income. The student's income is calculated in the same fashion. Again, the available income is the difference between income and allowances against income. For dependent students the only allowances are for taxes and a flat $2,200 as the income protection allowance. The student contribution from available income is 50 percent of his or her available income.

Student's assets. Calculation of the student's net worth is identical to that of the parents' net worth. The contribution from assets for the dependent student is 35 percent of net worth, and there is no education savings or assets protection allowance. Because the contribution rate is higher (35% as opposed to 12%) and none of the net worth is excluded, the effect on the family's EFC of an extra dollar of assets in the student's name is much larger than the effect of a dollar of assets in the parents' name.

Expected family contribution. The student's contributions from income and assets are simply combined, and the result is added to the parent's contribution to determine the expected family contribution. If the result is a negative number, the EFC is zero.

Theoretical Considerations: Access, Choice, Affordability, and Merit

Before embarking on the redesign of the financial aid system, I should discuss the theory behind such a system. Because I am an economist, my theory starts with an examination of the efficient allocation of costs and benefits, as illustrated in figure 4.1. The horizontal axis measures enrollment in higher education, the vertical axis measures the costs and benefits of higher education. The downward sloping line gives the marginal social benefits, and the upward sloping line the marginal social costs, for each level of college enrollment. The two lines cross at the socially optimal level of college enrollment, E^*. Any other enrollment level represents an inefficient allocation of society's resources.[1]

The figure allows a graphic definition of the concept "college qualified." A person is qualified to go to college if the marginal social benefit of providing a higher education to that person is at least as high as S^*, the marginal social cost of educating E^* students.

The social benefits of higher education are the sum of the private gains and positive spillovers to society at large that result from providing one year of higher education to one student. The marginal social benefit curve slopes downward because for each enrollment level it represents the optimal combination of students and institutions. At very low levels of total enrollment, the only students in the optimal student body would be those who could obtain the greatest benefits from higher education, and the only colleges and universities would be those that generate the greatest benefits to their students. As

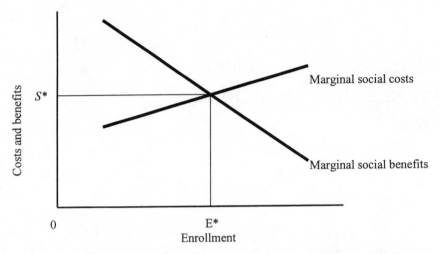

FIGURE 4.1. Efficient Allocation of Social Costs and Benefits in Higher Education

total enrollment increases, the higher education system adds less talented students and less effective institutions. As a result, marginal social benefits decline. At the optimum level, all student-institution combinations that yield marginal social benefits of S^* or greater are included in the national student body.

The marginal social cost curve in figure 4.1 is upward sloping, indicating increasing marginal social costs as the number of students enrolled increases, but this is not necessarily the case; it is possible that the marginal social costs of providing a higher education are constant over a large range of enrollments. However, the shape of the marginal social cost curve is not crucial for the argument to come. The point that deserves emphasis is that the marginal social cost curve leading to the optimal enrollment should contain only the essential costs of providing a higher education. Practices that add unnecessary costs have been eliminated from the marginal social cost curve in figure 4.1.

Choosing Students and Paying for Higher Education

The ideal mix of students and institutions would be one in which marginal social costs and benefits are in perfect balance—in figure 4.1, the point of intersection between the two lines. Both the way colleges and universities choose the members of their student bodies and the share of the cost of higher education students, as opposed to the government, have to pay influence the likelihood of achieving this point. It is instructive to consider a few options. Consider, first, a system in which the students who attend college are the winners of a lottery among all high school graduates, and the government pays all college expenses of the winners.[2] This would clearly be an inefficient system. Choosing students randomly would most probably send many students to college who would be unable to obtain marginal social benefits of at least S^*.

As a second possibility, consider a system in which the students who attend college are the winners of an auction, and the students have to pay the full costs of their education. This, too, would be an inefficient system. Choosing purely on the basis of ability to pay would exclude many students in the optimal student body and preclude the optimal placement of many students who would go to college.

The procedure actually used for admissions, relying on test scores, performance in precollege education, essays, and interviews, has much to recommend it over either a lottery or an auction. This admission procedure is designed to select the students most likely to succeed in college.[3] In theory, though probably not in practice, this type of selection procedure could yield exactly the student-institution combinations that lie on the optimal marginal social benefit curve.

The method used to pay for college, on the other hand, is a combination of the two payment methods considered above. The government and the student share in the expenses of a college education. In theory, though again probably not in practice, such a mixed system of paying for college could be consistent with efficient allocation.

On one side of the long-standing debate about who should pay for a college education are those who think that college students should bear the full cost of their education.[4] Supporters of this view think that the vast majority of the benefits of a higher education accrue to the individual receiving the higher education. According to this view, higher education will be overproduced (that is, more than E^* students will enroll) if it is subsidized. The opposing view claims that higher education provides a significant amount of spillover benefits to the society at large, benefits to society that will be underproduced (that is, fewer than E^* students will enroll) if higher education is not subsidized.[5] Owing to problems with identifying and measuring the societal benefits associated with higher education, this controversy is unresolved. The result is a mixed system relying on both subsidies from taxpayers and direct charges paid by students.

The argument over the importance of societal benefits in higher education does not cover all the relevant concerns. Even if one takes the position that the societal benefits of higher education dominate the private benefits by a large margin, one can still support significant tuition and fee expenses for higher education. Higher education is different from many other goods and services in a critical way: to gain the benefits of a higher education, an enrollee has to supply effort. (I switch terminology here from *student* to *enrollee* because I want to emphasize the distinction between enrollees who are students and those who are merely in attendance.) If people are willing to sacrifice resources to engage in an activity, it is a signal that they value that activity. If they do not have to sacrifice resources, they may or may not value the activity. Caroline M. Hoxby puts this well when she compares the performance of college enrollees with the performance of enrollees in primary and secondary schools. "Finally, and perhaps most significantly, college students and their families shoulder more of the burden of paying for their own educations than do their counterparts in the primary and secondary sector. This additional responsibility encourages better performance on the part of the students" (Hoxby 1999, 29).

It is possible that the forgone earnings of a college student, which are almost always higher than the out-of-pocket costs, would be a sufficient sacrifice to keep college enrollees motivated, but generally out-of-pocket costs are superior motivators.[6] This provides a rationale for including prices as a rationing device in higher education independent of any discussion of who receives the benefits.

Financial Aid: Access and Choice

A financial aid system is a necessary adjunct to a system in which students are selected on the basis of their ability to benefit from the education and required to pay a substantial portion of the expenses of that education. There will be some students who have the ability to benefit from higher education but lack the ability to pay for it. Given our selection and payment methods, targeted financial aid expenditures are necessary to obtain the optimal student-institution mix. The difficulty for the design of a financial aid system is to overcome the problems of those who are unable to pay while not destroying the important function that prices play in sorting out those who are unwilling to work hard enough to get the benefits of higher education. Starting with the programs created by the Higher Education Act of 1965, most federal financial aid has been need based, but the amount of need-based aid awarded is low enough that most of the costs of education fall on the students. From the standpoint of efficient allocation, this is sensible public policy.

The goal of financial aid is sometimes stated as providing sufficient aid so that every qualified student can afford to go to college. This can be interpreted to mean that the goal of financial aid is to ensure that total enrollment is E^*—that is, that the optimal number of students are enrolled. This is commonly called the access goal of financial aid and is grounded in the belief that all qualified students should have access to higher education. Clearly, this is part of the goal, but stated this way, the goal is too modest. More precisely, the goal of financial aid policy should be to facilitate the optimal set of student-institution combinations. This involves much more than ensuring that E^* students are enrolled. Under the assumption that students generally have the information for and the ability to make sensible decisions, this goal of financial aid will be met if students are given unrestricted choice in addition to access. Stated another way, the choice goal is satisfied if a student's choice of institution is not restricted by his or her financial circumstances.

In the United States, for the most part, allocations are the result of private decisions. In the case of the selection of colleges and universities, parents and students make the selection from the group of institutions willing to accept the student. The choice goal for financial aid therefore facilitates the optimal student-institution mix if we can rely on two decision makers: colleges and universities, on the one hand, and parents and students, on the other.

Colleges and universities face an inherently difficulty task in making their admission decisions. It is not easy, based on the information available, to forecast the maturation rate of eighteen- to twenty-one-year-olds. For a variety of reasons, a few students with excellent high school records and high test scores fail miserably in college, and some students with less than stellar high school records and low test scores do very well in college. Nevertheless, on average, the predictors used by admission offices are generally accurate.[7]

The information available to parents and students is more problematic. Depending on how comfortable the student is with the idea of being away from home, the number of institutions a student might qualify to attend and seriously consider could be as low as one and as high as twenty or thirty. To be sure that offering unrestricted choice is consistent with achieving the optimal student-institution mix, students and parents must have high-quality information. This means that the financial aid system should provide reliable information about the costs of attending various institutions and must provide that information in a timely fashion. As noted in chapter 1, the current financial aid system does a poor job in this respect. It is exceedingly complex, and those with little experience with financial aid find it difficult to comprehend. Moreover, institutions announce their financial aid awards only after students have applied and been accepted, at which point they have already made some irreversible decisions. Because of the confusion it creates, the current financial aid system may obfuscate rather than facilitate good choices.

Concepts such as the marginal social benefit of providing higher education are more than a little fuzzy. First, not everyone agrees on the constituent elements of the social benefits of higher education. Some argue that the benefits of providing a higher education to an individual accrue almost exclusively to the individual, others that the benefits accrue both to the individual and to society at large. Second, even if everyone could agree on a definition, measuring marginal social benefits is difficult. Third, even if everyone could agree on how to measure marginal social benefits, it is impossible to accurately forecast the marginal social benefits of providing an education for a given student based on what can be observed about the student as a senior in high school. This makes a direct application of the model especially difficult. Nonetheless, as I explain in the material that follows, some current financial aid practices are thoroughly inconsistent with an appropriate application of the model.

Affordability

Concerns with affordability should target the marginal social cost curve, and some attempts to make college more affordable are therefore misguided. If higher education is made more affordable through the use of devices such as tuition tax credits or subsidies from general tax revenues that provide lower net prices independent of financial need, the effect on the allocation per dollar of aid will generally be quite small. When the net price of higher education is reduced for all students, some students who would otherwise not be able to attend college will be now able to, but for the most part behavior will not be affected. In most cases, it will simply mean that the government is footing the bill for a greater percentage of the costs of higher education. Such policies could also reduce the effort that students put forth and thus may prove counterproductive.

Policies that lower the marginal social cost curve are another story. To lower the marginal social cost curve, colleges and universities have to become more efficient. Such a change would clearly affect allocation. A higher education would become more affordable, and the nation would have a larger optimal student body. Writing about increasing efficiency in higher education, however, is easier than doing it. The problem is clear. What looks like an efficiency increase in most of the rest of the economy looks like a quality reduction in higher education. In the rest of the economy, increases in output per worker are increases in productivity. In higher education, significant increases in output per worker can only be achieved by increasing average class size or by increasing the number of classes taught by each faculty member, and such changes would be perceived as quality reductions. The *U.S. News and World Report* rankings of American colleges and universities include student-faculty ratio (lower is better), the percentage of classes with fewer than twenty students (higher is better), and the percentage of classes with fifty or more students (lower is better) among its ranking criteria.[8] An institution that chose to increase average class size would suffer in the *U.S. News* rankings; and if it increased the number of classes taught by each professor, it would lose its top research faculty, so important to the "reputation score" in the rankings. One should not conclude that it is impossible to increase efficiency in higher education. It is, however, difficult.

The thrust of attempts to make a higher education more affordable should be to identify ways in which the education can be provided using fewer resources without sacrificing quality. It is possible that some of the innovations using computers and the Internet will be found to be more effective than large lecture classes, or that the availability of documents on the Internet will reduce the need to expand libraries. These are ways that a college and university education can be made more affordable. The key to efforts to encourage these changes is to provide benefits to institutions that are able to engineer the efficiency improvements. The current financial aid system, however, does not encourage such changes.

Merit Scholarships

The discussion to this point suggests that a program of need-based financial aid is sensible public policy. Most federal aid, and a significant portion of the aid offered by institutions, is based on financial need. Increasingly, however, financial aid provided by states and institutions is based on merit.[9]

Merit scholarships have two major benefits. First, to obtain the benefits of higher education a student has to be willing to work at it. This is also true for high school education, and many states have been attracted to merit scholarship programs as part of an effort to motivate students to work hard in high school. Such efforts have shown some success, though it is difficult to be completely sure that these programs have not just produced grade inflation. In addition, often students can keep their merit scholarships only if they maintain a certain grade point average, so the incentives for students to work hard (or at least to get acceptable grades, or for professors to give higher grades) continue in college. To the extent that they produce more than grade inflation, merit scholarships may enhance the efficiency of the higher education system through their effect on student effort.

Second, it is clear that fellow students are an important ingredient in higher education, in addition to as well as professors, facilities, and student effort. Other things being equal, the more talented and motivated one's classmates, the better will be a student's educational experience. It is easy to argue that the quality of the education at almost any institution would improve if the institution could recruit more talented students. Merit scholarships are a strategy that some institutions use to be sure that they attract at least a few truly talented students. If they use their scholarships intelligently, these institutions can recruit the few students who will make the difference in the classroom, as well as on the athletic fields, in the band, and on stage. This defense of merit scholarships argues that, left to their own devices, talented students would tend to cluster in a few institutions, lowering the marginal benefits curve. If used appropriately, merit scholarships could spread out the talented students, thereby improving the efficiency of the education system in general.[10]

There is a fairness concern with this second justification for merit scholarships. The benefits of a talented student attending a particular institution accrue most to the other students attending that institution. The effect on the quality of the talented student's education is problematic. He or she is being asked to give up some of the positive peer effects at the institution from which he or she is bid away, so the quality of his or her education may actually suffer. This makes a merit scholarship much fairer than a system that, for the good of a particular institution or efficient allocation in the society at large, assigned the student to that institution. Under this view, the merit scholarship to the talented student is essentially payment for services rendered. It would thus be unfair not to pay the student.

I have three questions about these benefits of merit scholarships. First, are they large? Second, can they really be attained? Third, are they offset by costs imposed by merit scholarships?

Regarding the size of the benefits, competitive admission already creates strong incentives for students to excel in high school, so there may not be large effects from the awarding of merit scholarships. Students who want to go to an Ivy League institution, or one with similar admission standards, have to work very hard in high school. In many states, admission to the premier state-supported institution (or institutions) is quite competitive. High school success often has a substantial payoff independent of any merit scholarship. Nevertheless, money is a powerful motivator, and there is added prestige to being awarded a merit scholarship, so merit scholarships may elicit increased effort on the part of high school students. If the continuation of the scholarship is contingent on college performance, merit scholarships may elicit more effort from students in college, as well. It is difficult, however, to ascertain the marginal effects on effort from merit scholarships.

The second presumed benefit of merit scholarships is that they can be used to distribute talented students across more institutions. This benefit assumes that the institutions at which these individuals would more naturally cluster allow other institutions to take the students away. Given the large excess demand for admissions slots at institutions such as Harvard, Yale, Princeton, and Stanford, it is likely that these institutions could afford to lose quite a few students before they took any action. Even here, however, there is a limit. Institutions just a bit below the ones I mentioned would be even less inclined to allow raids on their student bodies. Eventually, as its use expands, merit aid sets up a competition for the most talented students. It is folly to assume that the highest-quality institutions would not respond to such competition if it resulted in a significant dispersal of the most highly talented students. There is substantial evidence that these institutions aggressively compete with one another. I suspect that they will respond to competition from other fronts just as aggressively. This will make it difficult for merit scholarships to reduce the natural clustering of the high-quality students.

The costs of merit scholarships are twofold. First, often state merit scholarship programs are created with funds that would otherwise have gone to need-based financial aid. On net, this is unlikely to enhance efficiency. Many of the merit scholarships will have no effect on the margin. Merit scholarship winners are often from well-to-do families perfectly willing to fund college expenses. Such students are often highly motivated by peer pressure, and the possibility of a scholarship has little effect on their behavior. Because the need-based financial aid system is underfunded, poor students often have to go to extraordinary lengths to find the money to go to college, and many just give up. Extra need-based aid can be important to these students. If funding for need-based aid were sufficient to meet all financial need, merit scholarships might be a sensible extra expenditure to consider. As it is, however, funding for need-based aid should have a much higher priority.

The second cost of merit scholarships is that they open the door for the use of financial aid as a recruiting device. In a world in which students had sufficient financial resources to choose the best educational institution willing to admit them and sufficient information to make that choice, the student-institution mix would be close to optimal. The use of merit scholarships to try to alter the mix would be unlikely to result in an improvement. The result would most likely be a recruiting war using merit-based aid as the weapon of choice. In the long run, it is unlikely that this recruiting war would lead to a significant improvement in the student-institution mix. If the institution that attracts a student with a merit scholarship had actually been the best option for the student, given sufficient need-based aid the student would have chosen that institution in any case. Most merit aid would therefore be a transfer to the talented students.

Institutions will defend merit scholarships on the basis of imperfect information. "If students really knew what a great education we offer, they would come here without the scholarships. Our problem is that we are better than our reputation. Eventually our excellence will be recognized, and we will no longer have to use this type of recruiting device." Such an argument may be true, but generally one has to be wary of groups who always think they are better than everyone thinks they are.

More important, even if the basis of the argument—with full information, its scholarship students would have attended without the scholarships—is true, the rest of the argument would not follow. Consider the last sentence, "Eventually our excellence will be recognized, and we will no longer have to use this type of recruiting device." The difficulty with this forecast is that it ignores the reaction of the institution losing students to the institution claiming to be better than its reputation. It is highly likely that these institutions will retaliate by offering merit scholarships of their own, winning back some of the students. As other institutions retaliate with merit scholarships of their own, the institution will have to increase its merit scholarships to keep attracting the students it wants. It is exceedingly unlikely that, once it starts to use merit scholarships, an institution will ever be able to stop. In the long run, given the likelihood of retaliation, merit scholarships will have a small effect on the student-institution mix. They will, however, probably crowd need-based scholarships out of the picture for many institutions, so it is unlikely that the effect will be an improvement in the overall student-institution mix.

The kind of merit scholarships that do the best job of providing motivational improvements without creating problems are merit scholarships that are completely portable. Private charities are ideally suited to give these types of scholarships. National Merit Scholarships funded by entities other than a particular college or university are a good example. These scholarships can be used at the institution of the student's choice. They do not add to the competition among institutions, but they provide incentives to excel. States could also introduce such scholarships if they were willing to allow students to take the scholarships out of state.

Institutionally Funded Grants

Institutional grants occupy an important place in the financial aid system. However, for the following reasons, my proposed redesign recommends that their use be minimized. Institutionally funded grants confuse the process of college choice. They are funded with price increases. Need-based institutionally funded grants use a very narrow tax base, and merit-based institutionally funded grants are part of a socially unproductive competition for students with particular talents.

The Financial Accounts of an Institution of Higher Education

To help me explain the role of institutional grants in the financial aid system, I present a model of the way a college makes its financial decisions. My model relies on the notation used by Charles T. Clotfelter (1996), which closely follows the categories in which an institution is asked to report its current revenue and expense information to the National Center for Education Statistics. The budget equation for a nonprofit college or university is

$$TE + G + C + F = I + R + A + S, \qquad (5.1)$$

where T is the list-price tuition and fees per student, E is enrollment, G is gift and endowment income, C is external contracts and research grants, F is federal and state support earmarked for financial aid, I is instructional expenditures, R is research expenditures, A is administrative expenditures, and S is financial aid (scholarship) expenditures. In essence, equation (5.1) says that revenues, the left-hand side of the equation, have to equal expenditures, the right-hand side of the equation.

Tuition revenue and financial aid are handled in a peculiar way in these accounts. First, if T is the list-price tuition and E is enrollment, then TE is the revenue from tuition, under the assumption that every student pays the full list-price tuition. Because of financial aid, however, many students do not pay the full list-price tuition. Total financial aid expenditures are accounted for as S on the right-hand side of the equation. Some of the financial aid expenditures use outside funds, and F (federal and state support earmarked for financial aid) on the left-hand side of the equation accounts for this. With these accounting conventions, $S - F$ represents institutionally funded financial aid.

Clotfelter's notation was designed for the finances of a private institution. Only one addition is required for a state-supported institution. In this case, the institution's state support is accounted for by redefining G so that state appropriations are added to gift and endowment income.[1]

For the purposes of the model developed here I reorganize the equation so that the expenditures for which there are targeted revenues are expressed as net costs or net revenues. This requires two changes, one for financial aid and one for research monies. Thus scholarships and research revenues are subtracted from both sides of equation (5.1), yielding

$$[TE - (S - F)] + G = I + (R - C) + A. \qquad (5.2)$$

$S - F$ represents institutionally funded grants, and $R - C$ represents net institutional expenditures on research. I keep $S - F$ on the left-hand side of the equation because expenditure on scholarships, S, net of the federal and state support for financial aid, F, is essentially a discount on tuition.[2]

As the notation indicates, it is useful to divide the revenues on the left-hand side of equation (5.2) into two parts. The term in brackets, $TE - (S - F)$, represents the net revenue from tuition. Net revenue from tuition is the gross tuition revenue, TE, minus the portion of the tuition paid by the institution itself, $S - F$. To better understand this concept, consider the accounts for an institution for which all financial aid awards are from federal or state programs. The term $S - F$ would be zero for such an institution, and its net revenue from tuition would equal its gross revenue from tuition. If the institution funds any financial aid with its own money, then $S - F$ will be positive, and the institution will not be able to keep all of the tuition revenue included in TE.[3]

The term G, the second term on the left-hand side of equation (5.2), represents nontuition income. Nontuition income is important for state-supported institutions because it includes the state subsidy. It is also important for highly endowed private institutions because it includes endowment income. There are, however, some private institutions with small endowments and some state-supported institutions with small state subsidies. These institutions have to rely heavily on net revenue from tuition.

The right-hand side of equation (5.2) represents the institution's expenses: instructional expenses, I, plus the portion of research funded by the institution, $R - C$, plus administrative expenses, A. Equation (5.2) is written as an equation, but in reality the two sides can differ in a given year. Expenses and revenues are difficult to predict, and so most institutions are not able to balance their budgets exactly every year. It is not a good idea, however, for an institution to allow its budget to be out of balance for long periods of time. Its nonprofit status will be challenged if its revenues consistently exceed its expenses, and its existence will be challenged if its expenses consistently exceed its revenues.

A Model of Tuition and Quality Decisions for a Private Institution

The starting place for the model of institutional financial aid decisions is the model of the liberal arts college presented by David W. Breneman (1994) in his *Liberal Arts Colleges: Thriving, Surviving, or Endangered?*[4] The underlying decision-making process in this model has two steps. In the first, the institution determines its desired enrollment level and its desired level of educational resources. The desired level of educational resources determines the amount of net revenue from tuition and nontuition income the institution requires. In terms of the notation from the equations presented earlier, the first step of the decision process sets targets for normal enrollment, E_N, and the right-hand side of equation (5.2), $I + (R - C) + A$. This decision is made with a fairly reliable estimate of nontuition income, G, because endowment income and state support, the largest components of G, are relatively easy to predict in the short

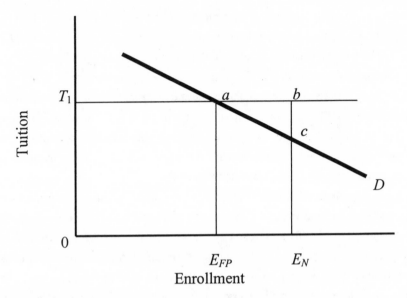

FIGURE 5.1. Demand Curve: Tuition Discounting. Source: Breneman 1994, 42.
Reprinted by permission of The Brookings Institution Press.

term. In the second step, the institution "seeks to enhance the quality of its students, faculty, and facilities" (Breneman 1994, 40). Figure 5.1 shows tuition setting, part of the second step.

D is the demand curve of the institution. It shows, for every tuition level, the number of students who will enroll at the institution. The (hypothetical) institution in figure 5.1 has a list-price tuition of T_1. If the institution were to charge every student its list-price tuition, T_1, it would not meet its enrollment target of E_N. Only E_{FP} students are willing to pay the list-price tuition. As a result this institution has to offer some financial aid. By cutting its price below T_1 for some students, the institution is able to attract a full class of E_N students.

The institution's accounts would show gross revenue from tuition, TE, equal to the area of the rectangle OT_1bE_N and institutionally funded financial aid, $S - F$, equal to the area of the triangle abc. Net revenue from tuition, $TE - (S - F)$, is area OT_1acE_N. The net revenue from tuition combined with the nontuition income, which the institution had previously estimated, yields the budget for the institution.

Given the demand curve in figure 5.1, the institution cannot meet its enrollment target and have revenue sufficient to purchase its desired level of educational resources unless it discounts tuition. Although the figure gives an accurate picture, it hides an important decision that a college has to make. It illustrates the choice of price for a given quality. In the second step of Breneman's model, among other things, the institution "seeks to enhance the quality of its students, faculty, and facilities." To capture the importance of quality, the model is amended by introducing quality as a choice variable.

The underlying objective function of an institution of higher education is complex. A variety of groups with many different motives have founded colleges and universities, a fact that has lead to considerable variation in institutional missions. I assume here that, given its mission, a college or university wants to maximize its prestige.[5] It wants to be known as the best at whatever it has set out to be. It could want to be the best research university, the best college for students preparing for the ministry in a particular religious denomination, the best small institution in the northwestern part of the state, or the best engineering school in the nation. I account for these differences as I develop the model.

In the amended model, I assume that institutions face an array of demand curves representing different student body qualities. Figure 5.2 presents a concrete example, measuring the student body's quality by its academic preparedness. Two demand curves are shown, for average SAT combined scores of 1,000 and 1,200, representing the demand for spaces in the institution that yield a particular average SAT score.[6] The demand curves are the result of a two-part process: First, for each tuition level, students willing to attend the institution are arrayed in descending order of SAT score. Second, the constraint of a particular average SAT score is imposed. A particular demand curve therefore indicates, for each tuition level, the number of students willing to attend, given the constraint that the average SAT score of the eventual class is fixed. The demand curve for an average SAT score of 1,000 is to the right of the demand curve for an average SAT score of 1,200 because, at each tuition level, fewer individuals are eliminated by its constraint than by the constraint of the average score of 1,200.[7]

These demand curves for average SAT scores assume that academic preparedness is the only constraint the institution places on its student body. More realistically, given varying missions, institutions place other constraints

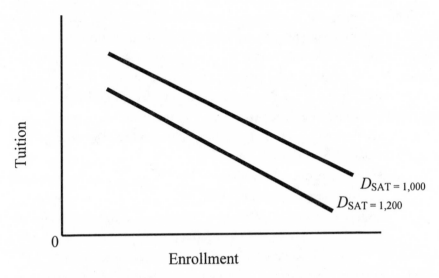

FIGURE 5.2. Demand Curves: Different Student Body Qualities

on their demand curves. For example, a college may want its student body to contain a certain percentage of minority students, or children of alumni, or children from wealthy families, or students with athletic prowess, or students from a particular state, or it may aim at a student body that exhibits socioeconomic diversity. As additional constraints are imposed, the demand curve for a particular SAT level shifts to the left. Moreover, other things being equal, increases in the reputation of the institution, increases in the perceived net tuition at other institutions, increases in the college-age population, or increases in the percentage of the college-age population that is inclined to go to college shift the whole family of demand curves to the right.[8]

Recognizing that a college faces a family of demand curves makes the interpretation of figure 5.1 more complex. The figure presents the simultaneous choice of a demand curve (student quality) and list-price tuition. How does an institution make such a choice? As it is drawn, figure 5.1 suggests two questions. First, why did the institution not try for a higher quality student body? If the institution had been willing to do more price discounting it could have moved to a lower (higher student quality) demand curve. The demand curve that intersects the horizontal axis at enrollment E_N represents the highest-quality demand curve that will meet the enrollment target. Why didn't the institution try to maximize student quality? Second, for a given demand curve, one could ask why the institution stopped with tuition T_1. Increases in list price above T_1 will increase the funds available to the institution. Why didn't the institution try to maximize revenue?

To answer the first of these questions, we have to recognize that not all quality-budget combinations are sustainable. Consider an institution that tries to maximize quality. It would be aiming for the demand curve that intersects E_N on the horizontal axis. As quality increases, the demand curve shifts to the left, and available tuition revenue declines. After a certain point the institution will not be able to sustain the level of quality required to sustain a demand curve. In other words, as an institution cuts its net tuition revenue by engaging in significant merit-based tuition discounting, it will attract a higher-quality student body. Because it has reduced its net revenue from tuition, however, it must present these students with a low-cost, low-quality education. Because of the low-quality education it offers, this institution will have a difficult time keeping the high-quality students it has attracted. Such a school might resort to deferring maintenance or increasing the rate at which it uses its endowment resources, but neither of these strategies represents a sustainable long-term policy. Eventually, the institution's reputation will suffer, shifting its family of demand curves further to the left.

Institutions of higher education are predominantly nonprofit enterprises whose mission statements include strong public service commitments, a fact that answers the second question. Such institutions will try to minimize their list-price tuition given their choice of student body size, student body quality, and level of educational resources. The current climate, in which the public has been critical of the rate of increase in tuition, reinforces the incentives for colleges and universities to be careful to limit tuition increases. Therefore, in most cases, institutions will halt the process of price discrimination before they have maximized revenues.[9]

In summary, the most accurate interpretation of figure 5.1 is that the choice of list-price tuition and financial aid it depicts yields sufficient revenue to sustain the student quality implied by the demand curve without providing excessive revenue to the institution. Figure 5.1 represents a decision that is contingent on other decisions. The institution has already determined its desired enrollment level and desired level of educational resources. It is also important to recognize that the college or university depicted in figure 5.1 is not maximizing its revenue. Colleges and universities try to maximize their prestige, and therefore do not always obtain the most revenue they can. For this reason, simple analogies to the behavior of profit-maximizing firms are often incorrect.

Application 1: Rankings and Merit Aid

The model helps explain some recent changes and tensions in higher education. Consider the rise in prominence of published rankings and the increases in the use of merit-based aid. College leaders spend a lot of time complaining about published rankings. At the same time, however, if an institution moves up in these rankings, its leaders are not at all ashamed to publicize that outcome. The love-hate relationship that college leaders have with the rankings is interesting to watch. Clever promotion has made many of these rankings popular, particularly those published by *U.S. News and World Report*.

The prominence of the rankings gives them a significant role in defining quality in higher education. The family of demand curves from which an institution chooses results directly from the number of constraints the institution imposes. Each additional binding constraint shifts the demand curve for each average SAT level to the left. The rankings put a premium on institutional characteristics that can be measured in a consistent fashion for all institutions. Thus the rankings focus on things such as SAT scores, percentage of freshmen in the top 10 percent of their high school class, and acceptance rates and do not place much value on other student body characteristics that may be important to the mission of a college or university. The only way, then, that an institution can play the ratings game as well as keep its commitments to, for example, minority students, poor students, alumni children, and students from various regions is to increase its tuition discounting. Alternatively, an institution could drop its commitment to one of the groups it had served, making it easier to attain a particular average SAT level. Such reactions to the increased prominence of rankings may well be part of the explanation for the observed shift away from need-based financial aid and toward merit-based aid.

Application 2: Price Discounts or Educational Investments?

In an influential article published in 1993, William G. Bowen and Breneman make a distinction between a *price discount* and an *educational investment*. They argue that institutionally provided financial aid is a price discount if the financial aid serves to attract more students. In this case, the institutionally funded grants have no cost to the institution. As the authors explain, in this case the institutions are acting as net revenue maximizers: "it is to the *financial* advantage of such colleges to provide price discounts in the form of scholarships" (Bowen and Breneman 1993, 29). If, on the other hand, institutionally funded financial aid does not attract more students, they argue, it is best thought of as an educational investment. Educational investments represent costs to the institution.

The motivation for Bowen and Breneman's 1993 article was the decision of Judge Louis C. Bechtle in the price-fixing case against Massachusetts Institute of Technology (MIT) as a participant in the Overlap Group discussed in chapter 2. Bowen and Breneman argue that MIT and the others in the Overlap Group were not giving price discounts (fixing prices); rather, they were making educational investments.

Other prominent researchers have accepted Bowen and Breneman's distinction. Charles Clotfelter cites Bowen and Breneman when he says that "some commentators have taken the view that financial aid is primarily a means of price discrimination whereby applicants with more choices are given a discount. While that characterization may be accurate for many less selective private institutions, for the selective institutions examined here, the commitment to this social contract made expenditures on financial aid a real cost of doing business" (Clotfelter 1996, 13). McPherson and Schapiro cite Bowen and Breneman in their discussion of financial aid at selective schools. "For these schools, student aid is a real cost, reflecting a choice by the institution to give up revenue from full-pay students to change the profile of the freshman class, aiming perhaps at socioeconomic or racial diversity or honoring a more abstract principle of admitting students without ability to pay" (McPherson and Schapiro 1998, 16).

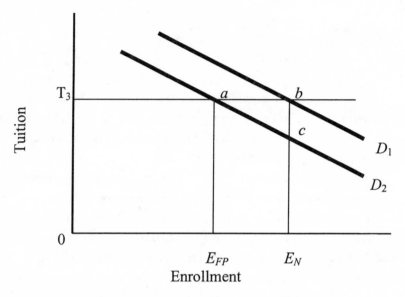

FIGURE 5.3. Demand Curves: Financial Aid As an Educational Investment

The key to the distinction that Bowen and Breneman make is contained in the test they propose. "A simple (conceptually at least) test allows us to tell whether student aid is a price discount or an educational investment. The key question is: does providing student aid increase or decrease the net resources available to the college to spend on other purposes?" (Bowen and Breneman 1993, 29). If providing financial aid increases net resources, it is a price discount because the college or university is using a pricing strategy designed to increase net revenue. If providing financial aid decreases net resources, then financial aid is an educational investment designed to obtain the type of students the institution thinks will constitute the best student body.

Figure 5.3 illustrates the demand curves that would exist in an institution that viewed financial aid as an educational investment. The institution in figure 5.3 could have chosen to have a student body represented by the D_1 demand curve and charged them all a tuition rate of T_3. Instead, the institution chose a student body represented by the D_2 demand curve. Bowen and Breneman argue that the financial aid, triangle abc, represents a cost to the institution that chose to be on the D_2 demand curve because the institution chose not to obtain this extra revenue. Such costs are often referred to by economists as opportunity costs.

Bowen and Breneman implicitly assume that the institution would set the same list price in the two situations. The model developed in the previous section suggests there is no reason for such an assumption. Figure 5.4 presents the analysis of the situation if the assumption of fixed prices is dropped. Without this assumption, the institution could achieve the demand curve D_2 by raising its list-price tuition to T_4.[10] As a result, it would have to provide more institutionally funded financial aid. It would have E'_{FP} rather than E_{FP} students paying full tuition. With the demand curve D_1, net revenue from tuition is area OT_3bE_N. With the demand curve D_2, net revenue is area OT_4dcE_N, and T_4 was selected so that these two areas are equal. In this situation, institutionally funded grants do not decrease the revenues available to the institution, so it does not make sense to talk about financial aid as an educational investment.[11]

The situation for which Bowen and Breneman reserve the term *educational investment* is inconsistent with my model. There is no reason for a highly selective institution to forgo any revenue because it wants to impose an additional constraint on its demand curve. The incentives in the *U.S. News and World Report* rankings reinforce this conclusion. An institution that decides

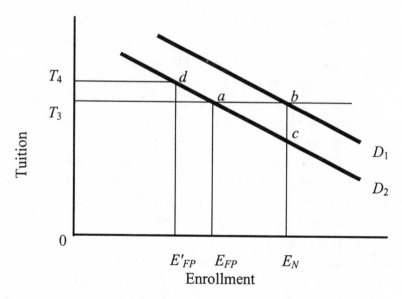

FIGURE 5.4. Demand Curves: Different Prices and the Same Net Revenue from Tuition

to decrease spending elsewhere in its budget to finance increases in institutional grants would harm its "financial resources rank" and therefore its overall rank. As the example above shows, an institution that chose to raise its tuition to fund additional financial aid could maintain its "financial resources rank."

The notion that institutions will be inclined to fund increases in financial aid with tuition increases is not novel. Ronald G. Ehrenberg and Susan H. Murphy (1993), for example, calculate the effect on tuition at Cornell University that resulted from the university's decision to increase the number of students from underrepresented groups. Ehrenberg and Murphy utilize a model much like the one suggested here. They clearly recognize that Cornell's was a decision to increase tuition, not one to decrease educational expenses. In slightly different contexts, Arthur M. Hauptman and Cathy Krop and Alan Reynolds make essentially this same point. "Institutions will respond as they have in the past to cutbacks in federal student aid—that is, they will raise their prices still further to generate more discounts for a student whose aid has been reduced" (Hauptman and Krop 1998, 72). Reynolds concludes that "a major reason why tuitions increased is that rising tuition from some students had to cover rising discounts to others" (Reynolds 1998, 109).

One interpretation of my rejection of Bowen and Breneman's terminology is that we have opposing views about the way selective institutions finance increases in institutionally funded financial aid. Bowen and Breneman assume that the expense of additional financial aid must be born by the institution (students, faculty, and staff) in the form of a reduction in expenditures. My model demonstrates that this need not happen. The additional financial aid could be funded by having a portion of the student body pay higher list-price tuition. In appendix A to this chapter, I present an analysis demonstrating that there is much stronger evidence for the notion that institutions use tuition increases to fund increases in institutional aid than for the notion that they use reductions in expenditures. The conclusion from the model and the evidence is that institutional grants are more appropriately thought of as price discounts than as institutional investments.

Although Bowen and Breneman's terminology is, in my opinion, poorly chosen, I would not dispute their basic premise that different institutions use institutionally funded financial aid for different purposes. I also agree that the ruling in the MIT case was unfortunate. The competition with financial aid unleashed by the breakup of the Overlap Group has had many adverse consequences for the financial aid system.

Institutionally Funded Grants Complicate Student's Choices

The structure of the financial aid system can be traced to the creation of the College Scholarship Service by the College Board in 1954. The College Scholarship Service set up the system of needs analysis and rules for the distribution of financial aid by colleges and universities. When the federal government inaugurated its financial aid programs with the Higher Education Act of 1965, it adopted the College Scholarship Service model. Under certain guidelines, colleges and universities determined the financial need of students and financial aid packages, including federal funds, offered to students. Because of this decision, the financial aid system in the United States is predominantly a campus-based system.

The creation of Pell Grants in 1972 changed the system slightly. Because the Pell Grant is not institution specific, students can plan their use of the grant before they actually receive a financial aid award from a college. In addition, most privately funded scholarships are administered off campus. Nevertheless, a significant portion of financial aid is campus based—students apply to a college or university, and the college or university makes a student-specific decision about a financial aid award. The recent growth in institutionally funded grants has reinforced the importance of on-campus financial aid.

Unfortunately, on-campus financial aid does a poor job of providing information to prospective college students. With such a system, students cannot make any meaningful price comparisons until after they have been admitted to the colleges they are considering and have been offered a financial aid package from each institution. Because applying to college is expensive, in both time and money, students apply to a limited number of institutions. Since on-campus financial aid hides the price of attendance, a student's choice of institutions to which to apply has to be based on assumptions about price. It is quite possible that these assumptions are incorrect. As a result, a student might not apply to the same group of institutions he or she would have applied to had he or she had perfect information.

Part of the reason that an on-campus financial aid system passes information so poorly is that institutional financial aid is increasingly being used as a recruiting device. If institutions acted as mere agents distributing federal funds, the fact they did so on campus would not be a problem. However, that is not the case; institutions give a considerable amount of their own financial aid. The recent trend toward using institutional financial aid as a recruiting device further complicates the matter. A growing fraction of this institutional aid is in the form of merit-based grants for students the institution would like to attract. In some cases, institutions make their definitions of financial need more generous or alter the structure of need-based aid packages, giving larger grants (and lower loans) to the students they want to attract.[12]

Because colleges and universities are "spending" their own money on financial aid, they want to be sure it is having the best possible effect. In the case of merit-based aid, the institution wants to ensure that its aid is going to the most meritorious students. The normal admission process provides it with just the type of information it needs. In the case of need-based aid, the institution wants to be sure its aid is going to those who are most needy. Many colleges and universities do not feel that the information, particularly the information on assets, collected to determine eligibility for federal financial aid is adequate. These institutions collect additional information on a family's assets using their own forms or forms made available by the College Scholarship Service. Families are allowed to make pleas for special consideration based on unusual circumstances. The variation in the information collected, as well as the way institutions react to a family's plea, can generate considerable differences in the financial aid offers a given student receives from various institutions.

In essence, in the current system a student determines a set of institutions to which to apply on the basis of an estimate of the net price of attending each institution. Once admitted, the student learns just how accurate these estimates were and makes a final choice with full information. In the end, the information problem is resolved. The adverse consequences of this type of system are twofold. First, the student may make a poor estimate and as a result eliminate from consideration the institution he or she would have most liked to attend. It is hard to know how often this happens. The second adverse consequence of the poor information flows is that the accurate information is hidden from everyone but the student and his or her parents. Those not familiar with higher education do not understand the financial aid system. Parents will commonly remark, "I couldn't afford to send my children to out-of-state colleges," whereas, given typical financial aid offers, the net cost of many out-of-state institutions is no higher than the net cost of the in-state institutions their children attend. Again, it is hard to know how often this happens. Both of these adverse consequences of an on-campus financial aid system would diminish if we minimized the role of institutionally funded financial aid.

Institutional Grants Raise the Level and Rate of Change of List-Price Tuition

Institutionally provided financial aid allows colleges and universities, like other retailers, to engage in price competition.[13] Unlike other retailers, however, many colleges and universities, particularly the well-known ones with headline-grabbing high tuition rates, are highly selective. They have a large surplus of willing buyers. They use price competition not to increase their sales but rather as a recruiting ploy designed to increase the quality of their student bodies. As the analysis above indicates, this price competition does not result in price reductions. Quite the reverse happens. Increases in institutionally funded financial aid create increases in list prices, allowing the institutions to selectively cut the price for students in high demand without suffering a decrease in revenue. In essence, these institutions have marked up prices so that they can discount them for some students. As the process has evolved, the prevalence of discounts has increased. At several colleges and universities, almost every student receives some type of scholarship or institutional grant—that is, a price discount. This makes these institutions' list price completely meaningless.

Because of the connection between institutionally funded grants and list-price tuition, the recent rapid increase in institutionally funded grants is a contributing factor in the precipitous rise in tuition. Increases in institutionally funded grants are only part of the story, of course. Nevertheless, if tuition increases from this source can be minimized, the overall rate of tuition increase will diminish. In fact, if we were to eliminate institutionally funded grants entirely, tuition rates would actually fall, at times by significant amounts.

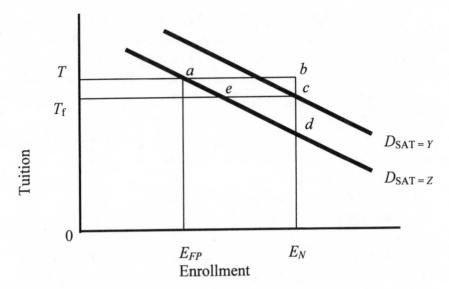

FIGURE 5.5. Demand Curves: Price Discounts and Equivalent Flat Tuition

Figure 5.5 illustrates two possible tuition policies: institutional grants and flat tuition. With institutional grants, the institution actually charges only E_{FP} students the full list-price tuition, T. The other students receive varying price discounts. In this case the institution has gross revenue from tuition given by the area $OTbE_N$ and net revenue from tuition given by the area $OTadE_N$. If this institution decided to charge a flat tuition rate—that is, to award no institutionally funded financial aid—it could set tuition at T_f and receive the same net revenue from tuition. Compared with the original situation, with tuition set at T_f the institution gains area ecd in net revenue, but it loses area T_fTae. Tuition level T_f was selected to make these two areas equal. The net revenue from tuition is therefore identical using the two different pricing strategies.[14] The difference between T and T_f is the difference in list-price tuition caused by price discounting.

Figure 5.5 also illustrates why an institution would engage in price discounting: price discounting allows the institution to increase the quality of its student body. In figure 5.5 the institution moves from the demand curve for average SAT = Y to the demand curve for average SAT = Z, where Z is greater than Y. Why is this practice at all objectionable?

There is no reason to object to an institution's attempts to increase the quality of its student body, but one could object to the method selected to accomplish this goal. There is no reason to object to an institution's attempts to upgrade the quality of its student body by hiring a better faculty or investing in improved facilities. This type of activity should be encouraged. There are, however, reasons to object to its using price discounts to improve the quality of its student body. There are two cases to consider. First, consider a student admitted to both Institution X and Institution Y who goes to Institution Y because Y offers a large price discount and X does not. If this student has financial resources sufficient to pay the full list-price tuition at either institution, institution Y is practicing what I call competitive price discounting. The difficulty with competitive price discounting is that Institution X will not stand by for long as Institution Y uses price discounts to attract the most talented students. In the long run, as more and more institutions start to offer competitive price discounts, it will become clear that the institutions are engaged in a zero-sum game. In this case, every institution could agree to charge flat tuition and suffer no decrease in quality as a consequence.

The alternative is social price discounting.[15] A social price discount is offered when the institution does not want to lose a student who meets its admission criteria simply because the student cannot afford to attend. In this case, T_f, which by construction yields the same net revenue from tuition as T, will not allow the institution to obtain the same student body it could obtain with tuition discounts. The price discounts serve a valid social objective of the institution—that is, they allow the institution to admit the most highly qualified students regardless of their ability to pay. Institutions that engage in social discounting will not be inclined to give up this practice unless they are assured that other funds will be available to ensure that all students who meet their admission criteria can afford to attend.

Both competitive and social price discounts are essentially reactive strategies. Competitive price discounts are a reaction to tuition discounting by other institutions. Given the behavior of its competitors, if the institution charges a flat tuition it will lose many of its high-quality students. Social price discounts are a reaction to government failures to fund need-based financial aid. If federal and state need-based financial aid were more generous, poor students would be able and willing to attend higher-priced institutions.

The practice of price discounting, it should be noted, does not increase the average net price. Because the net revenue from tuition is unchanged by adopting a flat tuition, and the size of the student body is unaltered, the net price per student is unaltered as well. For many purposes, net price per student is much more important than list price per student.

Why, then, do I emphasize list price per student? Net prices should be more important than list prices. Unfortunately, the number of people aware of that fact is not large. The rate of increase in list prices appears to be of great concern to many people. In 1997, alarmed by rising list-price tuition, Congress appointed a National Commission on the Cost of Higher Education. One of the commission's findings is that consumers are not well informed about college pricing practices, and its report goes to some length to clarify the difference between list prices and net prices.[16]

The news media are partly to blame for the attention given to list-price tuition. A headline reporting that the cost of attending Princeton is almost $40,000 a year, or the forecast that by a particular year the cost of a four-year education at an Ivy League institution will exceed $200,000, is a great way to grab the attention of readers.[17] Stanley Ikenberry and Terry Hartle (1998) find that the public dramatically overestimates the net price of attending college. These overestimates result from both overestimates of list prices and underestimates of the amount of financial aid available. The fascination of the news media with the high list prices at some institutions may well account for the overestimates of list prices.

Clearly, people are not well informed about colleges' pricing policies. As noted in chapter 3, many poor students who would benefit from higher education do not even attempt to attend college. It is likely that this is at least in part attributable to perceptions about college prices. Perceptions are important, and news about list prices affects perceptions. In such a world, policies that reduce list prices, even if they have no effect on net prices, can be beneficial.

It is also important not to lose sight of the first reason to minimize the use of institutionally funded grants: providing students more accurate information about college prices. The National Commission on the Cost of Higher Education clearly was concerned about this problem. Their second recommendation, to improve market information and public accountability, speaks to this concern. "The Commission recommends that the academic community provide the leadership required to develop better consumer information about costs and prices and to improve accountability to the general public" (National Commission on the Cost of Higher Education 1998, 17). This recommendation results in part from the commission's recognition that current financial aid practices obscure the prices that institutions actually charge.

A flat tuition strategy addresses the commission's concern. With flat tuition, it would be much easier for families to understand the costs of the colleges their children are considering. It would also be easier for them to evaluate changes in tuition. Currently, if an institution increases its list-price tuition, it is difficult to know whether it is really increasing educational inputs—for example, hiring more or better faculty or improving facilities—or simply increasing its "expenditures" on financial aid. Finally, with a flat tuition policy, an institution might be more inclined to hold the line on cost increases that do not increase educational quality because it knows that it will have to pass these costs on to all students. With selective price discounting, institutions can protect some students from price increases.

Institutionally funded grants affect not only the level of list-price tuition; they also influence the rate of change of list-price tuition. In appendix B to this chapter, I demonstrate that the rate of change of list-price tuition owing to a given rate of increase in costs will be larger for an institution that uses institutionally funded grants than for an the institution that does not. The logic for this result is fairly straightforward. The total amount of institutionally funded grants increases with the level of list-price tuition. When tuition increases, financial need increases, and an institution that meets need will have a larger financial aid bill. Given this, an institution that offers grants has to raise enough revenue from a tuition increase to cover both the cost increase and its larger financial aid requirement. In such a case, an institution that does not offer grants will have to raise only enough revenue to cover the cost increase. For a given rate of cost increase, the institution offering grants will have a more rapid rate of tuition increase than the institution that does not offer grants.

How Large Are Price Discounts?

How much money are we talking about? How much would tuition fall if institutions eliminated price discounting? By construction, the flat tuition—T_f in figure 5.5—is the net revenue from tuition divided by enrollment:

$T_f = [TE - (S - F)] / E.$

We are ultimately interested in the difference between T and T_f. This difference is given by

$$T - T_f = [TE / E - [TE - (S - F)] / E = (S - F) / E. \qquad (5.3)$$

Equation (5.3) shows that the difference between list-price tuition with discounts and flat tuition, under the assumption of equal net tuition revenue, is the amount of institutionally awarded financial aid divided by the size of the student body.

I use data from three sources to estimate equation (5.3): the Integrated Postsecondary Education Data System (IPEDS) data on institutional finances, the 1995–96 National Postsecondary Student Aid Survey (NPSAS), and the National Association of College and University Business Officers (NACUBO) Tuition Discounting Survey (Lapovsky and Hubbell 2000). The various data sets have their own advantages and disadvantages. The NPSAS 1995–96 survey looks at one time period, whereas the IPEDS and NACUBO data provide annual data. The NPSAS 1995–96 data allow me to measure price discounting for all types of institutions. For my purposes the only useful IPEDS data are those provided for private liberal arts colleges,[18] and the NACUBO data are collected only for independent institutions. Finally, the IPEDS and NPSAS 1995–96 data cover all students, and the NACUBO data have information

TABLE 5.1.   Distribution of Average Tuition Discounts, 1995–1996, Private Liberal Arts I Institutions

Tuition Discount	Number of Institutions	Percentage of Institutions
$1,000–1,999	5	3.2
$2,000–2,999	13	8.4
$3,000–3,999	17	11.0
$4,000–4,999	27	17.4
$5,000–5,999	25	16.1
$6,000–6,999	29	18.7
$7,000–7,999	24	15.5
$8,000 or more	15	9.7

Source: U.S. Department of Education, NCES, IPEDS, "Financial Statistics: Current Funds Revenues: Tuition and Fees," "Financial Statistics: Scholarship and Fellowship Expenditures: Institutional Scholarship and Fellowship Expenditures," and "Tuition Data: Undergraduate Tuition and Fees, In-State," 1995–96.
   Note: Private Liberal Arts I Institutions is a category of Carnegie Classification of Institutions of Higher Education.

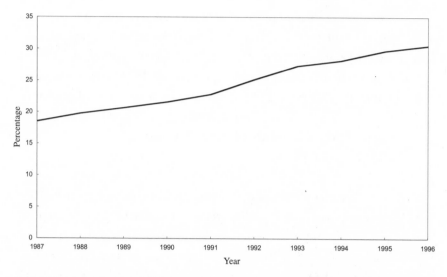

FIGURE 5.6. Institutional Aid As a Percentage of Tuition, 1987–1996, Private Liberal Arts I Institutions. *Source:* U.S. Department of Education, NCES, IPEDS, "Financial Statistics: Current Funds Revenues: Tuition and Fees," "Financial Statistics: Scholarship and Fellowship Expenditures: Institutional Scholarship and Fellowship Expenditures," and "Tuition Data: Undergraduate Tuition and Fees, In-State," 1987–96.

both on freshman and on all students. I first look at the IPEDS data, then the NPSAS 95–96 data, and end with the NACUBO data.

Integrated Postsecondary Education Data System Data

Table 5.1 presents the distribution of institutionally financed aid per student—that is, *(S – F) / E*—for private colleges in the Carnegie classification Liberal Arts I. The IPEDS data contain 156 institutions in this category. One of them, Christendom College, lists no institutional expenditures on financial aid. The other 155 institutions discount tuition. The table gives the distribution of the average tuition discount for these institutions. How much money is involved? At least for most of these private liberal arts colleges, the answer has to be quite a bit. More than half the institutions give average discounts of $5,000 or more.

All of the variables from the IPEDS data are available annually from 1987. Figure 5.6 presents the data on the average tuition discount as a percentage of list-price tuition for private Liberal Arts I institutions.[19] Clearly, tuition discounting has grown rapidly in this sector. In 1987 the average tuition discount was 18.5 percent of tuition; in 1996, it exceeded 30 percent.

National Postsecondary Student Aid Survey 1995–1996 Data

To get a broader picture of the higher education sector, I use the NPSAS 1995–96 average value per student of total institutional aid to compute the average price discount for public and private institutions by Carnegie classification. Table 5.2 gives these data by absolute amount and as a percentage of list-price tuition. Because of sampling and perhaps slight differences in definitions, the one overlapping data point does not quite match: my estimate for Liberal Arts I institutions (in figure 5.6) from the IPEDS data was 30.49 percent, slightly lower than the 31.87 percent obtained from the NPSAS data.

Not surprisingly, table 5.2 indicates that tuition discounting is much more prevalent in private than in public institutions. The percentage discounts are smaller, and the tuition is lower, at public institutions, yielding substantially lower average price discounts. The highest average price discount in the public sector is $671, compared with $4,585 in the private sector. Table 5.2 also indicates that the private Liberal Arts I institutions I investigated using the IPEDS data give, on average, the deepest discounts. The average discounts given by other private institutions, notably Research Universities I, are almost as high.

TABLE 5.2.   Average Price Discounts, 1995–1996, by Institution Type

Institution Type[a]	Public		Private	
	Amount	Percentage	Amount	Percentage
Research I	$427	12.86	$4,270	24.65
Research II	671	17.11	2,322	23.07
Doctoral I	475	15.52	2,148	20.44
Doctoral II	279	10.68	2,325	21.82
Comprehensive I	226	9.77	1,784	22.15
Comprehensive II	248	11.31	1,481	20.64
Liberal Arts I	38	1.74	4,585	31.87
Liberal Arts II	177	10.70	1,609	25.19

Source: U.S. Department of Education, NCES 1998.
[a]By Carnegie Classification of Institutions of Higher Education.

The prominence of private Research Universities I and Liberal Arts Colleges I in the rankings of institutional quality makes the fact that they provide large discounts particularly important. If these institutions were to adopt a policy of charging flat tuition, the headlines about the list-price reductions would be dramatic.

National Association of College and University Business Officers Data

The National Association of College and University Business Officers has surveyed independent institutions about their tuition discounting practices annually since 1990.[20] Lucie Lapovsky and Loren Loomis Hubbell (2000) summarize the results of the 1999 survey. The sample for 1998 and 1999 includes 348 institutions, 275 of which have been in the sample since 1990. The 1999 data indicate that the average tuition discount was $6,158, which is 37.3 percent of list-price tuition. The 1990 data indicate that the average tuition discount was $2,717, which is 24.1 percent of list-price tuition. These figures suggest that the extent of discounting in the NACUBO sample is not too different from that found among the private Liberal Arts I institutions. Interestingly, the NACUBO data include tuition discounting for freshmen. In their 1999 sample, this discount averaged $7,933, which is 48.1 percent of list-price tuition.

The practice of providing institutionally financed grants to some students clearly increases list-price tuition. It is easy to see why individual institutions operating in the current environment have been attracted to price discounting. Nevertheless, in some cases, they would lose little if they joined with their competitors in agreeing to outlaw this practice. In other cases, changes in government policy would be necessary to convince institutions to give up selective price discounting.

The data suggest that tuition discounts are quite large on average. The prevalence of tuition discounts has reached ridiculous levels at some institutions. Twelve institutions in the 1999 NACUBO data gave financial aid to 100 percent of their entering freshmen; 44.3 percent of the institutions gave financial aid to 90 percent or more of their freshmen, and 60.8 percent gave financial aid to 80 percent or more of their freshmen (Lapovsky and Hubbell 2000,

25). "One has to wonder what utility the tuition price can have in the situation where absolutely no entering student pays that amount" (ibid., 28). This is a good question. In these situations, colleges and universities have adopted the model of the automobile dealer. The sticker price is on the car, and the automobile dealer will accept a check for that price. However, if the customer shows any reluctance to pay that price, a lower price will be revealed. The sticker price is merely the starting price for a bargain. A proposal to eliminate tuition discounts asks colleges and universities to adopt a policy similar to what is called the "no-dicker sticker" policy adopted by Saturn that has been followed by some other car dealers.[21] This policy is also sometimes called the "most favored customer clause" because it amounts to a pledge that the institution will not have a lower price for any customer.[22]

Need-Based Institutional Grants Are Funded Inequitably

There are two principles of equity: horizontal equity demands that equals should be treated equally, and vertical equity requires that unequals should be treated unequally. Need-based institutionally funded grants violate the principle of horizontal equity, in that individuals with equal ability to pay are not treated as equals.

My argument is based on the widely held notion that the public interest is best served if a college education is available to everyone who is qualified regardless of ability to pay. Although this notion was not popular earlier in our history, few would argue with it now. Living in a society with appropriate access to higher education generates benefits both to the individual who receives the education and to the public at large.[23] In other words, there are positive externalities involved in the production of higher education. If this argument is granted, it follows that the costs associated with producing this public benefit should not fall on one group more than any other.[24]

In the case of federal financial aid, all taxpayers share the financial burden. In addition, when states provide subsidies to state-supported colleges and universities, all the taxpayers in the state share the financial burden. In the case of institutional grants, however, those who are comparatively well off and have children attending college carry a disproportionate share of the burden for financing this public benefit: they pay higher tuition so that those who are less well off and have children attending college can pay lower tuition. In essence, the tax base funding institutional grants is very narrow. This is likely to be inequitable. Students benefit from being educated at an institution with a socially diverse student body, so the children of these well-off parents receive more of the benefits than do those who are not students. Nevertheless, because these students do not receive all of the benefits and because some students carry large shares of the costs, there clearly are cases in which students and their families face inequitable burdens.

It is also important to note that most institutions offer students a highly subsidized education. In these cases students paying the full tuition simply receive a lower subsidy than students receiving institutional financial aid. In many cases even students paying full tuition are paying less than the total cost of their education.

The discussion here focuses on what I have called social price discounts.[25] As the name suggests, in the case of social price discounts, institutions are engaged in a socially beneficial activity. They are adopting a cause that the society as a whole has decided not to fully support. This happens frequently in American society. It is the foundation of private charity.

Social price discounting can be defended by saying that the family that pays the full price to send its son or daughter to one of the institutions engaging in social discounting is giving some of its funds to a private charity. In effect, this is what has happened, but few families are aware they are making a charitable donation through their tuition payments. One hallmark of true charity is that the contributor is fully aware that he or she is making a contribution, but in this case, all the parents typically know is that if they want their children to attend the institution, they have to pay the full tuition bill. Institutions are not inclined to tell those who pay tuition just how large a charitable contribution they are making, and the federal government does not allow the difference between T and T_f to be taken as an income tax deduction.

Some institutions that fund their grants from endowment income argue that their financial aid is funded entirely from voluntary private charity. Kim Strosnider reports on one of these institutions, Washington and Lee University. "Unlike many other institutions, which use tuition income to finance the bulk of their student-aid programs, Washington and Lee relies exclusively on endowment earnings and, to a lesser extent, gifts for the $8-million or so in institutional aid that it provides to students each year" (Strosnider 1998). The difference between institutions that fund institutional grants from gifts and endowment earnings and those that fund institutional grants from tuition revenue is illusory. In the end, dollars are fungible. Strosnider quotes Michael McPherson, the president of Macalester College, as saying that "all dollars are green. . . . Endowment for any core area is basically as good as for another core area" (ibid.).

For there to be a meaningful difference between funding financial aid from gifts and endowment earnings and from any other source, it has to be the case that those whose gifts support financial aid will give only for this purpose. It is difficult to know just how often this is the case. Helping needy students and helping the institution to attract the best students are appealing notions to prospective donors. Nevertheless, in many cases donors are willing to give for many purposes; it would be interesting to see what would happen to its endowment if a college or university were to decide to direct donors interested in financial aid to some other project within the institution. It is nonetheless true, however, that institutional grants raise list-price tuition and that this tuition increase falls unfairly on families with students currently in college. On the other hand, if institutions eschewing institutional grants were to lose donor support, they would not be able to reduce tuition by the full amount of the reduction in institutional grants. In this case, the institutions would have to make up the shortfall in endowment income and gifts with increases in net revenue from tuition.

The public, through state support for institutions and federal financial aid, makes a large financial commitment to higher education. The fact that institutions engage in social discounting implies, however, that these funds are inadequate. There are two potential sources of the inadequacy: a low total budget and poor distribution of the funds. It is easy to make the case for flaws in the distribution of public funds in higher education. Most state support is in the form of general subsidies to institutions, and, as many analysts have pointed out, this is a poorly directed subsidy. Many students who attend state-supported institutions would be willing to attend even if tuition were much higher, and state subsidy in no way affects the behavior of these students. Similarly, a large percentage of federal aid takes the form of loan subsidies, which are available to middle- and upper-income students as well as low-income ones, and tax credits, which are effectively available only to middle- and upper-middle-class families. Probably for political reasons, the recent emphasis in federal aid is affordability for middle-income families more than access for low-income students. Clearly, much of the need for social discounting could be eliminated by a redistribution of government support for higher education.

Some institutional grants are part of an income redistribution scheme. In many cases this income redistribution is designed to accomplish the socially desirable goal of insuring that all talented students have an opportunity to make the most of their talent. In the case of institutionally funded grants, this income redistribution is funded by a very narrow group—relatively well-to-do families with children in college. The benefits of living in a society with access to the best education for which one can qualify accrue to the entire society. Thus the burden of paying for these benefits is distributed inequitably.

Through private charities many individuals willingly contribute to help those less fortunate than they are. These private charities achieve social goals that local, state, and federal governments have decided not to undertake. The income redistribution implicit in the tuition and financial aid practices of colleges and universities are similar in effect. The major difference between private charities and colleges and universities is that those contributing to charities do so voluntarily, whereas few of those paying college tuition are aware that they are making a charitable contribution.

A system such as the current one might still be defended if the government money invested in supporting higher education were well directed but simply insufficient. Several private charities exist to fill in the gaps left by insufficient government attention to problems. However, much of the government's support of higher education is misdirected. A reallocation of government support might well eliminate the need for the private charity implicit in current tuition and financial aid practices.

Finally, there is a role for private charity in the financial aid system; its role is off campus. Private charities should be encouraged to give financial aid of all sorts. This aid, however, should be able to be used at any institution. In this way, the private financial aid would not confuse the student's decision about which institution to attend. The financial aid system should be designed to facilitate—not obfuscate—these decisions.

Merit-Based Institutional Aid Creates an Unproductive Competition for Students

Recent data on financial aid practices in higher education show a substantial increase in the amount of merit-based aid. Much of this aid is awarded to students as part of what I have called competitive price discounting. Table 5.3 presents data from the 1989–90 and 1995–96 National Postsecondary Student Aid Studies. These data indicate that non-need-based aid is clearly growing as a percentage of all financial aid.

The growth in the public sector has been especially rapid. It is worth noting that these data do not include the effect of the HOPE Scholarships in Georgia, which represent a major shift toward merit aid in the public sector. Peter Schmidt (2001) reports data that cover the 1998–99 academic year including Georgia's HOPE Scholarship program and its imitators. These data show that merit-based aid is growing more rapidly than need-based aid in the public sector. Merit-based aid increased 19 percent from 1997–98 to 1998–99, while need-based aid grew only 6.6 percent over the same period.

The essence of the argument against merit-based grants is that they are part of a zero-sum game, what Thomas Schelling (1978) calls a multiperson prisoners' dilemma. Ultimately, with or without institutionally granted merit-based grants, the same students go to college, and for the most part they go to the same colleges. Perhaps the prospect of a merit-based award encourages students to work hard in high school, but as merit scholarships proliferate this benefit withers away. Moreover, the competition for spaces at the most selective colleges and universities already keeps top students motivated, so there is little room for merit-based scholarships to have an effect.

The recent behavior of some well-known institutions that were members of the Overlap Group demonstrates how competition using aid has worked. Without the explicit collusion of the Overlap Group, despite their public commitments to need-based financial aid, many of its former members are starting to behave much more competitively. The financial aid policy changes that

TABLE 5.3.   Merit-Based Aid As Share of Institutionally Funded Undergraduate
Financial Aid, 1989–1990 and 1995–1996 (percentage)

Institution Type	Public		Private	
	1989–90	1995–96	1989–90	1995–96
Non-doctorate-granting	19.3	35.3	20.0	27.2
Doctorate-granting	20.3	24.0	14.1	19.6

Source: U.S. Department of Education, NCES 1998.

Princeton University announced in early 1998 were seen as a first sign of this change. Princeton changed its financial aid packages by increasing the grant-to-loan ratio for low-income students and eliminating the value of the family's home as a factor in determining financial need, a change that benefited middle-income students in particular.[26] The reactions to Princeton's changes revealed the new environment. Jim Belvin, the director of financial aid at Duke University, responded by saying, "We'll all have to think about this from a competitive perspective" (Gose 1998b). Yale University announced a similar change two weeks after Princeton's announcement (Gose 1998a). Stanford University soon followed suit, and "in a news release that followed the announcements by Princeton, Stanford, and Yale, Harvard said it would make 'competitively supportive' financial-aid offers this year" (Gose 1998c). The competition has been joined at the highest levels. The 2001 announcement by Princeton that it was eliminating loans from its financial aid awards represents the latest escalation of the competition.

McPherson and Schapiro present a good summary of the effects of the recent increase in merit-based aid. "Increased emphasis on merit scholarships in both private and public institutions suggests that opportunities will continue to be strong for our most accomplished and best-prepared high school graduates. But from the perspective of the nation, we must ask which groups are at the greatest risk of not being well served and which purposes of postsecondary education are most likely to be neglected under these changing conditions" (McPherson and Schapiro 1998, 134). This concern is well placed. A financial aid system that allows an increasing amount of merit-based financial aid will be very good for the students who have done well in high school and who do well on standardized multiple choice tests. Students with average high school records or difficulties on such tests, however—particularly those with limited means—will be less well served. The students with good high school records and high test scores have always been treated well by the higher education sector, however, and there is no good reason to improve their treatment. Students with limited means and less stellar records are another story. We should not leave these individuals behind.

Framing the Issue

My suggestion that the financial aid system minimize the use of institutional grants is admittedly radical and will face an uphill battle with many readers. Institutional scholarships, both merit based and need based, have a long history and enjoy great popularity. Most people deem it reasonable for institutions to give a price break to special students. A proposal to cut down on this practice will seem downright unnatural to many.

Part of the popularity of institutional scholarships, however, results from the way the transactions involved are framed in the minds of observers. A well-known example helps illustrate this. When credit cards other than gasoline company credit cards were first used at gasoline stations, a large number of stations raised their prices and offered "discounts for cash." Why didn't the gasoline stations keep their prices unchanged and require "surcharges for credit card purchases?" The answer is clear: although these two options yield identical prices, consumers would rather receive discounts than pay surcharges.

Institutional scholarships involve an identical choice: institutions have chosen to raise list prices and give selected students price discounts rather than keeping prices constant and charging some students surcharges. As with the gasoline stations, the logic behind this choice is clear: giving students scholarships, and thereby allowing them to pay less than the list price, sounds more appealing than imposing surcharges above list price.

Tuition discounts and tuition surcharges are two ways of describing the same system. A suggestion to minimize tuition surcharges would be a much easier sell than a suggestion to minimize scholarships. Modes of thinking about college financing are ingrained, and the way the debate has been framed places my redesign proposal at a considerable disadvantage. My hope is that pointing this out may eliminate some of the disadvantage. My proposal will succeed only if people realize the equivalence of tuition discounts and tuition surcharges. In summary then, let me say that I am solidly behind minimizing tuition surcharges, and I hope readers will join me.

Appendix A: Evidence on Tuition Increases versus
Expenditure Reductions

A proper test of the models in figures 5.3 and 5.4 would be a challenging exercise. The problem is the familiar one of identifying the model. Consider, for example, the effect of tuition discounting on tuition. I have argued that increases in tuition discounting increase tuition. It is also the case that, other things being equal, increases in tuition for any other reason at institutions that give need-based grants will increase the extent of tuition discounting. Similarly, a decision to increase the quality of the student body affects the amount of tuition discounting, which in turn affects the quality of the student body. All of the variables are simultaneously determined, and in such cases it is difficult to identify the structural relations. I do not attempt structural modeling.

For my much more modest exercise, I examined the behavior of institutions from the top forty national liberal arts colleges according to the 2000 *U.S. News and World Report* rankings. I chose these institutions for two reasons. First, the controversy focuses on selective institutions, and these colleges are highly selective. Second, the IPEDS data for institutionally sponsored scholarships and fellowships combine undergraduate and graduate financial aid. Focusing on institutions that are predominantly undergraduate institutions eliminates problems of different motivation for undergraduate and graduate financial aid.

I was able to collect complete data for thirty of these forty-two institutions covering 1987, the first available data for institutionally funded financial aid, through 1996, the last available data. The following institutions were in my sample: Amherst College, Bard College, Barnard College, Bryn Mawr College, Bucknell University, Carleton College, Claremont McKenna College, Colby College, Colgate University, College of the Holy Cross, Colorado College, Connecticut College, Davidson College, Dickinson College, Hamilton College, Haverford College, Keynon College, Lafayette College, Lawrence University, Macalester College, Pomona College, Sarah Lawrence College, Swarthmore College, Trinity College, Union College, University of the South, Vassar College, Washington and Lee University, Wellesley College, Wesleyan University, Whitman College, and Williams College.

Data are available for most of the variables in the financial accounts described at the beginning of this chapter. There is one difficulty with these data. The data for TE (revenue from tuition and fees) are for gross revenue—that is, they assume that every student pays the full list price. I require separate estimates for T (tuition and fees) and E (enrollment). Data for T are readily available, and for private institutions that have few, if any, graduate students, these data should represent the list-price tuition charged to all students, before application of financial aid (including institutional grants) to a student's account.[27] The most common approach to finding E is to use full-time equivalent (FTE) enrollment. It is standard to define an FTE student as one full-time student or three part-time students. Using the separate estimates for E, defined as FTE students, and T did not result in numbers that were sufficiently close to TE for my comfort. The errors in this exercise most likely came from the enrollment data. Given this, I decided to measure E as $E' \equiv TE/T$. "Number of tuition-paying units" is probably the best definition of the term E'.

Table 5.4 illustrates the relation between changes in the discount per student, ΔD, and percentage changes in tuition, instructional expenditures, and net tuition revenue. D is defined as $(S - F)/E$—that is, D is the amount of institutionally funded grants per student. All variables are measured as percentage changes from year to year. I restricted the sample to instances in which the discount increased and enrollment changed no more than 3 percent in either direction. There were 185 changes that met these criteria. The data in table 5.4 indicate that the more rapidly an institution increases institutionally funded financial aid per student, the more rapidly it increases its tuition. This is also what the analysis suggested. The relation is quite strong. The change in tuition increases monotonically with ΔD, and some of the differences are statistically significantly different from one another. The 95 percent confidence intervals for large increases in discounting, $15 < \Delta D < 20$ and $20 < \Delta D < 25$, do not overlap those for small increases in discounting, $0 < \Delta D < 5$ and $5 < \Delta D < 10$.

The larger tuition increases are not, however, sufficient to hold net rev-

TABLE 5.4.   Tuition, Instructional Expenditures, Net Tuition Revenue Changes, and Tuition-Discounting Changes

Category	n	Mean	95% Confidence Interval
$0 < \Delta D < 5$			
Tuition	25	5.968	5.379–6.558
Instructional expenditures	25	9.245	6.519–11.971
Net tuition revenue	25	7.137	5.759–8.516
$5 < \Delta D < 10$			
Tuition	49	6.100	5.564–6.635
Instructional expenditures	49	7.084	5.476–8.692
Net tuition revenue	49	6.480	5.523–7.435
$10 < \Delta D < 15$			
Tuition	56	6.671	6.191–7.149
Instructional expenditures	56	6.333	5.303–7.363
Net tuition revenue	56	4.959	4.081–5.837
$15 < \Delta D < 20$			
Tuition	23	7.681	6.815–8.547
Instructional expenditures	23	8.165	5.839–10.492
Net tuition revenue	23	5.786	3.770–7.804
$20 < \Delta D < 25$			
Tuition	18	7.980	6.909–9.051
Instructional expenditures	18	7.351	4.885–9.816
Net tuition revenue	18	5.127	2.084–8.170
$\Delta D > 25$			
Tuition	14	8.683	6.499–10.866
Instructional expenditurets	14	8.068	6.001–10.135
Net tuition revenue	14	1.692	–3.129–6.514

Source: U.S. Department of Education, NCES, IPEDS, "Financial Statistics: Current Funds Revenues: Tuition and Fees," "Financial Statistics: Current Funds Expenditures and Transfers: Instructional Expenditures," "Financial Statistics: Scholarship and Fellowship Expenditures: Institutional Scholarship and Fellowship Expenditures," and "Tuition Data: Undergraduate Tuition and Fees, In-State," 1987–96.

enue from tuition constant. There is a downward trend to the changes in net tuition revenue, but the relation between ΔD and net tuition revenue is not strong. In the range $10 < \Delta D < 25$, which includes three of the ranges given in the table, the mean for net tuition revenue is roughly constant. In addition, all of the 95 percent confidence intervals for net tuition revenue overlap, so none of the differences in the means are statistically significant.

Finally, instructional expenditure is not systematically related to tuition discounting. The percentage increase in instructional expenditures falls as ΔD increases from 0 to 15, but it then increases for larger values of ΔD. As with net tuition revenue, all of the confidence intervals overlap, so none of the differences in the means are statistically significant.

The conclusion from the data in table 5.4 is that larger increases in tuition discounting are associated with larger increases in tuition, but there is no statistically reliable association between increases in tuition discounting and either instructional expenditures or net tuition revenue. This evidence is by no means conclusive. The data come from a relatively small nonrandom sample of institutions and are based only on comparing means. They do, however, strongly suggest that it is inappropriate to maintain the assumption that tuition will be constant in the face of an increase in tuition discounting. As noted earlier, this is the implicit assumption in the model that justifies the use of the notion that institutional grants are an educational investment for highly selective institutions.

Appendix B: The Effect of Institutionally Funded Grants on the
Rate of Change in List-Price Tuition

I use the notation introduced at the beginning of this chapter to discuss the relation between institutionally funded grants and the rate of increase in list-price tuition. Typically, institutionally funded financial aid is positively related to the number of students and the list-price tuition level. I use a linear function similar to one used by Clotfelter (1996) to describe this relation:

$$(S - F) = (k + jT)E,$$

where $(S - F)$ represents institutionally funded grants, T is the list-price tuition, E is enrollment, and k and j are positive constants. The constant j represents the sensitivity of per student grant spending to the tuition level. Substituting this function into equation (5.2) yields

$$TE - (k + j\,T)E + G = I + (R - C) + A,$$

where G is gift and endowment income and $I + (R - C) + A$ represents the costs of the institution.

Solving the preceding equation for per student list-price tuition, T, yields

$$T = [1 / (1 - j)][I + (R - C) + A - G + kE] / E.$$

This equation allows us to discuss the effects of institutionally funded financial aid on the rate of increase of list-price tuition. Suppose that the costs of the institution, $I + (R - C) + A$, increase by a certain percentage, α, each year.

Other things being equal, the change in tuition, ΔT, attributable to the increase in costs is given by

$$\Delta T = \{(1 + \alpha) \, / \, (1 - j)\}\{[I + (R - C) + A] \, / \, E\}.$$

This equation demonstrates that the change in tuition increases with j, which measures the sensitivity of institutionally funded financial aid to the list-price tuition. If $j = 0$, either because the institution does not fund any grants or because all of the institution's grants are lump-sum grants, the increase in tuition from a given increase in costs will be lower than if $j > 0$. An institution that awards only lump-sum grants would be unusual. The presence of need-based aid would most certainly lead to $j > 0$, because as tuition increased the need of students would increase. Moreover, merit-based aid would not be an effective recruiting tool if it did not increase with tuition. Setting aside the unusual case of lump-sum grants, the general conclusion is that the presence of institutionally funded grants increases the rate of increase in list-price tuition.

Federal Loan Guarantees

The current system of financial aid in the United States relies heavily on federal guaranteed student loans. Federally supported lending started with the National Defense Student Loan Program in 1958. Title IV of the Higher Education Act of 1965 expanded the role of lending dramatically by incorporating the National Defense Student Loan Program in its mix of financial aid programs and adding the Guaranteed Student Loan Program. Supporters of need-based financial aid feared that tuition tax credits, which primarily benefit the middle class, would diminish funding available for programs for the more needy (see Gladieux and Hauptman 1995, 15–16), and federally guaranteed loans were included in the mix of student aid to counter proposals for tuition tax credits. Guaranteed student loans have grown in importance and are now, by a significant margin, the largest source of federal financial aid.

The guaranteed student loan program (known since 1972 as the Stafford Loan Program) has three objectives: to keep costs to borrowers low, to keep the return to lenders high, and to keep the costs to the federal government low (McPherson 1989, 12). These objectives are mutually contradictory, and at various points in the history of the program, the weights given to the three objectives have changed. Both lenders and students were initially wary of participating in the program. Most important, the program's interest rate ceilings, introduced to keep the loans affordable for students, made the loans especially unattractive to lenders. This problem was solved by the introduction of what is called the "special allowance," a government payment to lenders that makes up the difference between the market interest rate and the interest rate students pay on the loans. For the purpose of the special allowance, the market interest rate is assumed to be 3.5 percent above the yield on ninety-one-day Treasury bills. After the introduction of the special allowance, student loans became a profitable product for banks and other lenders.

From the very beginning the loans were not only guaranteed but also subsidized, because the government pays the interest on the loans while students are in college. The special allowance represented a dramatic increase in the subsidy and therefore in the costs of the program to the government. In the 1970s, pressure from the middle class and upper middle class to gain access to this affordable source of credit culminated in the passage of the Middle-Income Student Assistance Act (MISAA) of 1978, which dropped the financial need requirement for borrowers. The volume of loans, and the subsidy costs to the government, increased dramatically. It quickly became clear that the third objective for the program, keeping the cost to the federal government low, was not being met, and in 1981 need was reintroduced as a requirement for participation in the guaranteed student loan program.

Michael Mumper (1999) has noted that the current government guaranteed loan program has created a large industry. He lists five different types of firms in this industry. First, more than five thousand banks and other lenders directly provide Stafford Loans in the Federal Family Education Loan Program (FFEL). Second, secondary loan markets allow original lenders to use student loans as a liquid asset. The largest and most well known participant in the secondary loan market is the Student Loan Marketing Association, or Sallie Mae, which is now a fully private firm heavily involved in the student loan industry. Third, state guaranty agencies are the entities that monitor and collect the loans. Congress created these agencies in the 1970s in response to the U.S. Department of Health, Education, and Welfare's poor record in monitoring student loans. Fourth, a growing alternative loan industry offers loans to students who would like to borrow more than the federal programs allow. The College Board reports that "non-federal borrowing totaled $2.4 billion in 1998–99, up 25 percent over the previous years. While the amount of non-federal borrowing is small compared to the $35 billion in federal education loans, consistently large increases over the past three years reflect a growing interest in and reliance on alternative methods of paying for college" (College Board 1999b, 4). Finally, the complexity of the federal loan programs and the reporting requirements for federal financial aid in general have generated a large number of consultants and technology vendors who help colleges and universities administer the student loan program.

The student loan industry fell under attack in the 1990s. William D. Ford Direct Loans were created in 1993 to cure the perceived problems in the guaranteed student loan industry. Direct lending has taken a large portion of the business away from the industry. President Bill Clinton and other backers of direct lending had hoped that it would fully replace the traditional FFEL program, but direct lending seems to have leveled off at about one-third of total federal student lending. Mumper (1999) attributes the slowing in the growth of direct lending to two sources: the concerns of institutions that the federal government will not do a good job of running its loan program and improvements in the operation of the FFEL program. The FFEL program remains a controversial program. In 1998, Congress ordered the General Accounting Office to convene a group to try to determine ways of improving the program by introducing market forces. As Stephen Burd (2000b) indicates, this panel has had difficulty coming to agreement on a set of options to present to Congress.

My criticism of federal student loan programs is much deeper than the criticisms that led to the introduction of direct loans. Guaranteed student loans combine two features: subsidies and loan guarantees. Loan guarantees serve a useful purpose: without them, student access to credit would be dramatically reduced. I do not argue that loan guarantees are bad but rather that the government should not be the one providing the loan guarantees. In addition, the subsidies distort private decisions in unproductive ways. There is no reason to privilege borrowing over other means of paying for higher education. As I argue later in this chapter, federal involvement in student lending stifles innovation in the market for student loans. Because the government is guaranteeing the loans, they have a uniform structure. All these difficulties with guaranteed student loans could be eliminated if the responsibility for loan guarantees were shifted from the government to colleges and universities.

Government Loan Guarantees Introduce Moral Hazard

Placing the responsibility for loan guarantees with the federal government is an inherently flawed practice. The major problem, as I note in chapter 1, is one of moral hazard.[1] The classic example of moral hazard is fire insurance. Moral hazard exists if the insured person, by virtue of being insured, does not exhibit care in storing flammable materials or maintaining fire extinguishers. Because the insured carries fire insurance, he or she has little incentive to exercise sufficient care, and so the presence of fire insurance increases the likelihood of fires.

In the case of guaranteed student loans, two parties are at risk of moral hazard: the institution of higher education and the student. Suppose a college or university provides a mediocre educational experience to its students. At some time following graduation, many of the students who have financed their education through loans will find themselves unable to repay those loans. Lack of repayment will not affect the institution, however—it already has received its tuition payments—and there is therefore little incentive for the institution to improve the quality of its product. Alternatively, consider the case of a student who fails to expend appropriate effort at an institution that provides a worthwhile education to students who put forth a good-faith effort. Such a student may well not be able to repay his or her loans. Lack of repayment will affect the student's credit rating, so there is some incentive for the student to repay the loan, but a large number of students do not appear to be concerned with this prospect. In this case, the loan itself provides only limited incentive for the student to perform well, both in college and in adult working life.

The design flaw in a government-guaranteed student loan is that the government is not one of the parties involved in the production of the education. Because of moral hazard in government loan guarantees, one can predict that either there will be high default rates or monitoring and enforcement costs will be very high—or both. I am not alone in noting the moral hazard inherent in government guarantees for student loans. In 1992, the General Accounting Office (GAO) included the federal student loan program in its list of seventeen federal programs that it considered to be "high risk."[2] In selecting these high-risk programs the GAO identified "areas that are especially vulnerable to waste, fraud, abuse, and mismanagement" (GAO 1993, 1). According to the GAO's assessment, the guaranteed student loan program suffers from both mismanagement and severe structural problems. With regard to the latter, the GAO report finds that

the structure of the loan program is inordinately complex, and many participants have little or no incentive to prevent defaults. Lenders and guaranty agencies benefit from making loans, but generally do not bear any financial risk. Schools also bear little risk, and some use the program as a source of easy income, with little regard for students' educational prospects or the likelihood of their repaying the loans. Nearly all the risk falls to the federal government, whose only recourse is to pursue defaulters. (Ibid., 7)

Without using the term, the GAO clearly identifies the moral hazard problem in guaranteed student loans.

The typical solution to problems of moral hazard is to arrange the incentives so that each party to the transaction acts as the other parties would prefer. A significant deductible in a fire insurance contract provides part of the solution to the moral hazard problem in that example. The insured party who bears part of the risk will see that it is in his or her best interest, not just the best interest of the insurer, to be conscious of fire safety. The moral hazard in guaranteed student loans, however, cannot be reduced quite so easily. Limiting the availability of loan guarantees to officially accredited providers and eliminating institutions with poor default records, combined with threatening nonpaying students in various ways, does affect the loan repayment rate, but the fundamental problem remains.

The U.S. Department of Education and Congress have responded to the loan default problem in several ways since it was first identified in the 1980s. Figure 6.1 presents the data for default rates for all postsecondary institutions. These are cohort default rates—that is, they represent the percentage of borrowers who enter repayment in a certain year and default before the end of the following year. "Students are in default if they fail to make any scheduled payments on their loans for (1) 180 days, if repayment is made monthly, or (2) 240 days, if repayment is made less frequently" (ibid., 3). Default rates grew from 1988, one year after official default rates were first computed, until 1990 and declined thereafter.

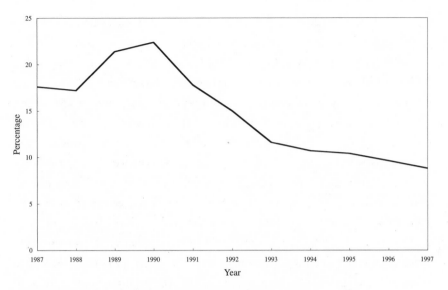

FIGURE 6.1. Cohort Default Rates, 1987–1997 (percentage)

The reduction in the default rate can be attributed to improvements in the overall economy and to the tougher response on the part of the Department of Education toward students, institutions, and, to a lesser extent, the state guaranty agencies. Adults who default on their student loans can find their federal income tax refunds attached, their wages garnished, their eligibility for federal aid for further study eliminated, and their access to other credit reduced because of a bad credit rating. More aggressive use of these options, made possible by increases in the department's ability to track students, is clearly part of the default rate reduction story.

The 1996 press release announcing the cohort default rate provides examples of the ways in which the department is getting tougher on students. It lists three pieces of information: "the department recovered $535 million in fiscal year 1996 by offsetting federal income tax refunds from 573,000 defaulters; the department's wage garnishment program increased from five thousand defaulters in fiscal year 1995 to twenty-five thousand in fiscal year 1996; [and] federal lawsuits against student defaulters increased from two thousand accounts in fiscal year 1995 to more than eight thousand in fiscal year 1996" (U.S. Department of Education 1996, 2). The data in figure 6.1 indicate that these efforts had an effect. It is also important to recognize that they represent a considerable expansion in the funds the Department of Education allocates for pursuit of loan defaulters.

The Department of Education and Congress have also gotten tougher with institutions. Most of the focus has been on what are called "gatekeeping procedures"—ways of eliminating eligibility for student loans for institutions with unacceptable default rate histories. There are two types of gatekeeping procedures. First, the Higher Education Amendments of 1992 mandates that institutions with default rates in excess of 25 percent for three consecutive years lose their eligibility for the guaranteed student loan program; institutions with default rates above 40 percent in any year face the same fate. By 1999 more than a thousand institutions had lost eligibility because of these provisions.[3] The 1998 amendments add a provision that removes these institutions from the Pell Grant Program, as well. Second, in 1992 Congress established the "85-15 rule," which requires that proprietary schools obtain no more than 85 percent of their revenues from federal student aid programs. The 1997 GAO report on the high risk of student aid programs suggests that there have been problems with the implementation of this rule.

Not all of the changes have involved aggressive government compliance efforts. In addition to the government stick, a small carrot is offered to schools with low default rates. Since 1998, institutions with default rates below 10 percent for the past three consecutive years receive loan money for their students more rapidly than other institutions (U.S. Department of Education 1999c, 2).

The final participant in the process is the state loan guaranty agencies. These agencies actually offer the guarantees to the financial institutions and make payments in the case of defaults. Before it began its efforts to reduce the default rate, the federal government covered 100 percent of any payments a state guaranty agency made in the case of default. In the mid-1990s this was reduced to 98 percent, providing some incentive for the guaranty agencies to assist in reducing default rates (GAO 1997, 23).

The percentages given in figure 6.1 are the aggregate default rates. Any study of student loan default rates has to recognize, however, that default rates vary by institution type. Table 6.1 gives the default rates for three years by type of institution. These data suggest four conclusions. First, the reduction in the

TABLE 6.1.   Default Rates, 1995, 1996, 1997, by Institution Type

	Public		Private		
Year and Category	Four-Year	Two-Year	Four-Year	Two-Year	Proprietary
1995					
Institutions	682	1,355	1,575	633	3,010
Participants	772,375	260,036	508,475	38,162	335,772
Default rate	7.1%	14.2%	6.9%	14.4%	19.9%
1996					
Institutions	673	1,296	1,578	612	2,924
Participants	844,276	279,630	549,798	37,553	330,124
Default rate	7.0%	13.2%	6.5%	14.0%	18.2%
1997					
Institutions	663	1,270	1,583	542	2,749
Participants	905,505	295,052	578,049	34,967	334,831
Default rate	6.8%	12.7%	5.8%	12.1%	15.4%

Source: U.S. Department of Education, 1999c.

overall default rate in these three years (from 10.4% to 9.6% to 8.8%) results from reductions at every type of institution. Second, there are clear differences in default rates by institution type. Default rates are much lower at four-year institutions than at two-year institutions, which are lower than default rates at proprietary (for-profit) schools.[4] These differences are large and persist across time. Third, the differences between private and public institutions are small. Fourth, part of the decrease in the overall default rate can be attributed to the changing mix of institutions and students. The number of two-year and proprietary institutions fell considerably (437 fewer institutions), while the number of four-year institutions decreased much less (11 fewer institutions). The number of participants at four-year institutions grew substantially more (202,704 students) than the number of participants at two-year and proprietary institutions (30,880 students). The elimination of institutions with high default rates probably accounts for a large portion of these changes.

Despite the magnitude of the problem, the academic literature has paid relatively little attention to default rates on student loans. Two studies are noteworthy. Laura Green Knapp and Terry G. Seaks (1992) estimate a probit model for loan default for 1,834 Stafford Loan borrowers at twenty-six colleges in Pennsylvania, and J. Fredericks Volkwein and Bruce P. Szelest (1995) estimate a logit model for loan default for 4,007 students from a national sample. These studies reach the same general conclusion: after they include factors measuring student characteristics, variables that measure institutional type are not significant in the regressions. The authors of both studies conclude that student characteristics, rather than institutional characteristics, determine the probability of loan default.

In their concluding sections both of these studies suggest that federal efforts to punish colleges and universities for high default rates are misguided. Knapp and Seaks use an interesting analogy: "No one would blame a hospital for a high mortality rate without conditioning the death rates on the complexity of its cases and the difficulty of its surgery. As one would expect a trauma center to have a higher death rate, a university that serves high-risk students is likely to have higher default rates" (Knapp and Seaks 1992, 410). Volkwein and Szelest also refer to this analogy. The point is well taken, but it should not guide our thinking too much. A college or university is a collection of students, and clearly a college or university with a higher-risk population will have higher default rates. It is a considerable leap from this, however, to the conclusion that a student's success is completely independent of the college he or she attends. Just as it is unlikely that a trauma patient has an equal probability of survival at every trauma unit, it is unlikely that a student has an equal probability of default at every college or university.

In fact, the studies in question do suggest that there are institutional effects on default rates. First, one of Volkwein and Szelest's regressions identifies two institutional characteristics, auxiliary expenditures per student and percentage of minority students, that affect the probability of default. Second, both studies find that earning a degree has a significant positive effect on the probability of repayment. They consider earning a degree as an individual characteristic, but it is not at all clear that this is the case. College graduation is the result of efforts both by a student and by his or her college. To graduate, the student has to pass a set of courses. To facilitate students' graduation, the college has to assure that these courses are available and provide students with sufficient support to succeed. There are clear differences in the amount of effort institutions expend in supporting their students. As the results regarding auxiliary expenditures suggest, when measures of support for students are included in the estimated model, they do affect default rates.

Clearly, government guarantees introduce a significant moral hazard problem into student loans. Given the expectation that the government will interceded in the case of default, lenders, guaranty agencies, colleges, and students have little incentive to minimize the likelihood of default. The government recognizes these problems and has instituted changes that increase the incentives of individual students and institutions alike to reduce loan defaults. These aggressive monitoring efforts have been successful: the loan default rate has decreased significantly. What, then, are the problems?

The first is that by the very nature of government, its solutions to incentive problems are arbitrary blunt instruments. For example, an institution must keep its default rate below 25 percent to avoid being dropped from the program. However, it receives no benefit from default rate reductions below 25 percent until its default rate falls to below 10 percent, and there are no further benefits beyond that point. The important default rates in the current system, 25 percent and 10 percent, are completely arbitrary, and because there are only two break points, the system is lumpy. An appropriate set of incentives would provide rewards for every reduction in the default rate.

The second problem is the expense associated with government monitoring of student loan repayments. Government expenditures have increased as the Department of Education has ratcheted up its monitoring and enforcement efforts. Moreover, because of mismanagement and errors in record keeping, the increased enforcement has also led to an expanded number of disputes. This further increases the costs of institutions that have to keep track of default rates and engage attorneys to challenge the Department of Education if they think they have been unfairly sanctioned. Many private citizens, as well, are currently involved in lengthy legal disputes with the government involving their student loans. These disputes are costly for both the government and the individuals involved.

As one of the two parties involved in the production of education, institutions are the appropriate guarantors of student loans. If they were responsible for guaranteeing their students' loans, they would have strong incentives to be sure that they do a good job of educating their students. There is a growing movement among state higher education administrators and legislators to tie funding for state-supported institutions to some measure of the performance of the institutions.[5] The rising popularity of performance-based budgeting reflects a sense that colleges and universities are not generally held accountable for their output. The response of colleges and universities—that they face a highly competitive market for students, a plethora of college ratings, and annual guidebooks that hold them accountable for the education they produce—has not been convincing. Giving institutions the responsibility for loan guarantees makes them accountable in a way that might speak more convincingly to legislators.

Loan Subsidies Distort Private Decision Making

The current government loan programs involve loan guarantees and interest rate subsidies. The rationale for loan guarantees is that without them, students would be unable to obtain loans to finance their education. The unwillingness of private lenders to make loans to students has several causes. Student loans are small; hence their administration costs are high relative to the lenders' return. Students cannot provide collateral, and lenders cannot repossess human capital. Students typically have no credit history that can be used to determine their creditworthiness. Loan guarantees are designed to overcome these barriers.

The problems that students have in credit markets, however, do not justify the interest rate subsidy. The rationale for interest rate subsidies should be the same as the rationale for other subsidies to higher education: the public benefits of higher education are greater than the private benefits, and without subsidies, individuals would underinvestment in higher education. This is the rationale for the general subsidies that states give to state-supported institutions. The state subsidies reduce the price to every student, encouraging college attendance.

It can be argued that access concerns—underinvestment on the part of low-income students—motivate the interest rate subsidies. There is evidence that low-income households are reluctant to take out educational loans.[6] To the extent that the interest rate subsidies, particularly the postponement of interest accrual until the student is no longer in college, make these families more comfortable with borrowing, they may encourage low-income students to attend college. It is difficult to know the strength of this effect. Most likely, however, the impact on access of a dollar spent on grants would exceed the impact of a dollar spent on interest rate subsidies.

Barry P. Bosworth, Andrew S. Carron, and Elisabeth Rhyne question the wisdom of tying higher education subsidies to loans. "Why," they ask, "should a low-income student be required to take out a loan as a precondition for receiving an educational grant?" (Bosworth, Carron, and Rhyne 1987, 131). This is a good question. In general, the solution to underinvestment and access problems should be a reduction in price, not a reduction in price contingent on a payment choice. The choice of whether or not to borrow for a particular purchase should involve a calculation concerning the point at which the purchaser chooses to limit his or her consumption. There is no particular reason to advantage those who limit their consumption after the purchase, by borrowing, over those who limit consumption before the purchase, by saving.

A case for interest rate subsidies can be made on the basis that those most likely to need financial aid will be most unfamiliar with and afraid of loans. This argument suggests that subsidizing the loans will make them more palatable to these students. The conclusion from this line of thinking is that subsidized loans are required to insure access.

There are good reasons to make sure that student loans are available. Students may not have parental resources they can use to pay college expenses. Either the parental resources may not exist, or the parents may not be willing to spend them on the student's education. For this reason, it is important that student loans be available. There is no argument from the access goal, however, that these loans have to be available at subsidized rates.

Financial aid policy is a bit schizophrenic in the signals it sends to savers. States and the federal government provide tax incentives to encourage families to save for college. At the same time, the formulas by which the expected family contribution is calculated place a considerable penalty on families who have accumulated assets. Tying financial aid to borrowing is a second example of the way in which the financial aid system discourages savings. Some families that save for the college expenses of its children decrease the future likelihood that they will be eligible to borrow at highly subsidized interest rates. It is likely that this factor explains some of the difficulty states have in attracting participants to their college savings plans.[7]

Federal expenditures on guaranteed student loans are large. In academic year 1998–99, there were $1,058 million in Perkins Loans, $6,039 million in subsidized William D. Ford Loans, and $11,969 million in subsidized Stafford Loans. Adding these yields a total of $19,066 million in subsidized loans made. Determining the budgetary impact of this lending activity is a complicated matter. Bosworth, Carron, and Rhyne provide an excellent discussion of the issues. There are four cost components: the interest payments the government makes for the student while he or she is in school, the "special allowance" payments the government makes to the lenders to compensate them for the low interest they receive on the loans, the net default costs, and the costs of administering the program. These costs are spread over the term of the loan. The authors calculate the present value of the costs of the loan (assuming a 9% Treasury bill rate and discount rate) as $443 for every $1,000 the government lends (ibid., 132). Using these assumptions, the cost to the federal government of its subsidized lending activity in 1998–99 was $8,446 million—an amount that exceeds the federal government's spending on Pell Grants.

Interest rate subsidies are not part of the proposal to make colleges and universities responsible for loan guarantees. The loan guarantee itself is a significant subsidy. It gives lenders the security necessary to convince them to lend to a group that they would not otherwise lend to. Because this provides significant incentives for families to finance higher education with loans, there is no compelling reason to provide additional incentives for borrowing. Support for poor students in the form of grants is much more effective.

The Government Stifles Innovation in the Market for Student Loans

McPherson and Schapiro note an additional problem with government loan guarantees. The current government loan guarantee system stifles innovation in markets for student loans. "The main features of loan agreement—length of repayment period, repayment schedules, fixed versus adjustable rates, and so on—are determined by the legislation authorizing the program" (McPherson and Schapiro 1991, 163).

Because the government guarantees the loans, it has insisted on uniformity in the types of loans. This is an understandable requirement, but it has the unfortunate consequence of eliminating the possibility of innovation in lending instruments. With the exception of the very small income-contingent repayment option, the loans from the three federal programs—Perkins Loans, Federal Family Education Loans, and William D. Ford Direct Loans—have the same basic structure. From the point of view of the student, the differences among these programs are of little consequence. The student does have four repayment options—the standard repayment, graduated repayment (lower payments early in the loan repayment period), extended repayment (payments over a longer time), and the income-contingent repayment—but these are the only choices available.

Other consumers interested in borrowing face a large array of possible types of loans. The loans can be short term or long term. The can carry variable interest rates or fixed interest rates. Various lenders are trying to find a niche in a crowded market, a situation that creates many options for most borrowers. Strong incentives encourage innovators in this type of market. The market for initial student loans has not shown the kind of innovation that has characterized other financial markets. One does not have to go far to find the reason for this. Changes in student loans are not the result of the quick actions of a lender with an entrepreneurial spirit. They are the result of acts of Congress, and Congress is likely to be neither quick nor innovative.

The problem is the result of the federal government's taking responsibility in what is essentially a private transaction. The rationale for this government intervention is clear: without loan guarantees, student loans would be available only to students who were unlikely to default, and thus poor students would be excluded from the market. My concern is not with the motivation for government action but rather with its result: the government has developed a clumsy one-size-fits-all system.

Institutionally Guaranteed Loans

Under my redesign proposal, private lenders would make the actual loans, as they now do in the FFEL program. To initiate the process, institutions of higher education would make it known that they were accepting bids on loan programs. The institutions would need to place only two restrictions on the bids that they received: the bids would have to be for loan options available on the same terms to any student in the student body, and lenders would have to be willing to lend up to the maximum amount authorized by the institution for each student. Optimally, the maximum loan amount would be the cost of attendance minus any grants the student might receive.[8] Based on the terms of the loans offered, institutions could then choose several lenders with which they were willing to work. It would be in each institution's interest to arrange the best terms for its students and to offer a variety of loan options.

Such a system would put the lenders in the position of having to study the financial health of the institution and the loan repayment history of its students. If the institution's finances prove to be sound, a lender will be assured that the institution can afford to make payments in the case of defaults, and other things being equal, the lender will be willing to offer loans on better terms than would be possible if the institution's finances were shaky. Similarly, if the institution's students have a good record of repaying student loans, lenders will be willing to offer loans on better terms than if the repayment record of its students is poor.[9]

The pressure of scrutiny by lenders will go a long way to allay the fears of some that the higher education sector is not accountable. In particular, the loan terms available at particular state institutions will give state higher education administrators and state legislators important information about the health of various institutions. In addition, lenders would take over the gatekeeper role now performed so clumsily by the Department of Education. If an institution's finances are sufficiently shaky or its students have a sufficiently poor history of repaying their loans, it is possible that no lender will be willing to bid to make loans to its students or that the only bidders will offer loans with exceedingly high interest rates. Such an institution will be eliminated from the loan program in a natural way. In this system there is nothing magical about a 25 percent default rate. Lenders will determine the highest acceptable default rate, and institutions with default rates close to that rate will pay a penalty for their high default rates. Institutions will benefit from every reduction in their default rate, not only once, when the rate falls below 10 percent.

There are potential problems with this system. First, it is possible that institutions will try to manage their admissions policies with an eye to minimizing their student loan default probability. In other words, they may shy away from admitting poor students, because these students would be graduated with large loan balances. An institution whose student body includes few students requiring large loans will be more likely to have a low default rate. An institution gains from a low default rate in two ways. First, other things being equal, because it does not have high expenses from covering defaults, it will be able to charge a lower tuition than institutions with higher default rates. Second, lenders will offer its students better loan terms than those offered to students attending institutions with higher default rates. In these ways institutions that do not admit poor students gain a competitive advantage over schools that do admit poor students.

I cannot deny this possibility. It points to the difficulty of designing a system with all the correct incentives. This problem may not represent a great change compared with the current system, however. In the current system an institution has to discount tuition to persuade low-income students to attend. This causes list-price tuition to increase, putting the institution at a competitive disadvantage compared with institutions that admit fewer low-income students. As a consequence, many institutions are currently using "need-aware" admissions policies, and so the objection that my proposal will force institutions to use need-aware admissions policies is not a major change.

There are reasons to believe that the proposed system might be an improvement over the existing system. If, as I propose, the government uses the money it now spends on guaranteed loans and other revenue on Pell Grants, the amount in loans student need to take out might be considerably reduced. To the extent that institutions minimize the use of institutionally funded grants, list-price tuition will be much lower. Finally, if an institution offers a valuable education to all its students, many of the poor students who require large tuition discounts under the current system will be financially successful and be able to repay their loans without difficulty. The institution will not need to raise tuition to cover a default, and the lender will not need to raise the interest rates it charges the institution's students. In summary, if the institution does a good job of selecting and educating its student body, it should have less to fear of admitting poor students under the proposed system than it does under the current system.

This is not to say that loan default rates will be unaffected by the choice of the student body. It is unlikely that any institution will be able to make the probability of graduation or postgraduate success equal for students from disadvantaged backgrounds and for equally talented students from more privileged backgrounds. An institution that takes on students from disadvantaged backgrounds will have to raise tuition to accommodate higher default rates. However, the effect on tuition of the institutional grants used to attract such students in the current system is likely to be higher than the effect on tuition of the loan defaults. Every student from a disadvantaged background has to be subsidized in the current system. Under the proposed redesign, only those who do not succeed will have to be subsidized.

It could be argued that the redesigned system would allow the rich to get richer and the poor to get poorer. Institutions with large endowments or large state subsidies generally attract more able students than institutions with smaller endowments or smaller state subsidies. Richer institutions will most likely experience lower loan default rates than poorer institutions simply because of the ability of their students. As a result, the richer institutions will have lower loan default expenses and will be able to offer more attractive loan terms than the poorer institutions. There is some merit in this objection. It is a common failure of proposals relying on market incentives: success in the market is easier for those who bring large amounts of money to the market than for those who have smaller amounts at their disposal.

The full redesign proposal, however, also calls for a significant increase in Pell Grants. This represents a major redistribution of financial aid dollars toward lower-income students. To the extent that low-income students tend to be concentrated in poorer institutions, the net effect of the full proposal on poorer institutions is difficult to determine. Their students may have relatively high default rates, but the larger Pell Grants will limit the amount those students need to borrow. Nevertheless, the requirement for institutions to make loan guarantees will most likely be a considerable burden for some poorer institutions. In defense of the proposal, I can only say that it will be a particular burden for poorer institutions that do a bad job of preparing their students. This is as it should be.

Eligibility for Financial Aid and Other Redesign Issues

For the most part, the existing system of financial aid is designed for an *Ozzie and Harriet* world in which students start college right after high school and parents take financial responsibility for the education of their children. Increasingly, this is an inaccurate picture of America. Many children are raised by a single parent, and many college students enter college well after they have completed high school. The changes outlined in this chapter are motivated by a desire to make the financial aid system responsive to the difficulties of those students who are not from *Ozzie and Harriet* families.

Intergenerational Decision Making

McPherson and Schapiro stress the importance of thinking of college finance in explicitly intergenerational terms (McPherson and Schapiro 1991, 174–77). They describe two pure systems: a student responsibility system, in which each generation pays for its own college education (through loans), and a parental responsibility system, in which each generation pays for the college education of its children (by parents' saving and sacrificing). In either system each generation pays for a college education; the difference is whose education is being paid for. Realistically, however, in the United States today neither of these pure systems can serve as a model for the financial aid system. The system has to be a mix, recognizing that some families will use a parental responsibility system and other a student responsibility system. The incentives in the financial aid system should not privilege one mode of paying for college over the other. The choice of payment should be up to the family and the student, and when possible, the participation of both parties should be encouraged.

For the most part, the current system assumes that parents should pay the college expenses of their children. The expected family contribution is based on current family—predominantly parental—income and assets, and awards of aid are based on the difference between the EFC and the cost of attendance. A large part of the aid is given in the form of subsidized loans, so some of the costs are shifted to the student, but the basic design of the system assumes that the student's parents are responsible for college expenses. The aid is really given to help parents pay for college expenses, not to help students pay for college expenses.

A parental responsibility system implicitly assumes the existence of willing parents (plural). Although this may have been a reasonable assumption in 1954, when the College Board first developed the needs analysis system, it is no longer so. Data from the Bureau of the Census show that in 1970 only 12.85 percent of families with children under the age of eighteen were maintained by one parent. In 1998, the percentage of families with children under the age of eighteen maintained by one parent had more than doubled, to 31.73 (Bureau of the Census 1998). Data from the Department of Education on opening fall enrollment indicate that in 1970, 27.78 percent of college students were above the age of twenty-four. By 1997, that number had grow to 42.87 percent (U.S. Department of Education, NCES 1999b, 204). Given the increasing number of students who come from single-parent families, or who live with grandparents, or are starting their higher education well after they have become financially independent of their parents, the assumption that a student is financially supported by two parents is increasingly an inaccurate assumption.

Even when a student has two parents, the current system does not distinguish between ability to pay and willingness to pay. The EFC is the "expected" family contribution, but in some cases parents are unwilling to make that large a contribution to their child's education. These children are not well served by the current system. Because there is no way to force parents to con-

should they be forced? What would that look like?

tribute to the education of their children, the system has to recognize the difficulties that arise when they do not.

To the extent possible, the financial aid system should be neutral with respect to the intergenerational payment choice. Some parents are able and willing to save and sacrifice for their children's college expenses. In other situations, either parents are not present or they are unwilling to pay, and the bulk of college expenses falls on the student. This means we need two kinds of financial aid: programs for parents who are unable to finance the education their children deserve and programs for students who are unable to finance the education they want to have.

Incentives and Disincentives

The costs of higher education are generally presumed to be met from four sources: a contribution from parents' or students' precollege income, aid for students with limited precollege resources, loans for the expenses not covered from the first two sources, and aid for students with limited postcollege resources to repay college loans. The objective of aid for students with limited precollege resources should be to reduce but not eliminate the amount students have to borrow. Even with generous aid, such a system will leave some students, particularly those from families with little willingness to pay, with substantial loan repayment responsibilities upon graduation. The existence of these responsibilities generates a need for government aid for students with limited postcollege resources.

The present system, however creates a number of disincentives. Need-based financial aid shares a problem with other social welfare programs: by awarding financial aid to students with low earnings and low asset levels, it creates disincentives to increase earnings and accumulate assets. Need-based financial aid increases with increases in tuition, and institutions' incentives to control tuition increases are thereby dulled. Need-based financial aid undermines the incentive for donors to fund private scholarships by imposing hidden taxes on those scholarships: if a student who receives such an award qualifies for need-based financial aid, the scholarship is counted as part of the student's assets, and her or his financial aid award is reduced. Finally, the need-based financial aid system compares current ability to pay with current educational costs; a system based on long-term income is more equitable.

Disincentives to Earn and Save

Federal financial aid as authorized under Title IV of the Higher Education Act is all need-based aid. Student, and usually their families, provide information on income and assets. Using this information, institutions determine the expected family contribution for each student and base their financial aid awards on the difference between the EFC and the cost of attendance.

Because the financial aid offer depends upon the family's income and assets, poorer families receive larger financial aid offers. As Edlin (1993) and Feldstein (1995) have observed, the rules that determine eligibility for federal financial aid act as a tax system. The precise parameters of the tax system are hard for students and families to understand because the amount of financial aid available is based upon complicated formulas and is subject to various limits. In addition, colleges and universities have considerable latitude in how they award federal as well as their own financial aid. In general, applicants with very low income or asset levels avoid these taxes because of various exclusions, and those with very high income or asset levels avoid the taxes because they do not qualify for financial aid. For those in the middle—and, as noted in chapter 3, it is a fairly broad middle—the tax rates can be very high.

My calculations in chapter 3 indicate that the marginal tax rate for income is between 25 and 35 percent for those with incomes above $50,000.[1] The tax continues until the family no longer qualifies for financial aid. The maximum income is quite high—above $130,000 for families sending their children to the most expensive private institutions. The income level at which the marginal tax rate is above 25 percent decreases for families with a significant amount of assets, other than home equity, IRAs, annuities, and pension funds.

Although clearly the implicit tax on earnings provides disincentives, most of the literature focuses on the effects on asset accumulation. In chapter 3, I discuss the effect of the implicit tax on asset accumulation for a family with one child in college. For this family, a dollar in assets will fall to 91.54 cents after the first year, 83.80 cents after the second year, 76.71 cents after the third year and 70.22 cents after the fourth year. Feldstein estimates the effect of these taxes on savings using the 1986 Survey of Consumer Finances. He summarizes his findings as follows: "The scholarship rules induce a typical household with a head aged 45 years old, with two precollege children, and with income of $40,000 a year to reduce accumulated financial assets by $23,124, approximately 50 percent of what would have been accumulated without the adverse effect of the scholarship rules" (Feldstein 1995, 566). This is quite a dramatic result. The financial aid system reduces accumulated financial assets by one-half.

Whether Feldstein's results, based as they are on 1986 data, are accurate today is difficult to tell. As he himself observes, his results are based on the savings behavior of adults who went to college, if they did at all, before 1972, when Pell Grants were introduced and the basic structure of the financial aid system was put in place. As more and more parents have had first-hand experience with the financial aid system, its measured effects may well grow. On the other hand, in 1992 the value of home equity was removed from the list of assets, and the asset protection allowance was raised.[2] These changes should diminish the effect of financial aid rules on savings. Most observers think that Feldstein's results overstate the effect of the financial aid system on savings (see Dick and Edlin 1997; Kane 1998).

Without further study, however, it is difficult to estimate the effect of the tax rates under the current rules on the actual amount of asset accumulation. Even if the effect on total asset accumulation is low, the high tax rates placed on particular asset categories are likely to affect the portfolio decisions of households. The financial aid rules contain a stiff penalty on holding liquid assets. The financial assets that are excluded—IRAs, annuities, and pension funds—all carry significant penalties for early withdrawal and often have lower yields than other financial assets. The other excluded asset, equity in the primary residence, is much more liquid, owing to the availability of home equity loans. The income tax system already privileges home equity loans, and the financial aid tax system enhances the attractiveness of this instrument. Thomas Kane concludes that "the impact on savings behavior is likely to be small, since the most alert parents, who would have been willing to adjust their savings behavior, avoid the tax by shifting resources into home equity" (Kane 1998, 4).[3] The conclusion is that the financial aid rules encourage an inefficient asset distribution for a large group of families. The changes these families might make to optimize their financial aid situations would result in portfolios that are less liquid than optimal and include overinvestment in home equity and pensions.

The argument here applies to need-based financial aid no matter who provides it and no matter what form it takes. The effect that can be traced to Pell Grants is, however, likely to be quite small. McPherson and Schapiro (1991) argue that the incomes of those who are eligible for Pell Grants are not high enough for them to save much.[4] Subsidized Stafford and Ford Direct Loans allow families with higher incomes to receive financial aid in the form of loan subsidies, increasing the likelihood of significant reductions in savings. Institutionally provided need-based grants stretch the eligibility for need-based financial aid further up the income scale, magnifying the adverse impacts on asset accumulation and portfolio structure.

One interesting aspect of this discussion is the clear inconsistency between the disincentives to save that are part of the needs analysis system and the clear encouragement of college savings in Section 529 of the Internal Revenue Code, which allows families to defer the taxes on the earnings in state-sponsored college savings plans. In addition, when the plans are eventually used to pay for college expenses, their earnings are taxed at the child's tax rates, not those of the parent. It is not surprising to find that the federal government has contradictory policies. It is schizophrenic about several matters. Nevertheless, it would be better if the federal government's programs all encouraged saving for college.

Disincentives to Control Tuition Increases

Financial aid awards depend on the difference between the cost of attendance and the expected family contribution. Thus increases in the cost of attendance increase the amount of aid awarded. Many institutionally funded grants have this property. Because of the structure of Pell Grants and limits on awards, however, not all federal financial aid has this property. An increase in the cost of attendance can increase federal financial aid in two ways: by increasing the aid for a student who was receiving less than the maximum amount of federal financial aid and by increasing the number of students eligible for federal financial aid.

Charles Clotfelter takes a close look at the finances at four top-flight institutions: Carleton College, Duke University, Harvard University, and the University of Chicago. His study provides considerable insight concerning the causes of increases in list-price tuition. In the concluding chapter, he explains why there is little price competition at the top of the heap in higher education. After arguing that high prices might not harm an institution because price itself might be an indicator of its quality, he continues:

The other, complementary aspect of competition in the market for students was the effective compact on financial aid to which all suppliers subscribed. Virtually all of the colleges and universities that competed with the sample institutions for the nation's top high school graduates had pledged to provide need-based financial assistance according to a fairly uniform formula. Each would offer applicants a package of loans, employment, and grants equal to the difference between the student's theoretical ability to pay and the total cost of attendance. Consequently, tuition increases largely would be cushioned, easing concerns that rising tuition would close the colleges' doors to low-income applicants. (Clotfelter 1996, 254–55)[5]

Colleges and universities, of course, want their doors open to the students who can best benefit from the education they have to offer. The great attractiveness of need-based financial aid is that it takes ability to pay out of the picture. The top institutions meet all demonstrated financial need and practice need-blind admissions. They admit the best students regardless of ability to pay and provide sufficient financial aid so that every admitted student can afford to attend. Under such a system, an increase in price falls only on those who can afford it. Recognizing this frees colleges and universities from one of the concerns they would otherwise have if they raised prices.[6] In effect, need-based financial aid makes institutions less willing to impose strict discipline on cost.

A similar argument holds for institutions that give institutionally funded financial aid on the basis of merit. In this case, tuition increases will not affect the net price for highly valued students. These institutions are freed of concerns about losing their top students if they decide to increase tuition.

The final link in the argument is the role of federal financial aid. Given the current limits on awards discussed in chapter 3, many students are already receiving the maximum federal aid, and increases in the cost of attendance will not increase their eligibility for federal financial aid. Other students are on the margin, either because they qualify for less than the full amount of a subsidized loan or because the increase in the cost of attendance will allow them to qualify for a subsidized loan. Table 7.1 presents data on full-time full-year undergraduate students' use of subsidized Stafford Loans by type of institution attended. A tuition increase could generate an increase in financial aid for two categories of students: students receiving less than the maximum Stafford Loan would definitely qualify for larger loans, and some of the lower-income students among those not currently receiving subsidized Stafford Loans would qualify for the aid.[7]

Table 7.1 suggests that federal subsidized loans could cushion some of the effect of tuition increases, both by increasing loan amounts for currently eligible students and by widening eligibility. Roughly one in six students receives less than the maximum subsidized Stafford Loan; an increase in tuition would most likely cause these loan amounts to increase. More than 70 percent of students at public institutions and more than 40 percent of students at private institutions do not receive subsidized Stafford Loans. Tuition increases could well cause some of these students to become eligible for subsidized loans.

Hidden Taxes on Private Scholarships

When the Rotary Club awards a $1,000 college scholarship to a local high school student, the Rotarians expect the scholarship to reduce the price of the student's freshman year of college by $1,000. Often, however, this is not the case. If the student qualifies for federal need-based financial aid, the outside scholarship is counted as part of the student's resources in the college's determination of the financial aid award. Regulations governing the federal financial aid programs prohibit overawards—that is, awards in excess of a student's need. If a student's financial aid package meets all of his or her financial need before the award of the Rotary scholarship, the federal portion of the award has to be reduced by $1,000 to avoid an overaward. If a student's financial aid package does not meet all of his or her financial need but the remain-

Why are outside scholarships counted? Is that fair?

TABLE 7.1.   Subsidized Stafford Loans, 1995–1996, by Institution Type
(percentage)

Institution type[a]	Public			Private		
	No Loan	Less than maximum	Maximum	No Loan	Less than maximum	Maximum
Research I	68.3	15.8	15.9	63.2	11.4	25.5
Research II	58.3	15.4	26.3	62.1	9.2	28.8
Doctoral I	63.3	18.3	18.4	46.5	19.0	34.5
Doctoral II	58.8	23.0	18.2	48.2	14.5	37.3
Comprehensive I	62.1	22.9	15.0	50.0	17.1	32.9
Comprehensive II	61.3	18.1	20.7	45.6	21.1	33.3
Liberal Arts I	68.2	25.7	6.1	54.1	19.9	26.0
Liberal Arts II	52.1	22.9	24.9	48.1	19.4	38.9
Two-year	86.1	7.0	7.0	43.9	25.9	30.3
TOTAL[b]	71.1	15.3	13.7	50.7	16.8	32.5

Source: U.S. Department of Education, NCES 1998.
[a]By Carnegie Classification of Institutions of Higher Education.
[b]Includes specialized schools (for examples, theological, art, music, and design).

ing unmet need is less than $1,000, the Rotary scholarship will also create an overaward, again requiring a reduction in the student's federal financial aid. The institution's financial aid officer has discretion as to how the award will be reduced.[8] In most situations, it is to the financial aid officer's advantage to reduce the SEOG. In any event, the federal prohibition of overawards greatly reduces the impact of outside scholarships for students receiving federal aid.

Students who do not qualify for federal financial aid but receive institutional need-based aid are not affected by the federal prohibition on overawards. Institutional policies on overawards vary. In most cases, institutional policies are not as strict as the federal ones. Some institutions place explicit taxes on outside scholarships that create overawards. For example, an institution might reduce a student's financial aid award by fifty cents for every dollar of outside scholarship. Alternatively, institutions count the entire outside scholarship in calculating the student's ability to pay but have a policy of reducing the self-help (loans and work-study) portion of financial aid awards for outside scholarship winners. In either case, the tax on the outside scholarship is less than the 100 percent tax levied by the federal government.

The Rotarians expect their $1,000 scholarship to reduce the price of the student's first year in college by $1,000. Unless they restrict their scholarships to students who do not qualify for federal or institutionally sponsored financial aid—that is, unless they restrict their scholarships to wealthier students—it is unlikely that their expectations will be met. It is quite possible that the

[Handwritten margin note, left side: "I don't find this very fair, they should be helping NOT hurting"]

$1,000 award will reduce the attendance cost to a poorer student by much less than $1,000. In effect, in many cases, the Rotary Club is giving part of its scholarship to the student, in the form of extra money, and part to the institution that the student attends, as a reduced financial aid burden.

This process is, in large part, hidden from the donors who fund outside scholarships. Many donors would be less eager to fund these scholarships if they realized the implicit tax. The intent of the donors is to reward a talented local student by helping with his or her college expenses, not to save some college or university money. To the extent that potential donors are aware of the implicit tax, the incentive to donate to outside scholarships is surely diminished.

It is hard to place blame in this case. One can sympathize with the federal government and the colleges and universities involved. An institution committed to awarding financial aid based on demonstrated financial need can hardly ignore outside scholarships. An outside scholarship represents funds specifically targeted to help the student meet the expenses of college, and those funds have to be included in the measure of the student's ability to pay. The federal system has strict rules about awarding more financial aid than required to meet the difference between the cost of attendance and the student's resources. Moreover, colleges and universities have incentives to minimize the amount of revenue they forgo in the form of institutionally funded financial aid.

[Handwritten margin note, left side: "Why?"]

Equity

Need-based aid fails the equitability test on both counts: It is horizontally inequitable, because individuals with equal abilities to pay are not treated as equals. It is also vertically inequitable, in that in certain circumstances those with more income are allocated more financial aid than those with less income; thus individuals who have unequal ability to pay are not treated appropriately. Although these two situations focus on different equity principles, the inequities they address have the same root cause. In both cases, the underlying flaw creating the inequity is the financial aid system's use of current ability to pay, rather than lifetime ability to pay, in determining eligibility for financial aid.

The first argument involves the timing of children. Two middle-class families, each with two children and with equal ability to pay, are not necessarily treated identically. If both children in one of the families are in college at the same time, the financial aid system divides the expected family contribution equally between the two children.[9] This dramatically increases the likelihood that this family will receive financial aid for both children. If the second family's children are in college at different times, the entire expected family contribution will be applied toward the cost of attendance for each student while he or she is in college. This family is much less likely to receive financial aid, or will receive much less financial aid, than the family with an identical ability to pay and two children in college.[10] If ability to pay is defined as ability over the lifetime of a family, these two families are not different, but the financial aid system treats them differently, violating of the principle of horizontal equity.

Borrowing allows consumers to meet large outlays that cannot be met out of current income. If all expenses had to be met out of current income, it might be sensible to say that the family with two children in college at the same time was more needy than the family that had two children separated by four or more years. Giving the possibilities of borrowing, however, this judgement makes little sense. I can think of no reason the financial system should encourage families to have their children closer together.

The second inequity is a violation of the principle of vertical equity. Consider two college students. The first, from a poor family, majors in electrical and computer engineering; the second, from a well-to-do family, majors in early childhood education. On the basis of the students' ability to pay at the point of entering college, it is easy to justify a transfer from student to the other. This is what the current system does. The well-to-do education student would not qualify for financial aid, but the less well to do engineering student would. Before college, the two students are not equals, and they are not treated equally. However, on the basis of the expected lifetime earnings of these two students, it is very likely that equity would suggest quite different treatment. From this view, any transfers involved should be from the engineering student to the education student.

It might seem odd to challenge need-based financial aid on equity grounds. Equity has been a paramount concern of those who designed the current financial aid system. As the last argument indicates, it is by no means clear that the approach to vertical equity adopted by the system's designers is the correct approach. In some cases, a system that redresses differences in income at the time of college attendance may be inferior, on equity grounds, to a system that redresses differences in lifetime earnings.

Redesign Proposal 1: Precollege Income Deficiencies

To address the problems stemming from low precollege income, I have three recommendations. First, to the extent possible, a long-term measure of income, not current income, should be used in determining the expected family contribution. Using a long-term income measure eliminates the need to include assets in the calculation. Second, the grants should be awarded on the basis of income, not need. A need-based grant increases as the cost of attendance increases, whereas an income-based grant would be insensitive to the cost of attendance. Third, given that the expected family contribution depends upon a long-term income concept, the application for federal financial aid could be moved up to the first semester of the student's senior year in high school.

Long-Run Income, Not Current Income and Assets

Designers of the financial aid system have long considered its reliance on current income a drawback, but for reasons of data availability, they have had no reasonable alternative. Aaron Edlin notes that the expected family contribution now depends, in fact, on the family's long-term income *and* what they have done with it. Under the current system, a family that saves a large percentage of its past income has a higher EFC than a family with the same income history who did not save at all. Edlin's suggestion is to base the EFC on a long-run view of income and to leave assets out of the calculation altogether. If the EFC were based on, for example, fifteen or twenty years of income or wage data,[11] Edlin suggests, college costs would continue to be low for students whose parents are poor because they have had low earnings, but those who are "poor" because they have lived high on the hog would face high costs (Edlin 1993, 156). Such a system eliminates some of the schizophrenia about savings in the current system. Those who contribute to state college savings plans and receive tax advantages from Section 529 of the Internal Revenue Code will not face the high taxes on those savings that are implicit in the rules governing federal financial aid. The system could not be completely based on long-term income; it would have to account, for example, for large unavoidable expenses, such as those involved with a protracted illness of a family member, that limit a family's ability to save.

Several difficulties are inherent in this plan. For many students, fifteen or twenty years of income or wage data may not be available. Separations, deaths, and divorces will complicate matters for dependent students. Other difficulties with data collection will arise for young independent students. Students from families with low current income and high long-term income will face access problems. Regarding the first three problems, which are essentially data availability problems, the system would have to be able to adapt to the data available for a particular student. The fourth problem is more resistant to solution. The objective of the plan is to encourage savings, and the reduction in access associated with a recent reduction in income is one of the costs of this change. The ready availability of loans would limit this cost, but it is a cost nevertheless.

A key element in my redesign of the financial aid system is a change in the way the expected family contribution is calculated. The EFC should be based on three things: the best estimate of the individual or family's long-term average income over the precollege years of the student, the number of children supported by the individual or family, and the existence of any special circumstances that have limited the family or individual's ability to save.

This proposal has several advantages over the present system. First, it eliminates disincentives to save. In the new system a family that saves a large amount will not have a larger EFC than a family with the same income history that does not save. Second, the timing of children will not affect the determination of the EFC. There are no advantages in the proposed system to the close spacing of a family's children. Third, with this proposal, outside scholarships will not affect the EFC. This removes all of the disincentives for donors to contribute to such scholarships. In a few circumstances this policy could lead to awards in excess of need because the student's combined resources from the EFC, the government grant, and the outside scholarship would be larger than the student's cost of attendance. Under the assumption that the government grant generally covers much less than the cost of attendance, even for the poorest student, this is not likely to not happen often. In my judgment, the encouragement it would provide to private charities to fund scholarships far outweighs the this limited danger.

Income Based, Not Need Based

Government grants should be based on the expected family contribution, which is determined by income, not by the financial need of the student, which is determined by the difference between the cost of attendance and the EFC.[12] My redesign proposes that the Supplemental Educational Opportunity Grant be eliminated and that all government grants be modeled on the current Pell Grant, which is designed to bring the combination of the EFC and the grant up to a certain level. The only way the cost of attendance comes into the picture for Pell Grants is through a rule that the total of the EFC and the grant cannot exceed the cost of attendance.

Need-based grants have the property that they increase with the cost of attendance, creating a climate that encourages tuition increases. Adopting the Pell Grant model removes the relation between the grant and the cost of attendance. If all grants were based on income, rather than need, an institution's tuition increase would inherently either increase the amount of loan that its students would need to take out or reduce the current consumption of the students' families. This should make the institution carefully consider any proposed increase in tuition.

One way to think of financial aid is that it should level the playing field for those with low income. Basing awards on income rather than need accomplishes this goal in a concrete way. The award is designed to bring the sum of the EFC and the government grant up to a level that makes a wide variety of colleges and universities affordable for a student who is willing to borrow. Unfortunately, such a system does not level the playing field for a student whose parents are unwilling to make the "expected" contribution. These students are a problem in any system based on parental contributions. Because it is impossible either to mandate or to ban parental contributions, no equitable solution for these students presents itself.

Timing of the Needs Analysis System

Because current income tax returns are not critical for determining long-term average income, the determination of the expected family contribution and the eligibility for federal grants could be moved to the first semester of a student's senior year in high school. Ideally, deadlines would be in the early fall, so that a student would know the size of the grant for which he or she qualified even before making early decision applications. This removes some of the information problem students currently face. With an early determination of the EFC and income-based grants, a student could make accurate predictions of the full cost of attending a large array of institutions. Institutional grants would be the only possible source of price confusion; and if these were eliminated, students would have all the price information they need before making any irreversible decisions.

Redesign Proposal 2: Postcollege Income Deficiencies

A college education is, on average, an excellent financial investment. As with any other investment, if the rate of return is high enough, investing is a wise decision, even if one has to borrow to do so. The data are quite clear that college graduates make significantly more than high school graduates, and the difference has grown recently. In 1980 a male with a college degree earned 19 percent more than his counterpart with only a high school degree, and a female earned 52 percent more than her counterpart with only a high school degree. By 1997 the advantage for a male had risen to 50 percent, and that for a female to 91 percent (U.S. Department of Education, NCES 1999a). Given the high rate of return to higher education, it makes economic sense for almost any student to borrow, even if he or she has to borrow all the expenses for a higher education. Given the existence of the government grants, few students will have to borrow the full cost of attendance. Some students, however, will graduate with loans covering a significant portion of their college expenses, particularly those whose parents have been unwilling to make the expected family contribution.

On average, students should be able to repay loans covering a significant proportion of their college expenses. For various reasons, what is true for the average student is not true for all students. Through no fault of their own, some students will have difficulty repaying loans after college. A system that relies heavily on loans should provide a safety net for these students.

Several noted economists, including two Nobel Prize winners, have suggested that this type of aid should be part of the financial aid system. Milton Friedman (1962) suggests such aid in *Capitalism and Freedom*. He advocates a system in which parents are not expected to pay for college. Students pay for their college education using loans, and government aid is given to students who have difficulty repaying the loans.

From 1971 to 1978, students at Yale University could utilize a tuition payment option designed by James Tobin. Under the Yale Tuition Payment Option, students borrowed the money they needed for college expenses directly from the university and agreed to repay Yale 0.4 percent of their yearly post-college income for every $1,000 they borrowed. The loan was repaid when all loans in the students' cohort (essentially a graduating class) had been repaid. Students with lower postcollege incomes were expected to repay less than the full amount, and students with higher incomes to repay more than the full amount, of their loans.[13]

Robert Reischauer (1989) has suggested a program in which students who take out college loans pay into a trust fund, similar to the Social Security trust fund, to repay their loans. The payments into the trust fund would be based on income, making the repayment burden lower for those with low postcollege incomes. The trust fund would then be available for loans to future students.

Thomas Kane (1999a) makes much the same suggestion when he advocates income-contingent tax credits for loan repayment. A student whose college loan obligation is above a certain level and whose income is below a certain level would qualify for a tax credit on federal income tax. Kane's tax credits are incorporated in the redesign proposals as the aid for students with limited postcollege income.

All of these proposals are similar to the existing income-contingent loan program.[14] With income-contingent loans, students agree to repay college loans with a fixed percentage of their annual postcollege income. In this case, an education major might repay less money than would an engineering major.

The income-contingent loan is a form of what Kane terms "forward-looking means testing." Because it is based on long-term income, it shares one of the features of the proposal to base the expected family contribution on long-term income. In this case the long-term income is long-term future income; in the other case it is long-term past income.

Through the Student Loan Reform Act of 1993, the federal government instituted an income-contingent loan repayment for the William D. Ford Direct Loans. This option was not part of the traditional Federal Family Education Loan Program, which relies on private lenders. The reluctance of private lenders to offer this option most likely can be traced to a concern over adverse selection: none of the engineering students would have been interested, but it is likely that all of the education students would have considered this option, and so the lender would probably have lost money in the exchange. Kane suggests that tax expenditures should be used as a way of overcoming this problem (Kane 1999a, 151, 152). Income-contingent tax credits for educational loan repayment would be available to taxpayers with student loans, but, again, they would be more likely to be used by education majors than by engineers.

One of the advantages of income-contingent tax credits for loan forgiveness is that they limit the likelihood of loan default. Institutions would be more willing to consider guaranteeing loans for their students under a system that included government aid in the form of tax credits for students with loan repayment commitments. Income-contingent tax credits would thereby mitigate the danger that institutions might limit their exposure to default risk by not admitting students who would need to take out large loans.

Moreover, income-contingent tax credits for loan repayments should decrease the pressure on students to consider economic concerns as the dominant factor in selecting a field of study. As our example of the engineering and education students indicates, there are clear predictable differences in the economic payoff to various college majors. In the absence of financial aid, the only students who could afford to pursue certain majors would be those from wealthy families; students with limited means would be limited to majors in more potentially lucrative fields. Financial aid in any form helps to improve the likelihood that students are not forced to make choices on exclusively economic terms. Their explicit focus on future income problems should make the income-contingent tax credits for loan forgiveness particularly effective in this regard.

Evaluating the
Redesign Proposals

It is time to bring the proposals described in the previous chapters together for an evaluation. This evaluation should focus on the objectives for a financial aid system set out in the first chapter. Because the proposal cannot meet all of the objectives, the conflicts among these objectives must be resolved, a step that involves a difficult process of compromise.

Incorporating the Redesign Proposals

To make my proposal concrete, I present a financial aid system that incorporates an extreme version of the redesign elements discussed in the previous three chapters. For the moment, I am putting aside any concerns about the legality or political feasibility of the changes required to move from the current system to this redesigned system. Discussion of legal issues and political feasibility is covered in the next chapter.

The redesigned financial aid system includes only four types of financial aid: federal Pell Grants, grants given by state governments and private organizations, institutional loan guarantees, and income-contingent tax credits for loan forgiveness. Major portions of the current financial aid system are missing from the redesigned system. There are no institutionally funded grants of any kind, and there are no tuition tax credits. The SEOG and work-study have been eliminated, as have all federal student loan programs.

Pell Grants will be much larger under the proposed redesign. All of the expenses associated with the federal programs eliminated under the plan—the SEOG, the Work-Study Program, the Perkins Loan Program, the Federal Family Education Loan Program, the William D. Ford Direct Loan Program, and the Hope Scholarship and Lifetime Learning tuition tax credits—will be shifted into Pell Grants and the income-contingent tax credits for loan forgiveness. This will allow for a significant expansion of the Pell Grant maximum.

Because Pell Grants are the only type of grant in the system, students will need to make only one application for financial aid. The application for financial aid will require information on the student's and his or her family's earnings from the Social Security records, so that the expected family contribution will be based on long-term income. Because there will no reason to wait until federal income tax returns have been file before applying for financial aid, families will be encouraged to make the application early in the student's senior year in high school. By submitting an early application for federal financial aid, students will be able to know the size of their Pell Grants before deciding on the group of institutions to which they will apply.

Institutions will take over the responsibility for guaranteeing student loans, contracting with private lenders who will make the actual loans. These loans will be available to any member of an institution's student body. Students will be allowed to borrow the difference between the cost of attendance and any grants they might receive. Lenders will communicate with institutions about the terms of the loans offered, so that the information can be included in college catalogues. It will be in the interest of institutions to contract with several lenders to provide students with a variety of loan options.

Under the new proposal, institutions neither determine financial need nor give out financial aid, so they will be able to dramatically reduce the size of their financial aid offices. Institutions will take on the administrative costs associated with the loan guarantees. It is hard to forecast the effects of this switch on total administrative costs for a college or university.

Meeting Objectives

The objectives for my proposed redesign of the financial aid system are discussed in detail in chapter 1 of this book. There are essentially six such goals:

access to higher education, choice in the selection of institution, simplicity, a halt in rising tuition rates, provision of appropriate financial incentives, and a neutral approach with respect to the intergenerational contract. How well does the proposed system meet each of these objectives?

Simplicity

Under my redesigned system, students will make only a single application for financial aid, and they will be notified of the size of their federal grants before applying to colleges. In addition to information on the costs of attendance, which they currently provide, college catalogues will have information on the loan options available to students. Because the Pell Grant can be used at any institution, students will be able to know the financial consequences of attending any institution using information in the catalogue and the results of their federal financial aid applications. Access to high-quality information in a timely fashion should facilitate better matches between institutions and students.

In addition, this system will be easily understood by potential applicants, especially freshmen and sophomores in high school. The system comprises essentially three elements. First, the Pell Grant is designed to supplement student and family resources so that each student will have at least a specified amount of resources to cover higher education expenses. This amount is called the maximum Pell Grant. Second, assuming willing parents, the maximum amount the student will have to finance through loans will be the cost of attendance minus the maximum Pell Grant, and each college and university will make these loans available to all its students. Third, after graduation, income-contingent tax credits for loan forgiveness will provide assistance to a debtor whose student loan burden is high and income low. These tax credits will allow the student to repay part of the loans with a reduction in federal income tax liability.

Financial Aid and Rising Tuition

The reductions in tuition resulting from the elimination of institutional grants will go a long way toward mitigating the concern that the general public has with college prices. This reform does not deal with many of the underlying causes of rising tuition, but it does generate one-time price decreases that will be beneficial. The data presented in chapter 5 indicate that in many cases the magnitude of the decreases in list-price tuition will be large. The headlines that would accompany these changes would be dramatic. In addition, a financial aid system with no institutional grants will lead to smaller increases in list-price tuition in response to increases in an institution's costs. Although the redesigned system by no means cures the problem of rising tuition, it will generate a one-time fall in tuition and a system with a lower rate of tuition increase.

Incentives in the Financial Aid System

The new system improves incentives in three ways. First, by shifting from federal to institutional loan guarantees, it greatly decreases the moral hazard problem in student loans. The increase in accountability associated with institutional loan guarantees should repair some of the recent damage to the public reputation of colleges and universities. Second, by eliminating assets from the formulas that determine the expected family contribution and by eliminating the interest subsidies on student loans, the system removes the disincentives to save that are endemic in the current system. Third, because Pell Grants represent income-based, not need-based, aid, the new proposal eliminates the link between financial aid and tuition. In this system most students will feel the effect of tuition increases; in particular, students who receive Pell Grants will face increases in the amount they have to borrow in the event of tuition increases. This concern will encourage institutions to carefully consider the impact of tuition increases on the socioeconomic diversity of their student bodies. They will not be in a position to use institutional grants to protect certain students.

A More Evenhanded Intergenerational Approach

Three innovations are important with respect to the intergenerational compact. First, basing the expected family contribution on long-term income eliminates the implicit taxes on family savings targeted for educational expenses. Second, by making loans available with institutional loan guarantees, the system avoids problems caused by limits on federal guaranteed loans currently faced by a student with parents who are unwilling to provide its share of the expected family contribution. Third, by offering income-contingent tax credits for loan forgiveness, students who decide to borrow and fare poorly in the postgraduation job market will be given assistance.

It comes as no surprise that the proposed system meets these objectives. It was designed, after all, with these objectives in mind. To be a viable proposal, however, it has also to meet the more traditional objectives of a financial aid system: access and choice goals.

The New Proposal and Access

The first concern for any reform of the financial aid system is to increase access to the higher education system. Susan P. Choy's (1999) finding that the proportion of college-qualified students who attend college is strongly related to income suggests that the current system is not meeting the access goal. If the proposed system is to improve access, it should be able to demonstrate that it improves the flow of aid to low-income students, thereby eliminating low income as a barrier to higher education.

One way to improve the situation of low-income students might be to increase federal spending on financial aid. In the end this may be required, but before coming to that conclusion I want to assess the increased availability of funds that would result from redirecting the federal resources from programs the proposal eliminates. To the extent that redirecting these funds increases the aid flowing to low-income students, it offsets the increase in federal spending required to meet the access goal.

The new proposal eliminates three forms of financial aid that currently cover need for some students: institutionally funded grants, guaranteed student loan subsidies, and tuition tax credits. Revenues freed by the elimination the federal programs—in the form of current expenditures on loans and revenue forgone from tuition tax credits—would be used to increase the funds available for Pell Grants. The elimination of institutionally funded grants will allow institutions to reduce tuition, thereby reducing financial need.

Table 8.1 lists approximations for the values of these changes. For the

TABLE 8.1.   Effect of Proposed Changes on Financial Aid Resources
(in millions of dollars)

Proposed Change	Loss	Gain
Eliminated need-based programs		
Need-based institutional grants	7,955	
Loan subsidies	5,415	
Tuition tax credits	3,858	
Proposed increases to Pell Grant funds		
Revenue from current expenditures on loans		8,446
Revenue from forgone tuition tax credits		7,460
Tuition reduction owing to elimination of institutional grants		6,164
TOTAL	7,307	22,070
Net surplus of resources directed to meet financial need		4,763

Source: Data from College Board 1999 and U.S. Department of Education, NCES 1998.
Note: The new proposal eliminates the SEOG program. Under the assumption that all of the funding from the SEOG program is transferred to the Pell Grant program, there is no need to account for this here. This switch in funds does not affect the amount of unmet need.

1998–99 academic year, institutional and other grants amounted to $12,209 million. (Grants by businesses and private charities will continue under the redesign.) The NPSAS 1995–96 data indicate that 90 percent of institutional and other grants are institutional grants. This leaves $10,988 million in institutional grants. Not all of these grants are need-based. In the NPSAS 1995–96 data, only 72.4 percent of institutional grants were need-based awards. This makes our estimate for need-based institutional grants, the first row in the table, $7,955 million.

To approximate the amounts for loan subsidies and current expenditures on loans, we need to evaluate the loan programs. In the academic year 1998–99, Perkins Loans made totaled $1,058 million, subsidized William D. Ford Loans $6,039 million, and subsidized Stafford Loans $11,969 million—a total of $19,066 million in subsidized loans that would be eliminated under the new proposal. The budgetary impact of this lending activity is a complicated matter to determine. Using the analysis in Bosworth, Carron, and Rhyne, costs of the loans (assuming a 9% Treasury bill rate and discount rate) equal $443 for every $1,000 the government lends (see Bosworth, Carron, and Rhyne 1987, 132). The first two of these costs, the interest paid while the student is in college and the special allowance that allows lending at a below-market interest rate, are a subsidy to the student. The present value to the student of this subsidy is $284 for every $1,000 borrowed. Using these assumptions, the lost subsidy from loans is $5,415 million, and the budget relief from ending loan activity is $8,446 million.

In chapter 3, I estimate that 48.29 percent of tuition tax credits go to individuals without financial need. The budget estimates for tax expenditures on the Hope Scholarship and Lifetime Learning Credits are $4,870 million and $2,590 million, respectively, for a total of $7,460 million (Executive Office of the President 1998, 333). This gives estimates of $3,858 million for the third row, the portion of the tax credits that reduce financial need, and $7,460 million for the fifth row, revenues available from the tax credits.

Under the assumption that institutions keep net revenue from tuition constant after the elimination of institutional grants, revenues from tuition payments will go down by the full amount of institutional grants—$10,988.1 million. Not all of the tuition reduction will benefit students with financial need, however. Data from the 1995–96 NPSAS indicate that 56.1 percent of all undergraduates have financial need. This makes our estimate of the amount of the tuition reduction that reduces financial need (the sixth row) $6,164 million.

Although the estimates in table 8.1 are crude, I do not think they are wildly inaccurate. The bottom line is that the new proposal generates more than enough in the form of the new Pell Grants and tuition reductions to make up for the need-based aid it eliminates. The new proposal reduces financial need by $4,763 million more than the current system.

The finding that the redesigned financial aid system does a better job of meeting financial need should not be surprising. Federal expenses from the loan defaults and administration of the loan programs are shifted to new grants, and the misdirected portion of the tuition tax credits is shifted to new grants. In addition, the tuition reductions from all grants, merit based as well as need based, are available to reduce the amount of financial need.

In chapter 1, I criticize the existing financial aid system because it results in the perverse relation between unmet financial need and income illustrated in figure 1.1. The new proposal should be immune to such criticism. There is one detail I need to consider. One of the peculiarities of the current system is that subsidized loans are included as part of aid in the definition of unmet financial need. Because in the new proposal loans are not subsidized, they are not included as financial aid. For this reason unmet need will appear to be higher in the new system. In the new system it is reasonable to think of unmet

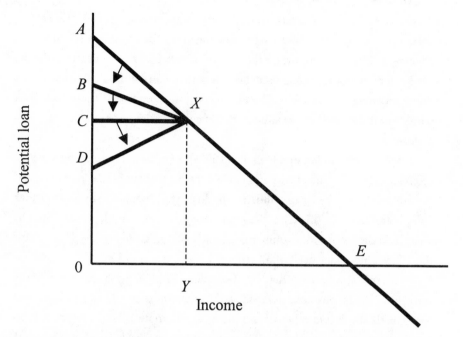

FIGURE 8.1. Relation between Potential Loan and Income, Dependent Students, under the Redesigned System

need as the "potential loan." I use this terminology because unmet need represents the amount the student would have to borrow, assuming that his or her family is willing to make an annual commitment equal to the expected family contribution and that he or she receives a Pell Grant if eligible. It is the "potential" loan because it is possible for a family to contribute more than expected. Figure 8.1 represents possible relations between unmet need (or potential loan) and income under the proposed redesign.

As figure 1.1 indicates, the current financial aid system yields a downward sloping relation between unmet and income. Such a relation would be given by AXE in figure 8.1. Under the new proposal, which targets financial aid toward those with limited ability to pay, the left-hand portion of the curve—representing incomes below Y—should bend downward, as the arrows in the figure indicate. I now turn to the question of how far downward this portion of the curve should bend.

Access is assured if the probability that a college-qualified student will go to college is unrelated to his or her family's ability to pay. This suggests two decisions. First, society needs to establish the importance it places on a college education—that is, it needs to determine the marginal social benefits of higher education. The more important the society considers higher education (that is, the higher the margin social benefit), the larger will be the Pell Grant maximum and thus the lower will be the maximum unmet need (point X). This would result in a higher probability that a college-qualified student will go to college.

Second, the design of the financial aid system should reflect the tolerance of college students and their parents for debt. It is possible that parents at all income levels feel that their children will do as well economically as any other college graduate. In this case, the financial aid system should be designed to yield the relation between unmet need and income given by line CXE. With line CXE, the unmet need of all students with incomes of less than Y will be identical. It is also possible that very poor families will have lower assessments of their students' postcollege incomes. These families will have less tolerance for debt than other families. If this view predominates, the appropriate relation between potential loan and income is given by line DXE. Although, as I have suggested, line DXE can be defended as the optimal relation between potential loan and income, gathering support for such a financial aid system would be politically difficult. The best we can realistically hope for is a line similar to CXE. This represents a significant improvement over the present system.

The Distribution of Financial Aid and Choice

Figures 1.1 and 8.1 show the relation between income and unmet need on average, but there will be a wide dispersion around the average. The relation between the maximum potential loan and income may be more important. Because of this, even if the new proposal moves the average relation in the desired direction, it cannot claim to reduce the net costs of attending college for all students with financial need. In fact, two types of students are likely to be worse off under the new proposal: students who are receiving merit-based institutional grants that exceed their financial need, and students who are receiving large need-based grants from relatively expensive institutions.

Merit-Based Aid in Excess of Need

The fundamental question regarding merit-based aid is how the behavior of students receiving these awards is likely to change under the new proposal. Institutional merit-based aid has developed into an arms race. By eliminating all institutionally funded financial aid, the new proposal will stop that arms race. Under the existing system, in extreme cases, a talented student can choose between several institutions, each of which is offering him or her a free ride. Such a student is free to choose simply on the basis of which institution offers the best-quality educational experience. In other cases, because of merit aid packages of different sizes and different underlying costs, a student faces different prices at the institutions under consideration. Such a student chooses the institution offering the best combination of net price and institutional quality. Under the new proposal, every student would face this choice.

I am considering students whose current merit grants exceed their financial need, so even without these grants, assuming sufficient need-based aid from the new system, access will not be a concern for these students. The question is then one of how the student-institution mix differs in the two systems. Under the current system, merit aid can affect a student's choice of which college to attend by making one institution much less expensive to the student than other institutions. In many cases, without the price break given by the merit scholarship the student would have selected a different institution. In effect, the merit scholarship allows the institution to attract a student it would otherwise have been unable to attract. Often this means that a student ends up attending an institution with an inferior combination of average net price and institutional quality compared with a competing institution. Is this likely to be an improvement in the student-institution mix? I think not. In most cases, increasing the relative importance of price in a choice that involves price and quality does not lead to better-quality choices.

Because of the way it changes incentives, the new proposal also improves the long-run situation by changing the strategies available for an institution that wants to increase the quality of its student body. Under the new proposal, an institution's best options involve either decreasing the real net costs of attendance for all students or increasing the quality of the education. In the long run, this should lead to a better set of choices for all students.

Large Need-Based Grants from Expensive Institutions

The effect of the elimination of large need-based grants from institutions is more complicated. Under the existing system, large institutional grants are required for some students to meet the costs at the more expensive institutions. Given the expansion of Pell Grants under the proposed system, these students will be able to afford to attend any one of a number of colleges. In this case, again, the question is not whether such students will attend college but rather how the new proposal affects the choice of institutions.

The argument made above suggests that the quality of the student-institution mix would deteriorate. Under the assumption that institutional quality and net price are positively related, institutional grants under the present system allow some low-income students to select a combination of institutional quality and net price that they could not otherwise afford. Under the new proposal these students would have to pay more to attend the same institution, and some of them will probably choose not to do so. From the viewpoint of the institutions, the new proposal takes away a strategy they use to meet their commitments to serve students from all socioeconomic groups. The effects on both student choice and institutional options are clearly regrettable, and it is unlikely that the institutions in question would favor the new proposal.

The problematic cases for the new proposal exist because the combination of the new Pell Grant and the tuition reduction may not be sufficient to meet all of the need met by current financial aid packages. This is likely to happen to low-income students at some expensive private institutions currently able to meet all financial need. It will be important for the new Pell Grants to be designed in such a way that these cases occur relatively infrequently. Fortunately, as demonstrated in chapter 5, the institutions in question, typically in the Carnegie classifications Liberal Arts I and Research I, will experience the largest decreases in tuition. This reduces the magnitude of the problem. Nevertheless, it is unlikely to be completely eliminated. Without institutionally funded grants, some institutions will have more difficulty making themselves affordable to students from all income groups.

This is not a small matter. As my discussion of the objectives of a financial aid system emphasizes, a financial aid system should facilitate the optimal student-institution mix. It should provide access to higher education and a full range of choice of institution for every qualified student. Unless the Pell Grants are much more lavishly funded than current expenditures would allow, under the proposed system, though all students would technically have the full range of choice, low-income students could attend some institutions only if they were willing to take out very large loans.

The issues surrounding choice are difficult. It is hard to argue that it is the public's duty to make a Rolls Royce or a castle affordable for every citizen; the public may want to ensure only that affordable transportation and housing are available. In like fashion, though the public may want to make sure that every qualified student has access to a higher education, it may not feel it is its duty to allow every qualified student the choice of an Ivy League education. Clearly, the concern over choice is a second-order concern compared with the concern over access. Nevertheless, if one gives up on choice, students at the high-priced institutions will be predominantly high-income students, and some low-income students who would be in the optimal student body for these institutions will attend other institutions. Moreover, to the extent that, as many people argue, the quality of the educational experience at an institution is positively related to the socioeconomic diversity of the student body, the quality of the education at our highest-priced institutions would decline.

It is important to see how large a problem the restriction of choice will be. Gordon C. Winston (1999) provides data that allow us to think about the distribution of net prices under the new proposal. Winston's data are from the 1994–95 academic year for 2,739 institutions—1,420 private and 1,319 public. He divides institutions into ten groups on the basis of the per student subsidy (from endowment, gifts, and state support). Table 8.2 presents the data. All of the dollar figures are expressed as per student averages.

In the absence of institutionally funded grants, every student will have to pay the average net price. The table shows the wide variety of financial situations faced by institutions.[1] The institutions with the highest average net price are those at the two ends of the subsidy distribution. The institutions in the first decile have the highest per student subsidies and offer a costly, presumably high-quality, education at a deep discount. Nevertheless, at $5,700, the average net price (tuition and fees) at these institutions is the second high-

TABLE 8.2.   Subsidies, Costs, Net Prices, and Price-to-Cost Ratios (1994 dollars)

Decile[a]	Average Subsidy	Educational Costs	Average Net Price	Price-to-Cost Ratio (percentage)
1	22,800	28,500	5,700	20.1
2	11,100	14,900	3,800	25.4
3	9,300	12,300	3,000	24.4
4	8,200	11,000	2,800	25.6
5	7,300	9,000	2,600	26.6
6	6,500	9,400	2,900	30.8
7	5,800	8,700	2,900	33.1
8	5,100	8,400	3,300	39.5
9	4,100	8,700	4,600	52.5
10	1,800	7,900	6,100	77.4

Source: Data from Winston 1999.
[a]Decile by per student subsidy from endowment, gifts, and state support.

est in the table. Interestingly, the highest tuition and fees under the new proposal are in the tenth decile, among the institutions that offer the lowest-cost education. These institutions have few resources with which to subsidize their students, and the only way they can survive is by charging high tuition.

Although table 8.2 gives us a look at the distribution of tuition and fees under the new proposal, it still hides quite a bit of variation. Each decile contains 274 institutions, and there will be considerable variation around these averages. The students of concern here are those who are qualified to obtain admission to a high-tuition institution but are unwilling to incur as much debt as that choice would entail. In the current system, many of these students receive sufficient institutional aid to attend one of these institutions. These institutions will not want to lose these students. Most of the problem will be experienced at the institutions in the top decile. The average net tuition and fees are quite a bit lower in the second decile and in a narrow range for the second through the eighth deciles.[2]

Facing Trade-offs: Solving the Choice Problem

For the new proposal to be acceptable, it has to eliminate its adverse effects on choice. This does not turn out to be an easy task. Ultimately, creating a system that provides complete choice compromises other objectives.

There are two possible ways to alter the new proposal to improve choice. First, colleges and universities could be allowed to give grants. Second, the structure of Pell Grants could be altered to allow them to increase with increases in the cost of attendance. Both alternative solutions have advantages and disadvantages.

Reintroducing Institutional Grants

The choice problem could be solved by allowing institutions to award their own grants. If these were limited to need-based grants, and federal Pell Grants were much larger (because they used the funds currently spent on loans and tuition tax credits), the institutionally funded grants allowed would be much smaller than they currently are. As a result, tuition could be reduced, though not by as much as the elimination of all institutional grants would allow. The reductions in tuition at institutions offering a large amount of merit-based grants would be substantial.

The major casualty of allowing institutional grants would be the simplicity of the system. The proposal without institutional grants describes a completely off-campus financial aid system in which all grants are portable. With portable grants, a student could use information in the catalogue and information from a single application for federal financial aid to determine the net cost of attending a given college or university. Institutional grants would not be portable. A student would only know the net cost of attending some institutions after the institutions had made admission and financial aid decisions. Because the cost of submitting applications for admission and financial aid are significant, students would not be able to have accurate information on as large a number of institutions. Moreover, if institutions followed current practices, students would probably have to make multiple financial aid applications. Currently, institutions have the freedom to make their own determination of a family's EFC for the purposes of awarding their own grants, and there is variation in the information they collect for this purpose. If institutions are putting their own money into institutional grants, they are likely to want to control the information used to determine its use. Reintroducing institutional grants clearly complicates the college choice decision for students.

It is ironic that the requirement that enough financial aid be available to facilitate choice causes changes that complicate the financial aid system. Providing high-quality information in a timely fashion makes it easier for students to make optimal choices. The proposal before us, reintroducing traditional need-based financial aid at those institutions that would be otherwise out of the financial reach of some low-income students, takes one step forward by making a broader range of choices financially feasible for low-income students. However, it also takes one step backward by complicating the financial aid process and delaying the distribution of accurate information about the costs of the options students face.

Other objectives are affected as well. With institutional funding, grants would become once again become need based—that is, they would be related to the difference between the EFC (or EFC plus the Pell Grant) and the cost of attendance. As such, they would increase with tuition increases. This would make institutions less likely to hold the line on tuition increases. With the ability to use institutionally funded grants, institutions will know that they do not have to sacrifice socioeconomic diversity if they raise tuition.

The final unfortunate aspect of allowing institutional grants is that it would reintroduce the possibility of competition using financial aid. Although the institutional grants would be awarded on the basis of need, not merit, institutions could compete by using different estimates of the EFC. Other things being equal, an institution using a lower estimate of the EFC will award a larger need-based grant. As a result, the institution would be more attractive to students and their families than an institution with a high estimate of the EFC. Given the current use of institutionally funded financial aid in recruiting, leaving it in the financial aid system is likely to continue the competition.

It might possible to restrict the form of institutional grants and regain some of the lost ground. For this to happen, institutions would have to give up a considerable amount of autonomy over their financial aid spending. Many institutions would resist this restriction. In any event, if all institutions would agree to utilize the federal needs analysis system and agree on the maximum allowable potential loan, a system based on institutional Pell Grant supplements could be instituted.[3]

Pell Grants are intended to bring a student's resources from the combination of the expected family contribution and the grant to a particular level. The Pell Grant given to a student with an expected family contribution of zero is considered the maximum Pell Grant. If federal Pell Grants were the only grant in the financial aid system, the highest potential loan at any institution would be its cost of attendance minus the maximum Pell Grant. Institutional

Pell Grant supplements would work in the following way. If the highest potential loan for an institution exceeded the agreed-upon maximum allowable potential loan, the institution would qualify to give institutional Pell Grant supplements. These supplements would be designed to reduce a student's potential loan to the maximum allowable potential loan. If such a system were universal, an individual student could group institutions into two categories: those at which his or her potential loan is below the maximum and those at which his or her potential loan is at the maximum.

The system that includes institutional Pell Grant supplements addresses the choice problem without complicating the system as much as the uncontrolled reintroduction of institutionally funded need-based grants would. In this system, institutions would not make assessments of financial need; they would instead rely on the calculations used to determine federal Pell Grant eligibility. Some students who are unlikely to qualify for federal Pell Grants but might qualify for institutional Pell Grant supplements would have to be encouraged to complete the Pell Grant forms to determine their expected family contribution, so the number of applications for financial aid would increase. Moreover, for the system to work well, institutions would have to agree to fully fund all students who qualify for an institutional Pell Grant supplement.

Institutional Pell Grant supplements simplify information gathering for students. Students need make only one application for financial aid, and they could do so early in their senior year in high school. They could easily predict the amount they would have to finance from sources other than their EFC, federal Pell Grant, and institutional Pell Grant supplement. Given the structure of institutional Pell Grant supplements, many institutions would offer effectively the same financial choices to a low-income student, and the choice problem would thereby be solved: students would make their decisions based on their evaluations of the educational experience they would expect from each institution. Finally, in this system, institutions would not be able to use financial aid as a tool in their competition for students.

Institutional Pell Grant supplements do reduce some of the benefits of the new proposal. First, the supplements would have to be financed on campus with increases in list-price tuition. Because institutional Pell Grant supplements would increase with tuition, the rate of increase in tuition would exceed the rate of increase in the costs of the institution. As with the existing system, the current students and parents would pay higher prices to overcome problems in the national income distribution. Nevertheless, as Winston's (1999) data suggest, many of the institutions that would offer large institutional Pell Grant supplements provide a highly subsidized education, one that many students would be willing to pay slightly higher prices to obtain.

A second cost of allowing institutional Pell Grant supplements is that it would reduce the incentives for institutions to control costs. By capping the potential loan amount, institutional Pell Grant supplements would eliminate price differences for needy students. In financial terms, several institutions would offer the same option to these students. Unfortunately, in such a system an institution could raise its price without having to worry that it would lose its low-income students, and thus one of the positive incentives in the new proposal would be diminished. However, the costs may not be high. Other things being equal, institutions that did not offer Pell Grant supplements would have a competitive advantage with low-income students over those that did. This would create an incentive for the institutions offering Pell Grant supplements to control costs so that their competitive disadvantage did not grow.

Changing the Basis of the Pell Grant Award

Another alternative is to change the rules for Pell Grants. Currently, the amount of a Pell Grant is based on the income of a student and is not sensitive to the cost of attendance. A Pell Grant simply increases the resources available to a needy student. The student can apply the Pell Grant to costs at any institution. One way to resolve the choice problem inherent in my redesign proposal is to increase the federal Pell Grant with increasing cost of attendance. In this way the net price of high-priced institutions could be controlled so that needy students would not be excluded.

This solution has difficulties of its own. First, for it to work, the government would have to commit itself to increasing Pell Grants as the costs of higher education increase; thus far, the government has shown an unwillingness to do so. Second, the variance of Pell Grants from one institution to another would make it harder for students to know the price they face at each institution. Third, this accommodation would negate the benefits of income-based grants over need-based grants: with need-based grants, the government absorbs some of any increase in prices that institutions decide to pass along to students, and the incentives for institutions to control costs are thereby diminished. Fourth, it relies on the government to determine the maximum potential loan, relieving institutions of higher education of the responsibility. The political arena may not be the best place for such a decision.

Conclusions and the Final Trade-off

Some parts of the redesign proposal survive the scrutiny I have given it. Although the discussion has naturally centered on those parts of the system that create trade-offs among the objectives, it is important to remember those parts of the proposed financial aid system that do not create such trade-offs and thereby have escaped scrutiny. The first of these I would mention is income-contingent tax credits for loan forgiveness. There is no reason to expect that any other objective of the financial aid system would be sacrificed if part of the funds identified in table 8.1 were used to finance such a program.

The second innovation that has escaped scrutiny in the discussion to this point is the proposal to base the expected family contribution on long-term income. Although this proposal does not create any conflicts among the objectives of the financial aid system, it would be feasible only if individuals were willing to give access to Social Security records and if the government were willing to allow such access. A second difficulty is that it requires institutions to rely on federal needs analysis for the distribution of their own funds. This will work only if institutions play a role in the determination of the new federal needs analysis system. Some of the complexity of the current system, however, derives from the dissatisfaction of many institutions with the federal needs analysis system. It will be important to try to develop a system that meets with the approval of all institutions.

The proposal to shift the responsibility for loan guarantees from the federal government to colleges and universities would not come about without controversy. For the most part, however, it does not conflict with any of the objectives I set out for a financial aid system. The one exception is the concern that institutions would try to control their default exposure by limiting the recruitment of low-income students. If this effect is strong, choice will be limited. Although it is hard to determine before the experiment is run, there is no reason to assume that the loss of choice from this practice will be any greater than the loss of choice from the current practice of need-aware admission policies. My confidence in this outcome would greatly increased if the income-contingent tax credits for loan forgiveness were also in place. Under the current system, institutions have to spend money, in the form of large grants, to be considered as an option to low-income students. With expanded Pell Grants, the amounts institutions have to spend to make themselves affordable to low-income students would decrease. Institutions would probably be more willing to take on low-income students if these costs were to go down by more than the expected value of default payments for these students. The existence of income-contingent tax credits for loan forgiveness makes this outcome much more likely.

Regarding the potential solutions to the conflicts in objectives identified in the previous section, my conclusion is that institutional Pell Grant supplements are the superior solution. There is one overriding reason for this conclusion: funding for institutional Pell Grant supplements would be much more reliable than the funding for need-based federal Pell Grants. The government has not always been responsive to the needs of low-income students. Colleges and universities, on the other hand, have strong commitments to fostering socioeconomic diversity in their student bodies, and institutional Pell Grant supplements would allow institutions to act on this commitment. A secondary consideration is that institutional Pell Grants would allow institutions to continue to raise private funding for financial aid. Clearly, some donors like to support financial aid. The existence of institutional Pell Grant supplements would give them a way to support both the institution and the efforts of needy students.

This leaves us with the final trade-off. Grafting institutional Pell Grant supplements onto the system gives us a financial aid system that meets most, but not all, of the objectives I have set out for it. What it does not do, however, is protect institutional autonomy. For the system to work, institutions would have to give up many long-standing practices. First, they would no longer offer merit-based grants. Many institutions are perfectly content with their current merit-based financial aid programs, and although they might agree that the competition using merit-based aid is ultimately not unproductive for the higher education sector, they would be more inclined to encourage others to abandon the merit-based aid than to take the pledge themselves.

Second, the proposal asks institutions to give up autonomy for their financial aid programs. There are three parts to this loss of autonomy. First, institutions would be spending funds in the form of institutional Pell Grant supplements, but they would have no role in determining a student's expected family contribution. Institutions currently have the option to accept the federal determination of a student's EFC, but most of the institutions that would be likely to use institutional Pell Grants supplements ask for additional information. These institutions feel they have good reasons to ask for this information, and they will not want to give up this privilege. The second loss of autonomy over the financial aid program is in the design of awards. Currently, institutions have the liberty to change the size of grants by changing the mix between grants and loans on a student-by-student basis. Under the proposed system, the grants they award would all be institutional Pell Grant supplements, of the same form for all students and for all institutions—a restriction institutions might well resist.

There is one benefit associated with these two losses in autonomy. The administrative costs associated with financial aid would be significantly decreased if institutions were not making independent determinations of the EFC or the form of aid awards. A financial aid office would still be necessary, to deal with student questions and changes in circumstances affecting financial aid awards such as study abroad, but the staffing level in financial aid offices could be dramatically reduced.

The third loss of autonomy is that institutions would have to abide by a jointly determined maximum potential loan. Without agreement on this parameter, institutional competition using financial aid would be rampant. To obtain this agreement, institutions will have to develop a mechanism that allows them to negotiate. In light of the case of the Overlap Group, it could be argued that the government frowns upon meetings of college officials in which they talk about matters such as financial aid. Setting the maximum potential loan would most likely strike the Antitrust Division of the Department of Justice as a form of price setting. Clearly, changes would have to be made in the antitrust laws, or at least in their interpretation, before this proposal could be workable.

In the final analysis, for the new proposal to work, institutions will have to make a decision to relinquish considerable autonomy. Some improvements within the structure of the current system are possible, but the toughest problems to deal with in the financial aid system derive from the fact that financial aid has become a competitive tool. It will be difficult to meet the objectives of a financial aid system unless institutions are willing to stop using financial aid competitively. To do so, some reduction in autonomy will be unavoidable.

On Political Feasibility

My redesign proposals call for several significant changes, and they will need champions, both in the national political arena and among colleges and universities. Who will initiate the switch in roles involving loan guarantees? Who will take the first step in minimizing the use of institutional grants? Finally, which of the proposals might be instituted independently of the others, given the difficult political battle in winning acceptance for this package of proposals?

The Program Switch

My redesign proposals call for the federal government and colleges and universities to agree to trade programs, the government taking on the administration of grants and institutions taking responsibility for the administration of student loans. Any proposal that involves a switch of duties will be difficult to initiate. Who goes first? Should the government make unilateral changes? Is it sensible for the federal government to eliminate the guaranteed student loan program and tuition tax credits and transfer the funding to Pell Grants? Would colleges and universities step forward and offer loan guarantees? Should it be the institutions that initiate unilateral changes? Should colleges and universities withdraw from the federal loan programs and replace them with their own? Would the federal government increase Pell Grants as its loan expenses decreased? Do the changes have to be coordinated?

The Government as Leader

First, consider the federal government as the leader. Suppose the federal government were to lead the way by instituting four changes: eliminating all student loan programs, eliminating the Hope Scholarship and Lifetime Learning tuition tax credits, eliminating Supplemental Educational Opportunity Grants, and using the funding from the eliminated programs to increase funding for Pell Grants. I think most colleges and universities would see the advantages of stepping into the void by creating their own loan guarantee programs. Loans would be next to impossible for many students to obtain without loan guarantees.

Although I am confident that colleges and universities would accept the responsibility for loan guarantees if the government were to leave a void there, I am much less confident that they would ever be given the opportunity. Clearly, the advantages offered by these changes would win the support of some political leaders. As illustrated by the budget negotiations in the fall of 2000, several members of Congress are concerned with the plight of students from poor families. These members of Congress lobbied for increases in the Pell Grant program larger than those the Clinton administration had requested.[1] The Bush administration initially appeared to be sympathetic to large Pell Grant increases, as well.[2] The new system should appeal to supporters of large Pell Grant increases in Congress and in the Bush administration. Second, as the report of the National Commission on the Cost of Higher Education (1998) suggests, several members of Congress are concerned about accountability in higher education. Giving the responsibility for loan guarantees to colleges and universities would increase accountability, a modification that could bring additional members of Congress into a coalition to support the changes.

Unfortunately, even with this support, it is unlikely that members of Congress or any administration would initiate the required legislation on their own. The program switch asks the federal government to abandon two popular programs. Guaranteed student loans have come to be viewed as a middle-class entitlement, and a small industry has grown up around them. Although the firms in this industry would most likely be able to find a role in a new system, they would probably lobby to keep the status quo. Tuition tax credits, like any tax privilege, are also popular. In 2000, the Clinton administration proposed an expansion of the tax credits, and the tax bill that passed early in the Bush administration increased the tuition tax credits.[3]

In the current climate, there is considerable support for expanding rather than contracting the aid offered to middle-class college students. Concerns over affordability seem to have more political clout than concerns over access. The programs to be eliminated are just too popular with the middle class (read "voters") for a plan to abandon them to gain the required political momentum on its own.

Colleges and Universities as Leaders

Although it is unlikely that the government will initiate a push for the switch in roles, colleges and universities are another story. A significant number of university leaders and higher education policy analysts have suggested similar changes. In many cases, these leaders would not have to change their position a great deal to start a lobbying effort for the switch in roles. Consider the advertisement that appeared in the *New York Times* on March 7, 2001, under the headline, "Just and Efficient College Finance." The ad, which was signed by a distinguished group of policy analysts and educational leaders, began with a listing of eight facts describing the growing access problem in higher education.[4] The policy analysts then presented three "policy implications":

1. Colleges and universities perform most effectively in the public interest when they concentrate their own financial aid on academically qualified but financially needy students, rather than using aid to subsidize financially able students to enroll at their campuses.

2. States bear the primary responsibility of assuring a supply of places and financial arrangements that permit all eligible students to enroll in college. States facing large enrollment increases in this decade bear a particularly heavy responsibility for supplying sufficient places for future students and meeting the increasing need for financial assistance.

3. The federal government has the principal responsibility of providing a solid foundation of need-based grants and loans. Priority should be placed on the restora-

tion of grants rather than the further expansion of loans for undergraduates or tuition tax benefits for families.

The American people clearly understand the vital importance of access to higher education in today's economy. The challenge facing the nation is not one of finding the resources but directing them to where the needs are greatest and using them most efficiently. We urge a national recommitment to this statement.

The third point suggests that this group might well be willing to support the switch in roles outlined in the redesign proposals. The switch in roles I propose goes much further, but their statement does a good job of addressing the "challenge facing the nation"—directing resources "where the need is greatest."

I would hope that many educational leaders could be easily convinced to take a slightly more radical position than the one presented in the *New York Times* statement. I would hope that the leaders of colleges and universities would call for and actively support legislation abolishing the government loan programs and tuition tax credits and redirecting the money freed up to Pell Grants and would also promise to replace the government loan programs with guaranteed loan programs of their own. The promise to accept the responsibility for student loan guarantees should be appealing to members of Congress. Typically, members of Congress deal with constituents looking for favors—for more money or advantageous program changes—but without offering more than political support or a campaign contribution in exchange. It would be a refreshing change for colleges and universities to express a willingness to take on more responsibility in exchange for the desired program changes. Moreover, this proposal is budget neutral: implementation would not require additional expenditures on the part of the federal government.[5]

Some colleges and universities will be reluctant to support this type of proposal. Proprietary and two-year institutions with histories of high default rates will not want to be saddled with loan guarantees. Supporters of the program switch will also have to allay fears that a system in which loans are guaranteed by institutions will encourage colleges and universities to more actively discriminate against students from poor families. The proposal clearly directs more of the federal aid toward needy students. The larger Pell Grants should be welcomed by those concerned about expanded need-aware admissions.

Including income-contingent tax credits for loan forgiveness in the proposal might well make this group of doubters more comfortable with the proposal, and there are good reasons to add them to the mix. In any event, it will be important to get support from a broad array of colleges and universities. Whether or not this can be done remains to be seen. It would be an effort worth making, however, and I hope considerable support for this position will be found among college and university leaders.

Minimizing the Use of Institutional Grants

The proposal also calls for colleges and universities to limit their institutional grants to Pell Grant supplements. The supplemented Pell Grants would leave no student with a potential loan larger than an agreed upon maximum.[6] To put this proposal in place, institutions would have to agree on the size of the maximum potential loan. Whether colleges and universities would be able to reach agreement on this important parameter is questionable, however. Institutions face a prisoners' dilemma of sorts: only if there is agreement among institutions will it be sensible for any one to make the changes required to minimize the use of institutional grants.

As the activities of the Overlap Group and the 568 Presidents' Working Group indicate, there is a demand for collusion of some sort on financial aid policy, especially among private institutions. Without interference from the Antitrust Division, the Overlap Group would probably still be operating today. In its absence, the 568 Presidents' Working Group has been meeting for the past several years to discuss the financial aid environment. In July 2001, twenty-eight institutions in this group reached agreement on a method of making uniform assessments of financial need (Hoover 2001).

Several commentators have traced increases in tuition discounting and merit-based aid to the downfall of the Overlap Group. Ronald Ehrenberg concludes that "while the consent decree [in the MIT case] has put more institutional grant aid in some students' pockets, it also has contributed to institutions' need to raise tuition levels by more than the rate of inflation" (Ehrenberg 2000, 79).[7]

McPherson and Schapiro (1999) advocate antitrust protection for colleges and universities. "Specifically, we should urge Congress to pass a law affirming that colleges can enter into agreements to apply common standards in assessing need and awarding aid without running afoul of antitrust laws" (McPherson and Schapiro 1999, A48). This desire to collude could find an outlet in support of the redesign proposals.

Several leaders in the higher education sector want to collude to insure that financial aid is not used as a recruiting devise. Merit aid is expanding rapidly, both in frequency of use and the amount awarded, and institutions are competing by making more and more generous assessments of financial need. Even under the Overlap Group and the 568 Presidents' Working Group arrangements, institutions can compete by increasing the ratio of grants to loans in their need-based financial aid awards for the students they would most like to attract. The redesign proposals give institutions a way to stop all of this competition.

To put this part of the redesign proposal in place, colleges and universities would have to agree to three things: to use a common assessment of the expected family contribution, to set a common maximum potential loan, and to limit their own financial aid to Pell Grant supplements. These three points should be part of a compact that institutions would be asked to sign. It would be interesting to see how many institutions could be convinced to sign such a compact.

The agreement on common standards for determining need by the members of the 568 Presidents' Working Group accomplishes the first point stressed in the *New York Times* statement. Although the proposal in chapter 8 suggests that the federal government be given sole responsibility for determining financial need, any system that standardized the assessment of need would work with the proposal. The apparent resistance of institutions (only twenty-eight agreed to the common methodology for determining need) and the institutional judgment allowed by the system suggest that this might be a sticking point for many institutions. To focus the discussion further, however, I will make the perhaps heroic assumption that this point is not a great stumbling block for most institutions.

The pricing agreement inherent in the new proposal is known among antitrust experts as a "most favored customer clause" or sometimes a "most favored nations clause" (see, for example, Kwoka and White 1999 and Baker 1996). In essence, it is an agreement to offer all students the lowest price it offers to any student. Although an individual firm may practice such a policy without violating the antitrust laws, serious antitrust problems arise when a group of firms collude to set up this or any other common-pricing policy. For the new proposal to move forward, therefore, it would need specific antitrust immunity. Unlike other instances of price fixing, there are compelling reasons to encourage this price fixing, and Congress should be persuaded to grant a specific immunity in this case.

The agreements needed for the new proposal will not be appealing unless they are coupled with a promise to increase government grants. With the current level of government grants, institutional Pell Grant supplements would have to be very large, and colleges and universities could reasonably expect the proposal for the program switch discussed to be successful in Congress.

Assuming that institutions find a way to agree on a common method for determining financial need, that the federal government grants a specific exemption from the antitrust laws, and that the switch in roles is accomplished, I now turn to the restrictions on institutional aid. Will institutions take the steps required to adopt the changes in their grant behavior?

An institution would have to make two critical assessments before agreeing to support these changes. First, it would have to believe that its enthusiasm for change was shared by other institutions. A college or university would not want to limit its grants unilaterally; it would want its close competitors to also limit their grants. One of the aims of this effort is to stop institutions from using financial aid in the competition for students. An institution will not be willing to agree to limit its grants if it thinks its competitors will be in a position to capture all of the high-quality students. It is likely that institutions will be risk averse, agreeing to the changes only if they are sure that their major competitors will follow suit.

The second assessment is perhaps more crucial. Institutions would have to be convinced that they and their students could flourish under the new rules of the game. The proposal cures many of the ills of the current financial aid system, but few cures are painless, and many institutions feel that the current system serves them well. According to the data presented in table 8.2, the institutions with the highest tuition, and therefore the greatest likelihood of having large institutional Pell Grants supplements, would be those at the extremes of the subsidy distribution. Average tuition would be $5,700 for institutions in the first decile, $4,600 for institutions in the ninth decile, and $6,100 for institutions in the tenth decile. Tuition at the other 70 percent of institutions would be, on average, between $2,600 and $3,800.

The institutions from the extremes of the subsidy distribution would most likely clash during negotiations to set the maximum potential loan. Institutions with large endowments or generous state subsidies currently are able to meet all of the financial need of each student, thereby limiting loans for their students. Princeton's recent announcement that it is eliminating loans altogether is an extreme case, but many institutions do not automatically award the maximum loan allowed under the federal programs. Institutions with meager endowments or limited state subsidies (or both) are another story. These institutions offer aid packages that, even including the largest possible loan, do not cover all of the financial need of all their students. Students attending these institutions often end their college careers with large debt burdens.

Clearly, the institutions offering educations with high subsidies will lobby for a low maximum potential loan, while those offering educations with low subsidies will argue for a much higher maximum potential loan. To think about how such a process might evolve, consider how these different institutions would react to a compromise that split the difference: neither group would be happy. Institutions from the first decile of the subsidy distribution would be unhappy because under a system with a high maximum potential loan, they would be offering less need-based grant aid to their students than they do now. With a maximum potential loan greater than zero, Princeton would clearly have to reduce its need-based grants. As the maximum potential loan grows, more and more of Princeton's close competitors would have to reduce their need-based grants as well. Many institutions would reject such a system. Institutions typically have a sense that they should do as much as possible to aid their students. It would not be easy for an administration to face its students or alumni after agreeing to a policy that would increase the indebtedness of all students with financial need.

On the other end of the subsidy distribution, institutions with low average subsidies would find that, as before, they could not meet all of the need of their students. Restricting institutional grants to Pell Grant supplements dramatically limits the strategies available to such institutions. Often these institutions rely on aggressive merit scholarship programs to attract their best students. Denied the ability to use merit scholarships and lacking the ability to meet all of the need of poor students, these institutions would be at a significant disadvantage. Some could raise more revenue by raising list-price tuition more aggressively, but such an effort would soon prove self-defeating because it would make the institution's financial aid offers relatively less attractive. Many of these institutions already offer a scholarship of one kind or another to most of their students, so there are relatively few full-paying students from whom to raise more revenue. Setting the maximum potential loan amount lower than the level they considered optimal would threaten the very existence of some of these institutions.

Many of the richest institutions will not see the proposed system as beneficial to their students, and without a greater ability to set prices than that allowed under the proposed system many of the poorest institutions will find their survival challenged. Will these issues cause sufficient dissent among colleges and universities that they cannot come to an agreement on a maximum potential loan? This is a serious concern. It is possible that political problems among the institutions will shoot down the proposal before it can get started.

Several arguments might be persuasive with some first-decile institutions, but it will be more difficult to deal with the problems of the institutions in the ninth and tenth deciles. First, consider the rich institutions. These institutions are very selective, as well as very wealthy. Although the new system offers their needy students lower grants than they now have, it does have some attractive advantages. The new system would offer more need-based aid nationally, so the average student with financial need would be better off—even if the students with financial need at some first-decile institutions will not be. The proposed system simplifies the financial aid process for all students, so students should be able to make better-informed decisions. The new proposal calls for the elimination of merit scholarships, but most of the first-decile institutions award very few, if any, merit scholarships.[8] Currently, these institutions are losing a growing number of talented students to other institutions with aggressive merit-based scholarship programs. Some first-decile institutions will see these as compelling reasons to adopt the new system.

The situation for the institutions at the bottom of subsidy distribution is much clearer. Their very existence will be threatened. The question now is whether this is a cost or a benefit of the new system. Clearly, the institutions at the bottom of the subsidy spectrum will be on one side of this issue. The institutions in the most trouble here are those that offer the lowest-cost education. On average, students in tenth-decile institutions pay $6,100 for an education that costs $7,900. Institutions in higher deciles offer a much more costly, almost certainly higher-quality, education and charge significantly lower prices. If the higher education system loses some of the tenth-decile institutions, the loss may not be that great. Firms that offer low-quality products at relatively high prices do not survive in most markets. It does not seem a good idea to give up any of the benefits of the redesign proposal to increase the survival odds of these institutions. The political difficulty, however, is that these institutions might then operate outside the system. If a sufficient number of institutions were to decide that the new system was detrimental to their well-being, it might be difficult to achieve the consensus required for the system to work.

It is difficult to know whether a limited collusion could survive. The Overlap Group contained only twenty-three institutions, and it survived for a long time. Several institutions, Stanford and Duke to name two prominent ones, have a significant admissions overlap with the institutions in the Overlap Group, and the absence of these institutions did not subvert the group's activities. The agreement of each institution would not be contingent on agreement by all institutions, but the collusion of some kind of critical mass of institutions would be required for the proposal to succeed.

The agreement reached by the members of the 568 Presidents' Working Group illustrates this same point. The twenty-eight institutions include some important institutions—Duke, Notre Dame, Rice, and Stanford—that were not part of the Overlap Group. Although all of the Ivy League institutions were members of the Overlap Group, only four—Columbia, Cornell, Penn, and Yale—have adopted common methods for determining financial need. Clearly, institutions are willing to join groups that do not include all their competitors.

The number of institutions that will agree to the compact is difficult to predict. The agreement should be attractive to institutions concerned about the acceleration in price discounting, particularly merit-based price discounting. It provides a mechanism to eliminate price discounting that is easy to monitor. Colleges and universities should feel a sense of urgency about the

issues involved. The financial aid system is clearly moving in the wrong direction. Colleges and universities are in an intense competition for the best students, and the use of financial aid as a competitive tool is expanding rapidly.
This competition is not beneficial to the long-run health of higher education.

Competition that expands the funds devoted to institutional grants is
counterproductive to the political support required to maintain the federal
commitment to access. Colleges and universities have to acknowledge the
competition for financial aid dollars. As tuition and fee charges have risen,
support for aid to the middle class has grown. Legislation authorizing tuition
tax credits was a result of this political dynamic. To shift the federal focus back
to access, colleges and universities have to do something about the rate of
increase of tuition and fees. Eliminating institutional aid would provide dramatic decreases in tuition and fees. Without the institutions' promise to decrease tuition, there is little likelihood that the government will abandon
tuition tax credits and subsidized loans. It is crucial for institutions to recognize that a continuation of the current system is not in their best interest.

The proposal to limit the use of institutional grants to Pell Grant Supplements is a long shot and will have considerable difficulty attracting support
from a large number of institutions. Without a sufficient number of participants, institutions that join the collusion will be putting themselves at a great
competitive disadvantage. There is clearly precedent for this gloomy forecast.
The Overlap Group, the strongest group ever assembled to limit competition
in the use of financial aid, was not able to eliminate all competition: members
of the Overlap Group could not use the size of their financial aid offers to compete, but they could change the mix between grants and loans in their aid
packages. It will be even more difficult for a new, necessarily larger group to
accomplish this.

Changes to Improve Intergenerational Decision Making

The proposals to improve intergenerational decision making also require significant changes in the legislation authorizing federal financial aid. Ideally, the
entire package would be enacted. However, each proposal also merits consideration on its own.

Changes in the Determination of the Expected Family Contribution

To increase the incentives for families to save, an estimate of long-term family income, rather than current income and assets, as the basis for determining the expected family contribution has several advantages. It rewards thrift, as opposed to penalizing it. By leaving out assets, it does not bias choices about how a family holds wealth; the current system exempts some assets, creating incentives to overinvest in these assets. The additional earnings of families who decide to finance college expenses by working more—for example, by taking on a second job or volunteering for more hours—will be taxed by the financial aid system at a much lower rate. Finally, families will be able to find out their expected family contribution much sooner than they can in the current system.

These advantages outweigh any disadvantages of the proposed system. Some will argue that the proposed system creates inequities for families with high assets and low income—students with trust funds being the most obvious example. Because they will not have to include their assets in the calculations of the expected family contribution, they may receive financial aid that is not needed. This will seem scandalous to some, and it is certainly unfortunate. Nevertheless, the livelihood of the vast majority of families is based on earned income. The improvements in incentives for these families outweigh any difficulties created by trust-fund children.

This change might seem difficult politically, but it really should not be. Members of Congress need to be made aware of the mixed signal the current system gives families. Many state governments have special college savings plans. Section 529 of the Internal Revenue Code gives tax advantages to these college savings plans. Clearly, such a policy is motivated by a desire to support saving for college. The current calculation of the EFC places high implicit taxes on savings. Although not all calls for government consistency are successful, past history does not indicate that all calls for consistency are futile. Consistency should be appealing. Often, inconsistent policies exist because there is no alternative that eliminates the inconsistency. The proposal to base the EFC on a long-term measure of income provides Congress with what it needs—a way to calculate the EFC that encourages savings.

Changes in the Basis for Determining Grants

The current Pell Grants are income based. If the switch is organized successfully, Congress will be presented with an opportunity to increase Pell Grants using funds freed up by the elimination of federal loan programs and the tuition tax credits. Although this change will occur naturally if the new proposal is adopted, it is worth lobbying for on its own. If the Supplemental Educational Opportunity Grants, which are given out on the basis of need, not income, were folded into the Pell Grants, the system would be improved. This would be a marginal improvement compared with adoption of the entire proposal, but it would be an improvement nonetheless. The SEOGs are a historical oddity, the remnants of a program that was deemed to be inferior to the Pell Grant program but one that Congress did not want to completely eliminate. Given the benefits of income-based grants over need-based grants, the existence of the SEOG program is difficult to support.

Income-Contingent Tax Credits for Loan Forgiveness

Under the existing financial aid system, many students leave school with a large amount of debt. Some of these students will have difficulties repaying that debt. Independent of any other changes, it would be a good idea to provide some aid to these students. The income-contingent loan repayment system currently offered is an attempt to provide this type of aid, so there has been support for this idea in Congress. The income-contingent tax credits for loan forgiveness suggested by Thomas Kane (1999a) would be an improvement, and the proposal could have a good chance of finding support in Congress.

From a political viewpoint, income-contingent tax credits for loan forgiveness have an interesting linkage with the remainder of the new proposal. In many cases the proposals would have to be enacted almost simultaneously. Income-contingent tax credits for loan forgiveness need not be part of this package of changes. In fact, it might be better if these tax credits were enacted before the remainder of the proposals or, as suggested above, at the time of the switch in roles. One of the concerns that many will have with shifting responsibility for loan guarantees to institutions is that the institutions might discriminate against poor students. I have argued that this should not be a large problem, and the existence of income-contingent tax credits for loan forgiveness plays an important role in the argument. If institutions know that this type of assistance will be available, graduating students with large loan repayment commitments will have less potential to be costly to the institution. To the extent that this argument is persuasive, the political momentum necessary for establishing the new system could be greatly enhanced if these tax credits were enacted as soon as possible.

Changes in the Spirit of the New Proposals

The redesign proposal represents a radical change. Although some of its components could be enacted by themselves, the most significant benefits depend on enacting the entire plan. Some other, less radical changes are nevertheless in the spirit of the new proposal.

Abandoning Merit Aid but Keeping Need-based Aid

The concern with tuition discounting among colleges and universities focuses more on merit-based aid than on need-based aid. Merit-based aid is part of a zero-sum game, and the more aggressively colleges and universities play that game, the more harmful it will become. Many leaders in higher education know this, but as in any game of this sort, the only solutions available are based on some form of collusion.

It is worth considering the changes that would be required to eliminate merit-based aid. Clearly, there would be support for such a proposal. The first policy suggestion in the *New York Times* statement bears repeating: "Colleges and universities perform most effectively in the public interest when they concentrate their own financial aid on academically qualified but financially needy students, rather than using aid to subsidize financially able students to enroll at their campuses." Because a large number of leaders in higher education would subscribe to these sentiments, the elimination of merit-based aid would meet broad support.

Suppose a large number of college and universities were to make a pledge to abandon merit-based aid. To forestall intervention by the Antitrust Division of the Justice Department, unlike the Overlap Group, these colleges and universities would not investigate the individual offers made to students. The obvious problem is that it would be difficult to enforce compliance with the pledge. The group would have only one legal enforcement practice available to them: by checking the records of each institution singly, it would be possible to determine aid awards in excess of financial need and to hold the offending institution up to ridicule as a violator of the pledge. Moral suasion would be their only enforcement tool. If the group tried directly to reduce aid awards it found objectionable, it would be operating dangerously close to price fixing.

All things considered, in the absence of more sweeping changes, the best bet may be to initiate the political groundswell necessary to get some institutions to sign a pledge to eliminate merit-based aid. If such a pledge were signed by several schools that use a large amount of merit-based aid, the resulting decreases in list-price tuition would be significant evidence of the seriousness of the problem.

Part of the problem with implementation of this plan absent the other proposals is that it does not restrict the form of need-based financial aid or make the assessment of financial need uniform. Although, in principle, distinguishing merit-based aid from need-based aid should be easy, it is sometimes more difficult in practice. Even if all aid given were need based, the use of financial aid in the competition for students would not be eliminated. For the purposes of defining need for their institutional aid, institutions could still use different formulas for the EFC, and they could manipulate the form of financial aid offered. As Princeton's recent action indicates, it is quite possible that wealthier institutions would offer better financial aid packages (more in grants and less in loans) than would less wealthy institutions. Some institutions may offer better financial aid packages to more desirable students.

Keeping the Old Formulas for Determining the Expected Family Contribution

It is possible to separate the determination of the expected family contribution from the remainder of the redesign proposal. Although the disincentives to save associated with the current method of calculating the EFC should be eliminated, none of the other components of the proposal hinge on this change. The major difficulty associated with this element of the proposal is the possible unavailability of the data required to make such an estimate. This would happen in two cases. First, the standard source for these data would be Social Security records. In some cases—for example, new immigrants or workers who are not covered by Social Security—it might not be easy to obtain a record of earnings over a long time span. In any case, newly independent students will have had an abbreviated work history. These are not insurmountable barriers, but they make the system much more likely to contain inequities. If these difficult prove insurmountable, there is no reason to abandon the entire set of proposals. The existing needs analysis system could be used.

Unilaterally Abandoning Institutional Grants

Interestingly, in some cases institutions might want to unilaterally abandon institutional grants even if the compact to support the new proposals does not succeed. The advantage for such an institution would be that it could reduce its tuition—in some cases, dramatically.

Some institutions have experimented with this type of policy change. Applications and enrollment rose in number at Waldorf College, a private two-year college in Iowa, after it cut both grants and tuition (Hamm 1995). Muskingum College, a private four-year college in Ohio, cut tuition dramatically in 1995 by reducing (though not eliminating) tuition discounting (Irving 2001). In both cases, the experience with this experiment has been positively viewed. Wells College, a women's college in upstate New York, followed Muskingum's lead by cutting tuition and fees 29 percent for the 1999–2000 academic year.[9]

These cases suggest that institutions should take a close look at how far tuition would fall if they stopped discounting tuition. The process follows a predictable course: The institution that drops both grants and tuition raises its appeal to students who are unlikely to receive tuition reductions at other institutions—the well-to-do who are only moderately talented. What happens at the institutions that lose such students to the renegade college that stops discounting tuition? Because they have lost a number of students paying full tuition, other things being equal, their students will probably have more financial need than before. To meet the increased financial need, the institutions would have to raise their tuition further. This would exacerbate their competitive position for the well-to-do students who are only moderately talented. These are the students whose tuition pays for the discounts that currently go to those with more talent or less income. Managing a system based on tuition discounting becomes difficult when the number of full-paying students declines, and some institutions may be forced to cut back on their grants. It would be interesting to see which type of grants they would reduce.

Although an institution that unilaterally eliminates institutional grants gains an advantage with some students, it is unlikely that many schools will be inclined to join the institution adopting such a strategy. The bold changes at Waldorf, Muskingum, and Wells have yet to induce similar changes by their competitors, and unless a large number of colleges and universities decide to adopt a "no-grants" strategy, such a movement is not likely to gain momentum. Even if a large number of institutions were to initiate this policy, it would be fairly easy for competing institutions to lure away the most desirable of their students with merit-based financial aid offers. Without a binding agreement among all institutions, eliminating tuition discounting may prove impossible.

Conclusions

It would be foolhardy to underestimate the political problems facing the changes I propose. There will be many battles along the way, and victory is by no means certain. Nevertheless, I think the battles are worth fighting, and they will generate valuable discussions. The current financial aid system is clearly not doing the best possible job, and generally the direction of change is not encouraging.

One bright spot is the action of the institutions in the 568 Presidents' Working Group. Their agreement to eliminate competition based on variations in the assessment of financial need is clearly a good first step, although the impact of a contract among such a small number of institutions is not altogether clear. On one hand—the glass is half full—twenty-eight of the nation's most prestigious institutions were able to come to agreement; on the other hand—the glass is half empty—many institutions who had an opportunity to join, including half of the Ivy League, decided not to do so.

The title of McPherson and Schapiro's 1999 editorial, "Gaining Control of the Free-For-All in Financial Aid," is apt. The practice of using financial aid as a competitive tool is escalating. The commitment to need-based financial aid using a uniform needs analysis system has been difficult to sustain, and it is rapidly disappearing. This is not the time to be timid. The stakes are high. At the very least, I hope the proposals offered in this volume generate a productive discussion about how the financial aid system can be improved. At best, it could be the vehicle that allows institutions and the government to take control of the financial aid system so that aid is targeted where it is most needed.

Final Thoughts:
Facing Trade-offs

The redesign proposals presented here call for colleges and universities to make major changes in their financial aid programs. Institutions are asked to take responsibility for loan guarantees, but the loans they will guarantee will be not be subsidized. They are asked to give up the determination of financial need for their students. Finally, they are asked to limit institutional grants to institutional supplements to the federal Pell Grants, which would follow a strict formula that institutions cannot change on their own.

Proposals calling for radical changes in behavior are often motivated by a sense that someone is misbehaving or has impure motives. This is not the case here. In many ways, colleges and universities are the heroes in the recent history of financial aid. My redesign proposals are not intended as punishment for bad behavior.

The proposals focus on two primary causes of the current problems in the financial aid system. First, for most of the 1980s and 1990s federal funding did not keep up with educational costs. Institutions dedicated to the idea of a diverse student body were forced to resort to increased use of institutional aid. The institutions financed the increases in aid by raising list-price tuition. The data clearly show that increases in institutional grants have accompanied the increases in tuition.[1] As a result of the political climate created by the tuition increases, the federal government lost its focus on access. The prime example of this loss of focus is the tuition tax credits. Tuition tax credits are aimed squarely at affordability, not access.

Second, the downfall of the Overlap Group, which enforced a prohibition against merit-based aid for its members, removed a stigma against the use of financial aid as a recruiting device. With only twenty-three members, the Overlap Group itself did not represent a large number of institutions or students, but the member institutions are opinion leaders in higher education. Their efforts in the Overlap Group, which demonstrated their commitment to the primacy of access in their financial aid policies, provided a powerful example for other institutions. After the forced breakup of the Overlap Group, its members began to use financial aid more competitively. This, too, provided a powerful example for other institutions. The result has been a mushrooming of the use of merit aid and more competition using variations in need-based aid policy.

If this is the appropriate diagnosis, the solution for the financial aid system cannot avoid changes in institutional behavior. Increases in federal spending on financial aid might have been a way of maintaining the primacy of access several years ago, but it is not a full solution now. The genie is out of the bottle. More federal money now will replace some institutional need-based aid, but in the current climate it is likely to merely free up funds that institutions will put into more aggressive merit aid programs. The redesign proposals are based on a conviction that a frontal attack on the use of financial aid as a tool in the competition for students is at least as important as changes in federal programs.

Focusing on changes in institutional behavior may seem unfair. In general, history shows that institutions have been the responsible parties in the financial aid system. A group of institutions developed the model for need-based financial aid in use today—more than a decade before the federal government had any financial aid program. One reason institutional financial aid has grown so rapidly is that federal spending for financial aid has failed to keep up with tuition growth. Although merit-based aid has grown rapidly in recent years, need-based institutional grants are still much larger in aggregate than merit-based institutional grants. In many ways the behavior of institutions should be applauded. In the final analysis, it is because I have faith in the motives of colleges and universities, not because I question them, that I think they should take the lead in the redesign of the financial aid system.

The Report of the Advisory Committee on Student Financial Assistance and the Redesign Proposals

The Advisory Committee on Student Financial Assistance was created by the Higher Education Amendments of 1986 as "an independent source of advice and counsel to Congress and the Secretary of Education on student financial aid policy" (Advisory Committee on Student Financial Assistance 2001, vii). The committee's most recent report, released in February of 2001, does a good job of outlining the case that access has become a serious problem in higher education. Among other things, the report cites Choy's (1999) research showing the strong relation between income and the rates of college attendance for college-qualified students.

The committee's recommendations for the financial aid system are contained in four major points:

- The nation's long-standing access goal must be reinstated, and federal student aid policy refocused on dramatically reducing current levels of unmet need.
- Need-based grant aid must be increased for low-income students by reversing the current policy focus on middle-income affordability and merit.
- The Title IV programs—their number, structure, and effectiveness—must be reaffirmed as the nation's long-term solution to solving the access problem.
- Access partnerships between the federal government, the states, and institutions must be rebuilt to leverage and target aid on low-income students (Advisory Committee on Student Financial Assistance 2001, 17).

The first recommendation, reinstatement of the primacy of the access goal, is vital. Access has slipped in importance relative to its position at the start of federal involvement in financial aid. An exhortation of this type is often useful, and it is important for officially sanctioned groups such as the Advisory Committee to keep the attention of Congress and the secretary of education focused on access.

The second recommendation, an increase in need-based grant aid, is also a good idea. The Advisory Committee criticizes changes in grant rules that inject merit into the process and calls for "full funding" of need-based grants.

Given that the committee's recommendations do not call for the elimination of any financial aid programs, in the end this recommendation is a call for additional federal funding for financial aid.

The third recommendation of the Advisory Committee praises all of the Title IV programs: Pell Grants, Supplemental Educational Opportunity Grants, Federal Work-Study, Perkins Loans, Federal Direct Lending, Federal Family Education Loans, and the Leveraging Educational Assistance Partnership program. "The Title IV programs, working together, are well-tailored policy instruments for solving the access problem at each stage of the educational pipeline" (ibid., 21). The only problem the Advisory Committee discusses is the underfunding of the programs. Obviously, at this point I break ranks with the Advisory Committee.

The fourth recommendation, rebuilding access partnerships among the federal government, state governments, and institutions, is the least well articulated recommendation in the report. The committee merely notes that "from an access perspective, the ideal partnerships involve integration, coordination, and cooperation to effectively ensure that low-income students are supported systematically and sequentially *through the entire education pipeline*" (ibid., 22). The committee's only concrete proposal here is to strengthen the Leveraging Educational Assistance Partnership program, the program that gives federal matching grants to states for need-based financial aid.

The redesign proposals I present provide a much more detailed and radical plan for change than the report of the Advisory Committee. Nevertheless, we share the goal of reinstating the primacy of the access goal for financial aid. It is interesting to investigate how we came to such different proposals to satisfy the same goal.

Information Flows

Reforms designed to improve information flows for prospective students are a major point of emphasis of the redesign proposals. I am by no means alone in making this type of recommendation; many others have suggested that the financial aid system should be simplified. The Advisory Committee, however, takes an interesting stance on efforts to improve the timing and quality of information on financial aid: "In light of the current record levels of unmet need, providing earlier and better information on financial aid is a double-edged sword, potentially dampening aspirations of low-income students" (ibid., vi). This is a point well taken. Nevertheless, more than anything else, this concern has to be interpreted as advice about ordering priorities—increases in funding should precede improvements in information flows. Unfortunately, the Advisory Committee's recommendations do not include any suggestions to improve information flows. They focus entirely on decreasing unmet need. Apparently, they did not recognize that if their fear about providing more and better information were well founded, any decreases in unmet need resulting from their recommendations would have a limited effect. If prospective students cannot find out about the current sorry state of affairs, how will they find out about an improved state of affairs?

The Advisory Committee's active discouragement of improving information flows is worrisome and locates the committee at the extreme margins on this issue. Thomas J. Kane, for example, goes so far as to suggest that focusing on information flows may be even more important than increasing funding. "Given the ambiguous evidence on the impact of Pell grants on college enrollment, dollars spent on simplifying the process of applying for aid may have larger effects on college enrollment than equivalent spending on raising the Pell grant maximum" (Kane 1999b, 70). The objectives of the Advisory Committee would have been better served if they had included advice on how to improve information flows. Their current stance on this issue will not be helpful to their cause.

Title IV Programs

The two proposals could not be more different in their treatment of Title IV programs. The redesign proposal calls for the abolition of all but one of the Title IV programs; only Pell Grants survive. In contrast, the Advisory Committee is completely uncritical; it supports increases in funding for all existing Title IV programs.

The biggest disagreement focuses on loans. The redesign proposals call for the elimination of all federal student loan programs, while the Advisory Committee wants to expand the loan programs. The Advisory Committee unquestioningly accepts the current set of student loan programs; in fact, they recommend that the government "eliminate origination fees and reduce interest rates for all students" (ibid., 24). Given the Advisory Committee's emphasis on access, I find their support of loan programs strange. There is no concern that default rates are excessive for some institutions or that further subsidies for loans reduce the payoff to saving for college. Most surprisingly, despite the report's strong emphasis on targeting financial aid to low-income students, the committee is not willing to suggest narrowing eligibility for subsidized student loans.

There is no good reason for the federal government to subsidize borrowing as a means of paying for college. The Advisory Committee seems to be confused here. "Finally," they say, "the Federal Direct and Federal Family Education loan programs must continue to subsidize the borrowing of low- and middle-income students and reduce debt burden to the lowest levels possible" (ibid., 24). Increasing loan subsidies will expand debt levels, not reduce them. Lending is unsubsidized in the redesign proposal, which should reduce debt levels. It is crucial to have loans available to students and families who want to spread the expenses of college over time, but there is no reason that policy should encourage borrowing.

The Advisory Committee's report recommends the expansion of the SEOG program. This program, the federal campus-based grant program, is an anachronism that should have been abolished with the introduction of Pell Grants in 1972, and it is one of the first to go in the redesign proposal. The advantages that come when all grants become portable are too large to rationalize continuation of the SEOG program.

Tuition Tax Credits

The Advisory Committee's recommendations do not say a word about the Hope Scholarship and Lifetime Learning tuition tax credits. Perhaps, because these tax provisions are not Department of Education programs, they fall out of the purview of the Advisory Committee. Nevertheless, the tuition tax credits represent the most significant change in federal financial aid in the last twenty years. These tax credits are federal tax expenditures that should be antithetical to any group with the strong emphasis on access permeating the Advisory Committee's report. The tuition tax credits are not need-based financial aid. The lowest-income students and families receive no benefit, and much of the benefits accrue to students and families with no financial need.

Institutional Aid

When it turns to institutions, the Advisory Committee report merely exhorts colleges and universities to stop giving merit aid and start giving more "integrated, coordinated, and cooperative" need-based aid. In my view, the financial aid activities of colleges and universities are crucial. They need more than exhortations of this type. They need a plan. A growing number of colleges and universities are doing quite well, thank you very much, aggressively discounting tuition for the students they want to attract. Other institutions are reacting with competitive aid of their own. An exhortation to unilaterally disarm will fall on deaf ears. Colleges and universities need a way to collude. Without some type of cooperative agreement, nothing will be done to reassert the primacy of need-based aid. This collusion will be the key to significant progress in the redesign of the financial aid system.

Although I share many goals with the Advisory Committee, I do not find their report useful. The Advisory Committee enthusiastically embraces the current structure of the financial aid system; but the system needs to be reformed, not embraced. Additional funding for the existing programs will help some students, but reform following the redesign proposals would be a much more effective way of meeting the committee's objective of focusing the financial aid system on the access problem.

Facing Trade-offs

As economists are fond of pointing out, there are few situations in this world in which one can escape trade-offs. To acquire more of one thing, one generally has to give up something else. The redesign of the financial aid system is by no means immune to this problem.

Political Trade-offs

The first trade-off is one between the thoroughness of the redesign and its political feasibility. I deliberately choose to lean toward thoroughness at the expense of political feasibility. Part of my goal is to stimulate discussion and motivate change; and the most effective way to get a discussion started is by staking out an extreme position and calling for radical change. However, there is more to it than that. I sincerely think the best possible financial aid system will be one that is radically different from the existing system, and I do not want concerns with political feasibility to cut off discussion about important issues.

There may be more politically palatable reforms, ones that maintain more of the existing programs, that would improve the financial aid system, but some elements of the existing system require more change. Policy often proceeds incrementally, because small changes are politically easier. The best solutions to the financial aid system, however, are not incremental, and therefore they will face an uphill struggle politically.

Political feasibility did influence my redesign proposals in two ways. First, to finance the increases in Pell Grants necessary to improve access, the redesign proposals suggest eliminating financial aid programs that are not well targeted—the SEOG program and tuition tax credits—and those that provide the wrong incentives—guaranteed student loans. This means that the redesign is largely self-financing—which should make it politically appealing. This attempt to limit the fiscal impact of the redesign may well be a political mistake. It might be easier to leave popular programs alone. A proposal that does not touch these programs and calls for an increase in spending on Pell Grants from general tax revenues may be more politically palatable.

The second political consideration is the concern that the public image of colleges and universities should be bolstered. Rapid increases in tuition and fees have caused many to wonder if colleges and universities are being fiscally responsible. In addition, though higher education has been spared most of the criticism leveled at kindergarten through twelfth-grade education, in several states there have been rumblings that higher education should be held more accountable for the tax dollars it spends. The redesign proposals deal with both of these concerns. A reduction in institutional grants would lead to an initial decrease in tuition, and thereafter rates of tuition increase will be somewhat lower. This should go a long way to allay concerns over rising tuition. If institutions were to take on the responsibility for loan guarantees, colleges and universities would become accountable for their activities in a concrete way. This should relieve some of the concern over the accountability of colleges and universities.

The Trade-off between Satisfying Need and Controlling Costs

One of the unfortunate consequences of a need-based financial aid system is that it dulls incentives for institutions to control costs. Most firms offering a product or service on a market have to control costs because they will lose customers as they increase prices to cover cost increases. If the government or anyone else automatically provides consumers with the extra funds to cover price increases, the incentives of the firm to control costs are considerably diminished. This is part of the problem in the health care sector. A need-based financial aid system introduces this problem in the higher education sector.

Many colleges and universities operate with persistent excess demand; in higher education terms, they are "selective." Given this, one of the things holding back tuition increases is the fact that these institutions want to serve talented students from all segments of society. If financial aid were awarded in the form of a lump-sum grant, insensitive to the cost of attendance, the more selective institutions would lose some of their low-income students if they increased tuition, and they would therefore probably make a greater effort to control costs. Nevertheless, some cost increases are unavoidable, and with lump-sum financial aid the highest-priced institutions would eventually have a hard time appealing to low-income students. For this reason these institutions award financial aid on the basis of need—including a sensitivity to the cost of attendance—rather than as lump-sum grants. One of the casualties of the adoption of need-based financial aid is that institutions lose some of the natural market incentive to control costs.

The redesign proposals faced this trade-off when it became clear that a system with only federal Pell Grants that are income based, not need based, would not be able to provide sufficient funds to meet the choice goal. The proposed solution is to reintroduce need-based grants in a controlled way. One of the casualties of this decision is a loss of some of the incentives for institutions to control costs.

Trade-offs Involving Choice

The third trade-off involves the goal of providing students the widest possible choice. The choice goal has two parts. First, students must have sufficient funds to afford to choose any college or university willing to accept them. Second, students must have sufficient information to make wise choices. If both of these conditions are met, the resulting mix of institutions and students will approximate the socially optimal one.

If all students were the same and all institutions were the same, there would be no choice problem. As it is, however, the reasons that students pursue higher education vary widely. Their abilities and temperaments vary widely, and their willingness to travel for higher education varies widely. This diversity in the national student body is unavoidable. At the same time, institutions of higher education have been founded by a wide variety of different groups for a wide variety of different purposes. Given the diversity of the national student body, the diversity of institutions strengthens the higher education system. Although change does not come easily at many colleges and universities, the system as a whole is fairly agile. It responds to changes in the needs and desires of students quite rapidly. In almost every case, there is at least one college or university that would be a good fit for any given student. The difficulty is providing the information required for the student to find the institution and, in some cases, the funds to afford that institution.

By its very nature, the financial aid system traditionally focuses on the problem of insufficient funds. This system was set up by institutions who wanted to be sure they would be in the choice set of highly qualified students from low-income families. These institutions have legitimate reasons to want socioeconomic diversity in their student bodies. The federal government's financial aid system was added to the existing system, and the resulting set of financial aid programs is complicated. Although it does a fairly good job of getting aid to students who fight their way through the system, the system is so difficult to understand that many prospective students and their parents are unable or unwilling to use it. In essence, the system that has evolved to ensure that students have sufficient resources to make good choices has lost sight of the importance of good information in the choice process.

The redesign proposals have followed a very different evolution. Initially, they took simplification of the financial aid system as a high priority, giving prominence to the information requirement for choice. As part of the simplification process, this proposal eliminated institutionally funded grants. Unfortunately, as a result it did not meet the funding requirement for choice. The trade-off between these two parts of the choice objective motivated the final shape of the redesign proposals.

The trade-off between the two requirements for choice is clearly unfortunate, but it may be unavoidable. The difficulty is finding a way to provide sufficient funding to facilitate choice without complicating the financial aid system more than is necessary. The redesign proposal's suggested solution is that institutional grants be in the form of supplements to the federal Pell Grants. This solution strictly limits the options of institutions. If more diversity is allowed in the form of institutional grants, the system becomes more complicated, and we lose ground on one of the requirements for choice. This solution itself brings up a different, perhaps more fundamental trade-off: to create a financial aid system that is easy to understand, institutions will have to give up some autonomy.

Trade-offs Involving Institutional Autonomy

The solution to the trade-offs between the components of choice, as well as other parts of the redesign proposal, clearly calls for institutions to give up autonomy. This is symptomatic of a more fundamental trade-off. I have characterized the competitive use of financial aid as a prisoners' dilemma similar to an arms race. In an arms race, it is in the interest of both countries jointly to disarm, but it is not in the interest of either country unilaterally to disarm. Competitive financial aid is similar. If all institutions stopped behaving competitively, the system would improve. List-price tuition would be lower, more aid would be available for low-income students, and it would be easier for students to determine the price of attending any institution. Some institutions have unilaterally abandoned the high-aid high-tuition strategy, but their bold move has not created a large following. Collective, not individual, action is required to slow down an arms race.

This means that the solutions to the financial aid problems we face require that institutions give up some autonomy. My redesign proposals are perhaps extreme in the amount of autonomy they suggest be relinquished. It is possible to design reforms that would allow institutions to keep more autonomy—for example, a system that would not allow merit-based grants but would not control the form of need-based aid—but no long-term solution for the financial aid system is likely to allow institutions to keep all of their autonomy. The problems are collective ones, and they will require collective solutions.[2]

Conclusions

The financial aid system chronically underperforms; it is not in a crisis. In this case, a crisis might be a good thing: it would demand reform of the financial aid system. Most likely, however, the underperformance will continue indefinitely. Students from low-income families will have to overcome ever greater financial barriers to attend college. As a result, many college-qualified low-income students will not attend college. Unfortunately, for the most part, the loss to these students and to the nation will escape notice. Lost opportunities just do not speak as loudly as they should.

The academic community should not allow the problems in the financial aid system to continue. Groups such as the Advisory Committee on Student Financial Assistance, the university leaders and policy analysts who placed the advertisement in the *New York Times* in March 2001, and the 568 Presidents' Working Group are sounding the alarm and working to change the system. The financial aid system can only be improved through conscious effort. All of the players—the federal government, state governments, private charities and other groups offering scholarships, and institutions of higher education—will have to be involved in the reform effort. The institutions of higher education should take the lead in this effort.

Any reform proposal faces trade-offs. There are no magic bullets for the financial aid system. The sooner the participants start talking about how to deal with these trade-offs and begin to repair the system, the better off the country will be. I hope the redesign proposals presented here will be a catalyst for these discussions.

Notes

1 | Introduction

1. Michael S. McPherson is the president of Macalester College, and Morton Owen Schapiro is now the president of Williams College, though he was not at the time of the 1999 article.

2. The data for independent students suggest a similar pattern, although the average unmet need for independent students is generally higher than that for dependent students.

3. The data for figure 1.1 were collected before tuition tax credits were introduced in 1997. In chapter 3, I present simulations of the effect of these tax credits on unmet need. As these simulations demonstrate, the line has an even steeper slope after the introduction of tuition tax credits.

4. For the purpose of this analysis, *college-qualified* is defined based on an index from the National Education Longitudinal Study (NELS) of 1992. This index combines high school grade point average, senior class rank, scores on a NELS aptitude test, scores on the College Board's Scholastic Aptitude Test (SAT) and the American College Testing's (ACT) assessment test, and a measure of the academic rigor of the high school program. See Choy 1999 for more details.

5. The Advisory Committee on Student Financial Assistance emphasizes the importance of this finding in its February 2001 report.

6. See Schmidt 2001 for a discussion of the trends in state spending on financial aid.

7. Throughout this book, I define *financial aid* to include scholarships of any kind as well as other grants. Some people distinguish between scholarships and financial aid, but I do not find the distinction useful. The distinction is typically between a need-based grant and a merit-based scholarship.

For example, one speaks of a Pell "grant" and an athletic "scholarship." I find it much easier to refer to both as grants and to distinguish between need-based and merit-based grants when that distinction is important.

8. Grants awarded to children of the employees of some firms do not neatly fit my distinction. In some cases it is hard to describe the student's talent or ability as anything more than having the good fortune to have a parent working for the firm. Nevertheless, I would include these grants in the merit-based category unless they were explicitly awarded to cover unmet financial need.

9. Under this practice, often called "preferential packaging," the more meritorious students are given the preferred financial aid packages (larger grants and smaller loans).

10. South Dakota provides no grants to its students, so it shows up in both lists.

11. Colleges and universities represent the vast majority of the spending in this category.

12. The tax legislation passed in the spring of 2001 increased the amount of the credit and the income limits for eligibility; see Hebel 2001 for the details.

13. The source of these estimates is Executive Office of the President 1998, 333.

14. Chapter 5 gives details on the size and prevalence of institutional grants. It is not uncommon for these price discounts to be as high as $5,000 per student.

15. As I demonstrate in detail in chapter 6, when loan default rates were first calculated in 1987, they were very high, and they continued to be high until the Department of Education started to monitor the repayment of student loans much more aggressively.

16. This follows because of the string of late payment and nonpayment that generally precedes default.

17. The terminology "parental responsibility system" and "student responsibility system" is mine, but the basic ideas are clearly from their book; see the section titled, "College Finance as an Intergenerational Compact," 174–77.

18. There are still incentives in the current system that encourage students to become independent. Most important, parental income and assets are not included in the determination of the EFC for independent students, making it advantageous for some students to become independent.

2 | The History of Financial Aid in the United States

1. This story, which is supposed to be true, was used as a sermon illustration by Pastor Beth McCrary of the Williamsburg (Virginia) Presbyterian Church.

2. Eells 1958 (4–14) lists all the colleges and universities founded in the seventeenth and eighteenth centuries.

3. Rainford 1972 (15–28) discusses the controversies surrounding the idea of a national university.

4. At Harvard, "the Democrats regarded the College as a haven of smug aristocracy" (Morison 1936, 286). Similarly, in the 1820s "it was unfortunate that Princeton had acquired the reputation of being a rich man's college where expenses were excessive" (Wertenbaker 1946, 178).

5. According to Samuel Eliot Morison (1936, 295), separate endowments, such as those founded by Lady Mowlson, had previously been intermingled with other funds and lost their identities as endowments for scholarships.

6. "An early, perhaps the first, institution to resort to this device was the University of North Carolina in 1789, but the heyday was in the years 1835–60, when perpetual scholarships became the last resort for many of the sectarian institutions. In these years the scholarship scheme commended itself to the governing boards of Cumberland, Lafayette, Wesleyan, New York University, Dickinson, Antioch, Hamden-Sidney, Wofford, Kenyon, DePauw, Ohio University, Ohio Wesleyan, Oglethorpe, Oberlin, Columbia, Vermont, Emory, Denison, Genesee, Hanover, Indiana University, and unquestionably also dozens of other small struggling colleges" (Rudolph 1990, 190–91).

7. Howard R. Bowen comes to the same conclusion: "Before the war [World War II], the theory and practice of higher education finance had been quite settled. The finance of students was primarily the responsibility of parents, and of students themselves through part-time earnings. . . . Working one's way through college was the accepted and respected model of student aid" (Bowen 1974, 12).

8. The College Board action reflected the opinion of the time. The 1952 report of the Commission on Financing Higher Education of the Association of American Universities concludes that "if by democracy we mean equality of recruitment among the intellectually able without regard to the limitations of their purses, American colleges and universities would welcome an extension of it" (Hofstadter and Hardy 1952, 107).

9. Several commentators have pointed out that a financial aid system based on state subsidies gives financial aid to many students who do not need the aid. I return to this issue later.

10. The title (and content) of a 1969 report of the U.S. Department of Health, Education, and Welfare, *Toward a Long-Range Plan for Federal Support for Higher Education,* suggests the Johnson administration quickly became aware of the need for revisions to the 1965 act.

11. "The debate leading up to the Education Amendments of 1972 indicated that both interest groups and policy-makers wanted a clearer answer to a fundamental question of strategy: should the federal government henceforth concentrate its higher education efforts on programs that assisted institutions or on those that provided aid primarily to students?" (Finn 1978, 60–61).

12. See Hansen and Weisbrod 1973 and Carnegie Commission on Higher Education 1973 for studies of the costs and benefits of education that reveal the thinking at the time.

13. According to Sandra R. Baum, "The main problem in this area is the distribution of public subsidies, rather than the level of public subsidies. Too many of the dollars subsidize relatively affluent people, who should be taking more private responsibility for funding their own educations" (Baum 1994, 101).

14. Titles such as *Condemning Students to Debt: College Loans and Public Policy* (Fossey and Bateman 1998) are not uncommon. Lawrence Gladieux and Arthur Hauptman list "the growing reliance on loans" as the first concern in a section titled "Policy Drift" (Gladieux and Hauptman 1995, 23–27). Finally, Michael Mumper laments that "insuring that middle- and upper-income students have a choice of colleges, through the availability of federal student loans, has replaced providing lower-income students access through grants as the fundamental value advanced by the student aid programs" (Mumper 1996, 251).

15. The institutions in the Overlap Group were Amherst College, Barnard College, Bowdoin College, Brown University, Bryn Mawr College, Colby College, Columbia University, Cornell University, Dartmouth College, Harvard University, Massachusetts Institute of Technology, Middlebury College, Mount Holyoke College, Princeton University, Smith College, Trinity College (Connecticut), Tufts University, the University of Pennsylvania, Vassar College, Wellesley College, Wesleyan University, Williams College, and Yale University (see Jaschik 1992).

16. See Jaschik 1992 for a chronology of the case against MIT.

17. The institutions agreeing to the new policy were Amherst College, Boston College, Bowdoin College, Claremont McKenna College, Columbia University, Cornell University, Davidson College, Duke University, Emory University, Georgetown University, Haverford College, Macalester College, Massachusetts Institute of Technology, Middlebury College, Northwestern University, Pomona College, Rice University, Stanford University, Swarthmore College, the University of Chicago, the University of Notre Dame, the University of Pennsylvania, Vanderbilt University, Wake Forest University, Wellesley College, Wesleyan University, Williams College, and Yale University.

18. The other members of the Overlap Group did participate in the discussions of the 568 President's Working Group, but they did not agree to the common set of rules for determining financial aid.

19. See Burd 1998a for a full listing of the changes.

20. These thirteen states are Alaska, Arkansas, Florida, Georgia, Kentucky, Louisiana, Michigan, Mississippi, Missouri, Nevada, New Mexico, South Carolina, and Washington; see Selingo 2001 for more details.

21. See McPherson and Schapiro 1998 for a discussion of the strategic use of financial aid.

22. See Winston 1999 for a discussion of the subsidies implicit in private school tuition.

3 | The Financial Aid System

1. The details of the calculation of the EFC are in U.S. Department of Education 1999a. Sandy Baum (1999) provides a detailed discussion of the issues involved in need analysis that interested readers will find useful.

2. The appendix to this chapter gives this formula. The highest marginal rate is 47 percent of adjusted available income for incomes above $221,000. The maximum tax rate on parental assets is thus 5.64 percent (47% of 12%).

3. The EFC is calculated differently for two other student types: independent students without dependents other than spouse and independent students with dependents other than spouse.

4. The value of home equity, pension funds, annuities, noneducational IRAs, Keough plans, and life insurance are excluded from the assets under consideration.

5. I discuss the behavioral effects of these taxes in chapter 7.

6. That is, 47 percent of discretionary net worth (in this example, 12 percent of net worth plus the 6 percent interest those assets earn); thus 47 percent times 18 percent of net worth. The 47 percent figure is the marginal effect on EFC of an additional dollar of adjusted available income (see the appendix to this chapter for the details).

7. This analysis assumes that none of the assets were used to meet the contribution from income—that is, that the family did not draw down its assets beyond its contribution from assets.

8. This means that 35 percent of students' net worth is added, compared with 5.6 percent (47% of 12%) for parents with the highest incomes.

9. There are income tax advantages to having assets in the name of minor that also affect this decision. Combining these considerations with the fact that the assets of siblings are ignored in the calculation of the expected family contribution suggests that there is a considerable advantage to a family's having a child younger than the college student.

10. The presence of qualifying assets would cause the line to shift to the left. Changing the state of residence or the assumption about the number of children or the standard deduction would also affect the exact position and height of the line. The basic picture would, however, be similar.

11. See U.S. Department of Education 1999a for the complete details of the calculation of cost of attendance.

12. In the 1998 reauthorization of the Higher Education Act the reasonable expenses for the documented rental or purchase of a personal computer was added to this category.

13. See U.S. Department of Education 1999b (11–12) for these loan limits.

14. Sixty-two percent of respondents "strongly agreed" or "somewhat agreed" with

the statement, "When I think of college financial aid, I am mostly thinking of grants and scholarships, not student loans" (Ikenberry and Hartle 1998, 46).

15. Because the maximum for subsidized student loans increases for students in the later years of their education, the maximum would have been $13,625 for a second-year student and $15,625 for a third- or fourth-year student.

16. This number would have been $6,625 for a second-year student and $8,625 for a third- or fourth-year student.

17. It is important to recognize that the discussion here is about grants; if we include loans, the federal government gives much more financial aid than do private institutions.

18. See Internal Revenue Service Form 8863 for the regulations that cover the Hope Scholarship and Lifetime Learning Income Tax Credits.

19. Eric A. Hanushek comes to the same conclusion about the subsidy package that includes the tax credits: "The best information currently available, however, suggests that few new students will be attracted to college as a result of the subsidy package—implying that this should be viewed mainly as a transfer to students who would otherwise attend college, not as a program designed to change the human capital development of our youths" (Hanushek 1999, 26).

4 | Theoretical Considerations

1. Those unfamiliar with this type of argument might review, among others, Gramlich 1990.

2. For most students the opportunity costs of forgone earnings are the largest cost of attending college. To keep this example simple, assume that the government covers these costs as well as the out-of-pocket costs.

3. Continuance requirements for students already enrolled have much the same purpose. Those who are not allowed to continue have indicated with their classroom performance that they will not benefit sufficiently from continuing their higher education at the present time.

4. Milton Friedman (1968) presents this position forcefully.

5. See, for example, Enarson 1974. This view appears to win the argument in many countries, and it is the leading view in many states in the United States.

6. For good discussions of evidence that economic agents often undervalue opportunity costs, see Thaler 1980 and Thaler, Kahneman, and Knetsch 1992.

7. I recognize that I am abstracting from the controversies surrounding practices such as the use of SAT scores and affirmative action. This is purposeful. Doing justice to the arguments here would take us too far afield from our focus on financial aid.

8. The U.S. News ranking criteria also include spending per student on instruction, research, and education-related services averaged over the three previous years. Higher

spending per pupil raises an institutions ranking, so in this way, too, inefficiency is rewarded.

9. See Selingo 2001 for an interesting discussion of the rapid growth of state merit-based aid programs.

10. Although the terminology differs, this argument is essentially the same as that made by McPherson and Schapiro (1998, 107–15).

5 | Institutionally Funded Grants

1. The accounts also differ because of the treatment of capital expenditures. In the National Center for Educational Statistics accounts for a private institution, expenditures on capital are included in I, R, and A in equation (5.1), but there are separate capital accounts for state-supported institutions.

2. The term $R - C$ could also be on the left-hand side of the equation. Institutions that do a large amount of sponsored research use the overhead recoveries from this research as a significant source of revenues. The position of this term is not important for the discussion that follows.

3. The division chosen here ignores the fact that scholarships funded by some institutions use income from endowments that are dedicated to financial aid. This model essentially assumes, therefore, that the institution recognizes the fungibility of money. Alternatively, I could subtract a separate term for scholarships funded from endowment income from both $S - F$ and G.

4. Breneman's model is derived from Hopkins and Massy 1981.

5. Dominic J. Brewer, Susan M. Gates, and Charles A. Goldman (2002) make a distinction between institutions seeking to enhance their prestige and those seeking to enhance their reputation. For my purposes the distinction they make between prestige and reputation is not important.

6. In this example, SAT is used as a shorthand to mean a combination of test scores, grades, the rigor of the high school curriculum, and other things that determine the academic preparedness of a prospective college student.

7. Operationally, the admissions office has the task of finding the students who meet the constraints that the institution chooses. This is often a difficult task.

8. In addition, the availability of financial aid from sources other than the institution may have an effect on the whole family of demand curves. I consider the effects of financial aid in detail below.

9. In the language of economics, William Bowen and David Breneman's (1993) model is one of a first-degree price discriminator who has decided not to take all of the consumer surplus. This behavior is inconsistent with profit maximizing, but that does not concern most colleges and universities.

10. Figure 5.4 assumes that T_4 is below the point at which the demand curve D_2

intersects the vertical axis. However, this may not always be the case. Institutions that already discount the tuition to a large number of students will not be able to use the strategy described here. I am assuming that MIT and the other members of the Overlap Group are not among this group. They have many students who do pay full price.

11. It is possible that an institution might find that one of the constraints it imposes on its demand curve yields a student body that is more expensive to educate. In this case its desired educational resources increase, and it will have to recover more net revenue from tuition. It might be sensible to use the term *educational investment* for the extra expenditures of the institution in this case, but this is not the way Bowen and Breneman use this term.

12. Princeton University has recently upped the ante in this competition by eliminating all loans from its financial aid packages; see Brownstein 2001.

13. Colleges and universities would never admit to price competition. They would be more inclined to say that they were engaged in "enrollment management"; see McPherson and Schapiro 1998 for a discussion of the increase in this practice.

14. To see that this is possible, start with demand curve $D_{SAT = Z}$ and consider shifting the demand curve to the right and maintaining a fixed-price strategy. Start with a very small demand curve shift. In this case the fixed price will yield less revenue than the initial strategy. Larger and larger shifts will yield more revenue, and T_f is selected because it yields the same amount of revenue as the initial situation.

15. It is tempting to equate competitive price discounts with merit-based grants and social price discounts with need-based grants. In many cases this will be correct. The difficulty comes in the case of a merit-based grant awarded to a student who does not have sufficient income to afford college. In this case a portion of the merit-based aid serves the purpose of a social price discount.

16. See National Commission on the Cost of Higher Education 1998, fig. 1.

17. The news media are not the only ones to blame for the importance given to list-price tuition. A recent report by Joseph Stiglitz, Laura Tyson, Peter Orszag, and Jonathan Orszag (2000), titled *The Impact of Paying for College on Family Finances*, emphasizes the rate of increases in list-price tuition to support its major finding that few families are saving enough to cover the costs of college.

18. In essence, the reason is that we need a reliable measure for enrollment, and we can find such a measure only for institutions that charge one and only one tuition. This eliminates state-supported institutions, which charge different prices to in-state and out-of-state students, and institutions that have graduate programs, which often charge different prices to undergraduate and graduate students.

19. This average was computed as a weighted average, the size of the student bodies being used as the weights.

20. The NACUBO data have the disadvantage that they are not a random sample of private institutions. There is a possibility that the institutions that answer the

NACUBO survey are those most involved in, and therefore most interested in, tuition discounting. For this reason, these data may be biased.

21. See Perloff 2000 (9–12) for a discussion of the strategy at Saturn.

22. This language is taken from international trade. A "most favored nation clause" is a provision that says that the nation in question will be able to export at the lowest existing tariffs. Under the new system, colleges and universities would have such a policy for all their students: that is, institutions would agree to offer the lowest possible price to all students.

23. Bowen 1996 provides a good discussion of the social value of providing unhindered access to higher education; see also Friedman 1968 and Enarson 1974 for different views on this issue.

24. "Financing the education of lower-income students *is* fundamentally a national responsibility" (McPherson and Schapiro 1991, 197).

25. Social price discounts and need-based institutional grants are not quite synonyms. Some merit-based aid could be a social price discount. Consider an athlete from a poor family who receives an athletic scholarship. The athletic scholarship would be classified as a merit-based scholarship, but given the fact that the student would not have been able to afford college without the scholarship, the price discount could also be considered a social price discount.

26. The changes discussed here do not represent a change toward merit-based aid, because the more generous interpretation of need is available to all Princeton students with financial need. Nevertheless, this practice might make institutions competing with Princeton turn to merit-based financial aid awards.

27. This illustrates why it would be difficult to use our methodology for an institution that charged a different price for graduate and undergraduate students or for a state-supported institution that charges different tuition for in-state and out-of-state students.

6 | Federal Loan Guarantees

1. See Kreps 1990, 577–85, for a good discussion of moral hazard.

2. The other sixteen programs were the Farmers Home Administration's farm loan programs, the bank insurance fund, the Resolution Trust Corporation, the Pension Benefit Guaranty Corporation, Medicare claims, Department of Defense weapons systems acquisition, Department of Defense contract pricing, Department of Energy contract management, Superfund program management, NASA contract management, Department of Defense inventory management, Internal Revenue Service receivables, custom service, overseas real property, Federal Transit Administration grants, and asset forfeiture programs.

3. The legislation included an exemption for historically black colleges and univer-

sities, tribally controlled institutions, and Navajo community colleges, but this exemption ended on July 1, 1999.

4. The consistent poor performance of proprietary schools demonstrates why they would be targeted by the 85-15 rule.

5. See Carnevale, Johnson, and Edwards 1998 for a discussion of this phenomenon.

6. See, for example, Campaigne and Hossler 1998.

7. This is probably not an important explanation for low-income families, but it could be important for middle- and upper-middle-income families who send their children to out-of-state institutions or private institutions. The analysis in chapter 3 indicates suggests these families have a good chance of qualifying for need-based aid, much of which would be in the form of loans.

8. I explicitly decided not to include the expected family contribution in this discussion. As mentioned in the chapter 1, some parents are unwilling to pay the expected family contribution, so this funding may or many not be available to a given student. I want to be sure that these students are served well by the redesigned system.

9. Because of the string of nonpayments and late payments that typically precede a loan default, loans that eventually default are much more expensive to carry than loans that are repaid.

7 | Eligibility for Financial Aid and Other Redesign Issues

1. It is important to remember that these calculations are based on the federal methodology for calculating financial need. Many institutions use a different methodology for the purposes of awarding institutional aid.

2. Most private colleges continue to include home equity in the set of assets that they consider when determining eligibility for institutional grants. As mentioned in chapter 5, in 1998 some institutions, led by Princeton University, removed home equity from the set of assets they consider.

3. Many private institutions include the value of home equity in their calculations of the expected family contribution. The behavior suggested by Kane will not work in this case.

4. See Case and McPherson 1986 for additional details.

5. Richard Fossey makes a similar point when he notes that "although some higher education officials would deny it, it seems likely that the easy availability of student loans reduces the incentives for colleges and universities to contain their costs" (Fossey 1998, 182).

6. Although the number of institutions that meet all financial need is small, the effects of their high prices on the public's perceptions of the cost of a higher education are large.

7. Some of the students who qualify for larger Stafford Loans than they receive do

so because the institution they attend chooses to award a lower loan amount. In these cases it is not clear what the effect of a tuition increase would be. It is possible that these students would receive a larger grant rather than a larger loan.

8. Pell Grant funds are not affected by outside scholarships.

9. This is an instance in which the federal methodology differs from the methodology used by many private institutions. The institutional methodology calculates the EFC for a family with two children in college at 120 percent of the EFC for a family with one child in college. This eliminates some of the inequity under discussion.

10. Expressed somewhat differently, "The result of this process is a substantially higher tax on accumulated assets for a couple with two children spaced with a four-year interval than for a couple with twins" (Feldstein 1995, 555).

11. Data availability would be crucial for making the decision between income or wage data. If income totals from income tax records could be easily retrieved, these data would be preferable. If not, lifetime data on wage earnings are available from the Social Security Administration. Although these data do exclude nonlabor income, they are preferable to a short time series of income data.

12. McPherson and Schapiro (1991) also advocate government grants that are based on income, not need; see their discussion under the heading "Needs Testing and Income Testing" (134–36).

13. The Yale Tuition Payment Option has met with less than universal approval by its participants; see William M. Buckley, "Some Alumni of Yale Realize That They Owe College a Lasting Debt," *New York Times,* February 23, 1999.

14. See Johnstone 1972 for a discussion of income-contingent loans.

8 | Evaluating the Redesign Proposals

1. The discounts implied by the price-to-cost ratio are discount over cost. These discounts should not be confused with the tuition discounts discussed in chapter 5.

2. Tuition and fee payments produce most of the variance across institutions in the cost of attendance. Charges for room and board, books and supplies, and so forth do vary across institutions, but this variance is much smaller than the variance in tuition and fees.

3. At this point I should reiterate that by assumption I am ignoring any constraints involving the legal system or political feasibility. I recognize that the amount of cooperation required for institutional Pell Grant supplements would violate the antitrust laws. In addition, it would require a degree of agreement on financial aid matters than might not be politically realistic. These issues are discusses in the following chapter.

9 | On Political Feasibility

1. See Burd 2000a for a discussion of the members of Congress who supported an increase in Pell Grants. Quinn 2000 supports increases in Pell Grants over expanded tuition tax credits.

2. See Burd and Southwick 2001 for a discussion of the initial Bush proposals.

3. See Hebel 2000 for a discussion of the reaction to the Clinton administration proposal. Increased tuition tax credits are also prominent among the proposals Vice President Albert Gore made as a presidential candidate; see Burd 2000a. Finally, see Hebel 2001 for a discussion of the new tax legislation.

4. The twenty signatories of the advertisement were Sandy Baum (Skidmore College), David W. Breneman (University of Virginia), Patrick M. Callan (National Center for Public Policy and Higher Education), William C. Chance (Northwest Education Research Center), Joni E. Finney (National Center for Public Policy and Higher Education), Lawrence E. Gladieux (education and public policy consultant), Donald E. Heller (University of Michigan), D. Bruce Johnstone (State University of New York at Buffalo), Dennis P. Jones (National Center for Higher Education Management Systems), Thomas J. Kane (Harvard University), Glenn C. Loury (Boston University), Mario C. Martinez (New Mexico State University), Michael S. McPherson (Macalester College), Jamie P. Merisotis (Institute for Higher Education Policy), Thomas G. Mortenson (Center for the Study of Opportunity in Higher Education), Michael Nettles (University of Michigan), Michael A. Olivas (University of Houston Law Center), Gary Orfield (Harvard University), Morton Owen Schapiro (Williams College), and Robert Zemsky (University of Pennsylvania's Institute for Higher Education Research).

5. I do not say this because I am in any way convinced that the current level of funding for federal programs is adequate. I do, however, want to separate the issue of the adequacy of funding from the structural issues the switch in roles addresses.

6. The potential loan is the difference between the cost of attendance and the combination of expected family contribution and any grant awarded.

7. See Gose 2000 for others who give prominence to the case against the Overlap Group in their explanations of the increase in tuition discounting and merit-based aid.

8. Some of these institutions have Division I athletic teams, and Division 1 institutions, except for those in the Ivy League, do offer merit-based athletic scholarships.

9. Bethany College in West Virginia made a similar decision. Bethany did not abandon grants, but they decided to lower list-price tuition by 42 percent, from $20,650 to $12,000. This change was at least partially motivated by a desire to reduce financial aid expenditures. The *Post* article lists North Carolina Wesleyan, Bluefield College in Virginia, and Pine Manor College in Massachusetts as institutions that had made similar dramatic tuition reductions; see Michael A. Fletcher, "One College's Cutting Reply:

Losing Students Because of Rising Costs, Tiny West Virginia School Trims Tuition 42 Percent," *Washington Post,* December 10, 2001, A1, A4.

10 | Final Thoughts: Facing Trade-offs

1. The causation clearly runs two ways here. I have emphasized the effect grants have on tuition, but clearly tuition increases affect spending on grants as well.

2. The formation of the Overlap Group and later the 568 President's Working Group demonstrate that many institutions are aware that they face a collective action problem. The limits the antitrust laws place on the activities of these institutions are unfortunate.

References

Advisory Committee on Student Financial Assistance. 2001. "Access Denied: Restoring the Nation's Commitment to Equal Educational Opportunity." Washington, D.C., February, www.ed.gov/offices/AC/ACSFA/access_denied.pdf (March 8, 2002).

Archibald, Robert B., and Michael BeVier. 1998. "Imposing Market Discipline on Public Colleges and Universities." Policy Paper 3. Sterling, Va.: Virginia Institute for Public Policy, October.

Baker, Jonathan. 1995. "Vertical Restraints with Horizontal Consequences: Competitive Effects of 'Most-Favored-Customer' Clauses." Paper presented to Business Development Associates, Inc., Antitrust 1996 Conference. Washington, D.C., September 28, www.antiturst.org/law/US/bakerMFN.html (February 28, 2001).

Baum, Sandra R. 1994. "Financing Liberal Education in America: Public and Private Responsibilities." In *America's Investment in Liberal Education,* edited by David H. Finifter and Arthur M. Hauptman. Jossey-Bass.

———. 1999. "Need Analysis: How We Decide Who Gets What." In *Financing a College Education: How It Works, How It's Changing,* edited by Jacqueline E. King. Oryx Press and the American Council on Education.

Blum, John Morton. 1965. *From the Morgenthau Diaries: Years of Urgency, 1938–1941.* Houghton Mifflin.

Bolton, Roger E. 1968. "Burdens and Bargains in Higher Education." *Public Interest* 11 (Spring): 123–26.

Bosworth, Barry P., Andrew S. Carron, and Elisabeth H. Rhyne. 1987. *The Economics of Federal Credit Programs.* Brookings.

Bowen, Howard R. 1996. *Investment in Learning: The Individual and Social Value of American Higher Education.* Transaction Press.

Bowen, William G., and David W. Breneman. 1993. "Student Aid: Price Discount or Educational Investment?" *Brookings Review* 11 (Winter): 28–31.

Breneman, David W. 1994. *Liberal Arts Colleges: Thriving, Surviving, or Endangered?* Brookings.

Brewer, Dominic J., Susan M. Gates, and Charles A. Goldman. 2002. *In Pursuit of Prestige: Strategy and Competition in U.S. Higher Education.* Transaction Press.

Brownstein, Andrew. 2001. "Upping the Ante for Student Aid." *Chronicle of Higher Education* (February 16): A47.

Burd, Stephen. 1998a. "The Higher Education Amendments of 1998: The Impact on Colleges and Students." *Chronicle of Higher Education* (October 16): A39.

———. 1998b. "Republicans Put a Moderate Stamp on the 1998 Higher Education Act." *Chronicle of Higher Education* (October 16): A38.

———. 2000a. "Democrats Push White House to Seek Additional Increase for Pell Grants." *Chronicle of Higher Education* (September 29): A31.

———. 2000b. "The Role of Market Forces in Providing Student Loans." *Chronicle of Higher Education* (April 28): A34–A36.

———. 2001. "Private Colleges Seek to Extend Antitrust Exemption for Aid Talks." *Chronicle of Higher Education* (March 16): A25.

Burd, Stephen, and Ron Southwick. 2001. "Bush's Budget Calls for Substantial Increases for National Institutes of Health and Pell Grants." *Chronicle of Higher Education* (March 9): A26.

Campaigne, David A., and Don Hossler. 1998. "How Do Loans Affect the Educational Decisions of Students?" In *Condemning Students to Debt: College Loans and Public Policy,* edited by Richard Fossey and Mark Batemen. Teachers College Press.

Carnegie Commission on Higher Education. 1972. *Institutional Aid: Federal Support to Colleges and Universities.* McGraw-Hill.

———. 1973. *Higher Education: Who Pays? Who Benefits? Who Should Pay?* McGraw-Hill.

Carnegie Foundation for the Advancement of Teaching. 1932. *State Higher Education in California.* California State Printing Office, June 24.

Carnevale, Anthony P., Neal C. Johnson, and Anne Ruffner Edwards. 1998. "Performance-Based Appropriations: Fad or Wave of the Future." *Chronicle of Higher Education* (April 10): B6.

Case, Karl E., and Michael S. McPherson. 1986. "Does Need-Based Student Aid Discourage Savings for College?" Washington Office of the College Board.

Choy, Susan P. 1999. "College Access and Affordability." NCES 199-108. U.S. Department of Education, Office of Educational Research and Improvement.

Clotfelter, Charles T. 1991. "Financial Aid and Public Policy." In *Economic Challenges in Higher Education,* edited by Charles T. Clotfelter, Ronald G. Ehrenberg, Malcolm Getz, and John J. Siegfried. University of Chicago Press.

———. 1996. *Buying the Best: Cost Escalation in Elite Higher Education.* Princeton University Press.

Cohen, Arthur M. 1998. *The Shaping of American Higher Education: Emergence and Growth of the Contemporary System.* Jossey-Bass.

Coleman, James S. 1968. "Benefits, Costs, and Equity." *Public Interest* 11 (Spring): 118–22.

College Board. 1999a. *Trends in College Pricing, 1999.*

College Board. 1999b. *Trends in Student Aid, 1999.*

de Vijlder, Frans J. 1994. *Financing Higher Education in the United States* (Ministry of Education of the Netherlands). Quoted in Lawrence E. Gladieux and Arthur M. Hauptman, *The College Quandary: Access, Quality, and the Federal Role* (Brookings, 1995), 1.

Dick, Andrew W., and Aaron S. Edlin. 1997. "Implicit Taxes from College Financial Aid." *Journal of Public Economics* 65 (3): 295–322.

Edlin, Aaron S. 1993. "Is College Financial Aid Equitable and Efficient?" *Journal of Economic Perspectives* 7 (2): 143–58.

Eells, Walter Crosby. 1958. "Baccalaureate Degrees Conferred by American Colleges in the Seventeenth and Eighteenth Centuries." Circular 528. U.S. Office of Education, May.

Ehrenberg, Ronald G. 2000. *Tuition Rising: Why College Costs So Much.* Harvard University Press.

Ehrenberg, Ronald G., and Susan H. Murphy. 1993. "What Price Diversity? The Death of Need-Based Financial Aid at Selective Private Colleges and Universities." *Change* 25 (4): 64–73.

Enarson, Harold L. 1974. "A University President: Where Do We Go from Here?" In *Exploring the Case for Low Tuition in Public Higher Education,* edited by Kenneth E. Young. ACT Publications.

Executive Office of the President. 1998. *Budget of the United States Government, Fiscal Year 1999.* U.S. Government Printing Office.

Farrand, Max. 1911. *The Records of the Federal Convention of 1787.* Vol. 2. Yale University Press.

Feldstein, Martin. 1995. "College Scholarship Rules and Private Saving." *American Economics Review* 85 (3): 552–66.

Fels, William C. 1954. "The College Scholarship Service." *College Board Review,* no. 23 (May 1954): 428–34.

Finn, Chester E., Jr. 1978. *Scholars, Dollars, and Bureaucrats.* Brookings.

Fossey, Richard. 1998. "Condemning Students to Debt: Some Conclusions and Reflections." In *Condemning Students to Debt: College Loans and Public Policy,* edited by Richard Fossey and Mark Batemen. Teachers College Press.

Fossey, Richard, and Mark Bateman, eds. 1998. *Condemning Students to Debt: College Loans and Public Policy.* Teachers College Press.

Friedman, Milton. 1962. *Capitalism and Freedom.* University of Chicago Press.

———. 1968. "The Higher Schooling in America." *Public Interest* 11 (Spring): 108–12.

Gladieux, Lawrence E., and Arthur M. Hauptman. 1995. *The College Aid Quandary: Access, Quality, and the Federal Role.* Brookings.

Gladieux, Lawrence E., and Thomas R. Wolanin. 1976. *Congress and the Colleges: The National Politics of Higher Education.* D. C. Heath.

Gose, Ben. 1998a. "Following Princeton's Move, Yale Increases Size of Student-Aid Packages." *Chronicle of Higher Education* (February 13): A54.

———. 1998b. "Princeton Plans Major Increases in Aid for Middle- and Low-Income Students." *Chronicle of Higher Education* (January 30): A35.

———. 1998c. "Recent Shifts on Aid by Elite Colleges Signal New Push to Help the Middle Class." *Chronicle of Higher Education* (March 6): A43.

———. 2000. "Tuition Discounting May Rankle, but It Has Become Widespread." *Chronicle of Higher Education* (February 18): A62.

Gramlich, Edward M. 1990. *A Guide to Benefit-Cost Analysis.* Prentice Hall.

Hamm, William E. 1995. "The Waldorf Tuition and Grants Reduction Experiment." *Rethinking Tuition and Student Aid Strategies: New Directions for Higher Education,* no. 89 (Spring): 41–52.

Hansen, Janet S. 1991. "The Roots of Federal Student Aid Policy." In *New Directions in Higher Education: The Changing Dimensions of Financial Aid,* no. 74 (Summer): 3–19.

Hansen, W. Lee, and Burton A. Weisbrod. 1973. *Benefits, Costs, and Finance of Public Higher Education.* Markham Publishing.

Hanushek, Eric A. 1999. "Budgets, Priorities, and Investment in Human Capital." In *Financing College Tuition: Government Policies and Educational Priorities,* edited by Marvin H. Kosters. AEI Press.

Hauptman, Arthur M., and Cathy Krop. 1998. "Federal Student Aid and the Growth in College Costs and Tuitions: Examining the Relationship." In National Commission on the Cost of Higher Education, *Straight Talk about College Costs and Prices.* Oryx Press.

Hebel, Sara. 2000. "Clinton Tax-Break Proposal Favors the Middle Class, College Officials Say." *Chronicle of Higher Education* (February 4): A34.

———. 2001. "Colleges Praise Many Provisions in Tax Bill, but Worry That It May Limit Federal Spending." *Chronicle of Higher Education* (June 8): A25.

Hitch, Charles J. 1968. "The Need for New Guidelines." *Public Interest* 11 (Spring): 126–28.

Hofstadter, Richard, and C. DeWitt Hardy. 1952. *The Development and Scope of Higher Education in the United States.* Columbia University Press.

Hoover, Eric. 2001. "Twenty-eight Private Colleges Agree to Use Common Approaches to Student Aid." *Chronicle of Higher Education* (July 20): A33–A34.

Hopkins, David S. P., and William F. Massy. 1981. *Planning Models for Colleges and Universities.* Stanford University Press.

Hoxby, Caroline M. 1999. "Where Should Federal Education Initiatives Be Directed?" In *Financing College Tuition: Government Policies and Educational Priorities,* edited by Marvin H. Kosters. AEI Press.

Ikenberry, Stanley O., and Terry W. Hartle. 1998. *Too Little Knowledge Is a Dangerous Thing: What the Public Thinks and Knows about Paying for College.* American Council on Education.

Irving, Carl. 2001. "Muskingum College's Gutsy Move." *National Crosstalk* 9 (1): 3–6.

Jaschik, Scott. 1992. "Judge Rules MIT Violated Antitrust Law as Member of Twenty-three-College 'Overlap Group.'" *Chronicle of Higher Education* (September 9): A22.

———. 1993. "Appeals Court Gives MIT Another Chance." *Chronicle of Higher Education* (September 29): A25, A29.

Johnstone, D. Bruce. 1972. *New Patterns for College Lending: Income-Contingent Loans.* Columbia University Press.

Kane, Thomas J. 1998. "Savings Incentives for Higher Education." *National Tax Journal* 51 (3): 609–20.

———. 1999a. *The Price of Admission: Rethinking How Americans Pay for College.* Brookings.

———. 1999b. "Reforming Public Subsidies for Education." In *Financing College Tuition: Government Policies and Educational Priorities,* edited by Marvin H. Kosters. AEI Press.

Keppel, Francis. 1987. "The Higher Education Acts Contrasted, 1965–1986: Has Federal Policy Come of Age?" *Harvard Educational Review* 57 (1): 49–67.

Kerr, Clark. 1968. "The Distribution of Money and Power." *Public Interest* 11 (Spring): 100–4.

King, Jacqueline E. 1999. Conclusion to *Financing a College Education: How It Works, How It's Changing,* edited by Jacqueline E. King. Oryx Press and the American Council on Education.

Knapp, Laura Greene, and Terry G. Seaks. 1992. "An Analysis of the Probability of Default on Federally Guaranteed Student Loans." *Review of Economics and Statistics* 74 (3): 404–11.

Kreps, David M. 1990. *A Course in Microeconomic Theory.* Princeton University Press.

Kwoka, John E., and Lawrence J. White. 1999. *The Antitrust Revolution: Economics, Competition, and Policy.* 3d ed. Oxford University Press.

Lapovsky, Lucie, and Loren Loomis Hubbell. 2000. "Positioning for Competition." *NACUBO Business Officer* (March): 22–30.

Levine, David O. 1986. *The American College and the Culture of Aspiration, 1915–1940.* Cornell University Press.

McPherson, Michael S. 1989. "Appearance and Reality in the Guaranteed Student Loan Program." In *Radical Reform or Incremental Change? Student Loan Policy Alternatives for the Federal Government,* edited by Lawrence E. Galdieux. College Board.

McPherson, Michael S., and Morton Owen Schapiro. 1991. *Keeping College Affordable: Government and Educational Opportunity.* Brookings.

———. 1998. *The Student Aid Game: Meeting Need and Rewarding Talent in American Higher Education.* Princeton University Press.

———. 1999. "Gaining Control of the Free-for-All in Financial Aid." *Chronicle of Higher Education* (July 2): A48.

Moos, Malcolm. 1968. "The Need for Direct and Substantial Aid." *Public Interest* 11 (Spring): 134–36.

Morison, Samuel Eliot. 1936. *Three Centuries of Harvard.* Harvard University Press.

Mumper, Michael. 1996. *Removing College Price Barriers: What Government Has Done and Why It Hasn't Worked.* State University of New York Press.

———. 1999. "The Student Aid Industry." In *Financing a College Education: How It Works, How It's Changing,* edited by Jacqueline E. King. Oryx Press and the American Council on Education.

National Commission on the Cost of Higher Education. 1998. *Straight Talk about College Costs and Prices.* Oryx Press.

Perloff, Jeffrey M. 2000. *Microeconomics.* 2d ed. Addison-Wesley Longman.

Quinn, Jane Bryant. 2000. "New Money for College." *Newsweek,* October 9, 41.

Rainsford, George N. 1972. *Congress and Higher Education in the Nineteenth Century.* University of Tennessee Press.

Reischauer, Robert D. 1989. "HELP: A Student Loan Program for the Twenty-first Century." In *Radical Reform or Incremental Change? Student Loan Policy Alternatives for the Federal Government,* edited by Lawrence E. Galdieux. College Board.

Reynolds, Alan. 1998. "The Real Cost of Higher Education: Who Should Pay It and How?" In National Commission on the Cost of Higher Education, *Straight Talk about College Costs and Prices.* Oryx Press.

Rudolph, Frederick. 1990. *The American College and University: A History.* University of Georgia Press.

Schelling, Thomas C. 1978. *Micromotives and Macrobehavior.* W. W. Norton.

Schmidt, Peter. 2001. "Boom in Merit-Based Scholarships Drives 8.8 Percent Rise in State Funds for Student Aid." *Chronicle of Higher Education* (April 21): A39.

Selingo, Jeffrey. 2001."Questioning the Merit of Merit Scholarships: The Awards Beggar Need-Based Aid, and Many Recipients Require Remediation." *Chronicle of Higher Education* (January 19): A20.

Sharpe, Russell T., George B. Risty, William S. Guthrie, and Harold B. Pepinsky. 1946. "Financial Assistance for College Students." American Council on Education Studies, series 6, *Student Personnel Work* 10 (7).

Stiglitz, Joseph E., Laura D. Tyson, Peter R. Orszag, and Jonathan M. Orszag. 2000. *The Impact of Paying for College on Family Finances.* SEBAGO Associates, November.

Strosnider, Kim. 1998. "A University Relies on Its Endowment to Cover the Costs of Financial Aid." *Chronicle of Higher Education* (June 12): A37.

Thaler, Richard H. 1980. "Toward a Positive Theory of Consumer Choice." *Journal of Economic Behavior and Organization* 1 (1): 39–60.

Thaler, Richard H., Daniel Kahneman, and Jack L. Knetsch. 1992. "The Endowment Effect, Loss Aversion, and Status Quo Bias." In *The Winner's Curse: Paradoxes and Anomalies of Economic Life,* edited by Richard Thaler. Princeton University Press.

Truman, David B. 1968. "Autonomy with Accountability." *Public Interest* 11 (Spring): 104–7.

U.S. Department of Commerce. Bureau of the Census. 1960–1998. *Statistical Abstract of the United States.* U.S. Government Printing Office.

———. 1975. *Historical Statistics of the United States: Colonial Times to 1970.* U.S. Government Printing Office.

———. 1998. *All Parent/Child Situations, by Type, Race, and Hispanic Origin of Householders or Reference Person: 1970 to Present,* December 11, www.census .gov/population/socdemo/hh-fam/htabFM-2.txt (September 19, 2000).

U.S. Department of Education. 1996. "National Student Loan Default Rates Hit All-Time Low." Press release, January 22, www.ed.gov/PressReleases/01-1996/def96 .html (April 12, 2000).

———. 1999a. *1999–2000 SFA Handbook.* U.S. Government Printing Office.

———. 1999b. *Student Guide: Financial Aid, 1999–2000.* U.S. Government Printing Office.

———. 1999c. "Student Loan Default Rate Drops, Again; 8.8 Percent Is Lowest Rate Ever." Press release, October 5, www.ed.gov/offices/OPE/Data/97default.html (April 12, 2000).

———, National Center for Education Statistics (NCES). 1998. *NPSAS, 1995–1996: National Postsecondary Student Aid Study.* CD ROM, Public Use Data. NCES 98-074.

————. 1999a. "The Condition of Education," nces.ed.gov/pubs99/condition99/indicator-12.htm (March 19, 2002).

————, Integrated Postsecondary Education Data System (IPEDS) Survey. n.d. caspar .nsf.gov (March 19, 2002).

————. 1999b. *Digest of Educational Statistics 1999*. NCES 2002-031.

U.S. Department of Health, Education, and Welfare, Assistant Secretary for Planning and Evaluation. 1969. *Toward a Long-Range Plan for Federal Financial Support for Higher Education: A Report to the President*. U.S. Government Printing Office.

U.S. General Accounting Office. 1993. *High-Risk Series: Guaranteed Student Loans*. GAO/HR-93-2. U.S. Government Printing Office.

————. 1997. *High-Risk Series: Student Financial Aid*. GAO/HR-97-11. U.S. Government Printing Office.

U.S. House of Representatives. 1985. Committee on Education and Labor. *Higher Education Amendments of 1985: Report Together with Supplementary and Dissenting Views*. 99th Cong., 1st sess. H. Rept. 99-383.

U.S. President's Commission on Higher Education. 1947. *Higher Education for Democracy*. Vol. 2. U.S. Government Printing Office.

Volkwein, J. Fredericks, and Bruce P. Szelest. 1995. "Individual and Campus Characteristics Associated with Student Loan Default." *Research in Higher Education* 36 (1): 41–72.

Wertenbaker, Thomas Jefferson. 1946. *Princeton, 1746–1896*. Princeton University Press.

Winston, Gordon C. 1999. "Subsidies, Hierarchy, and Peers: The Awkward Economics of Higher Education." *Journal of Economic Perspectives* 13 (1): 13–36.

"Year 1990 Annual Guide: America's Best Colleges." 1999. *U.S. News and World Report*, August 30, 1999, 62–107.

Index